Responsibility Sharing in International Refugee Law

International Refugee Law Series

VOLUME 23

The titles published in this series are listed at *brill.com/irls*

Responsibility Sharing in International Refugee Law

Towards Common but Differentiated Legal Obligations

By

Elizabeth Mavropoulou

BRILL | NIJHOFF

LEIDEN | BOSTON

Library of Congress Cataloging-in-Publication Data

Names: Mavropoulou, Elizabeth author
Title: Responsibility sharing in international refugee law : towards common but differentiated legal obligations / by Elizabeth Mavropoulou.
Description: Leiden ; Boston : Brill Academic Publishers, Inc, 2025. | Series: International Refugee Law Series ; volume 23 | Includes bibliographical references and index.
Identifiers: LCCN 2025029965 | ISBN 9789004546691 hardback | ISBN 9789004547711 epub
Subjects: LCSH: Refugees--Legal status, laws, etc. | Responsibility to protect (International law) | Climatic changes--Law and legislation
Classification: LCC K3230.R45 .M387 2025 | DDC 342.08/3--dc23/eng/20250702
LC record available at https://lccn.loc.gov/2025029965

Typeface for the Latin, Greek, and Cyrillic scripts: "Brill". See and download: brill.com/brill-typeface.

ISSN 2213-3836
ISBN 978-90-04-54669-1 (hardback)
ISBN 978-90-04-54771-1 (e-book)
DOI 10.1163/9789004547711

This book is printed on acid-free paper and produced in a sustainable manner.

To my son, Renaldo

Contents

PART 2
A Proposal

Foreword

The responsibility sharing of refugees is a critical global challenge that requires coordinated international cooperation. While the 1951 Refugee Convention is built on the right to seek asylum and the enjoyment of rights and standards of treatment, the practical implementation of these rights and standards falls disproportionately on low- and middle-income countries, creating significant strain on their resources and infrastructure. This book offers a comprehensive and lucid analysis of how the concept of responsibility sharing emerged and evolved in the refugee context, drawing compelling parallels with the principle of 'common but differentiated responsibilities and respective capabilities' from environmental law. Looking to the Paris Agreement on Climate Change as a model, Dr. Elizabeth Mavropoulou proposes a Protocol on Refugee Responsibility Sharing that would complement the Refugee Convention, as a legally binding solution to the responsibility sharing gap. This timely book advances our understanding of refugee law and offers much needed practical solutions to one of today's most pressing humanitarian challenges. The book makes a valuable contribution to both scholarly discourse and policy development in refugee protection, and will no doubt establish itself as a cornerstone in international refugee law.

Professor Hélène Lambert
Director, Peter McMullin Centre on Statelessness
Melbourne Law School, Australia

Acknowledgements

This book has been a long time in the making and there are a number of people who have contributed to it in various ways. First and foremost, I would like to thank my partner Renaldo Scheepers who made the doctoral research possible through his generous financial support. I would not have had the opportunity to research and write this book without him.

My first encounter with the study of international refugee law dates back to my postgraduate degree at the University of Westminster in 2014 where I met Prof. Hélène Lambert. Lucky for me, three years later Hélène became my Ph.D. Supervisor offering rigorous academic support and advice throughout the course of the research encouraging me along the way. I would like to thank Hélène for reading multiple drafts of the Thesis and the book proposal and for believing in the work. I will never forget the early mornings or late evenings Zoom meetings as we tried to reconcile our times zones from different hemispheres.

I would also like to thank my second Ph.D. supervisor and now colleague Ruth McKenzie for helping me navigate the field of international environmental law so as to draw parallels to my research. I thank Ruth for reading the thesis and advising on the book.

Special thanks go to Dr. Emma McClean, another dear colleague, who introduced me to enlightened legal positivism and the importance of method. Emma gave her time generously over the course of my doctoral research by reading parts of the thesis, providing invaluable comments and encouraging feedback to raw ideas. I thank Emma for being the internal examiner of my Ph.D. Thesis and for her support.

There are also scholars whom I met along the way and with whom I had the opportunity to discuss and test some of my ideas and arguments during academic events and conferences. It would be impossible to list them all here. I want to thank in particularly Prof. David Cantor and the Refugee Law Initiative (RLI) for being a second academic and intellectual home. Through various RLI events I have met junior and senior RLI affiliates, experts in the field with whom I embarked upon intellectual encounters that benefited the research of this book greatly.

Special thanks go to Dr. Harriet Samuels and Prof. Luke Mason from Westminster Law School for encouraging me to complete the manuscript and for facilitating with editorial assistance. My heartfelt thanks go to Mr. Napoleon Gonzales (LL.M.) for his diligence and work ethic in going over the manuscript. All errors and omissions remain of course my own.

An important intellectual debt is owed to Prof. Marco Roscini who introduced me to the study of international law in the course of my postgraduate degree at Westminster. Marco's teachings infused in me a passion for the discipline.

It is the wish of every scholar that the outcome of their research contributes to the furtherance of the discipline and if possible, beyond. I would also hope that the ideas in this book provoke debate on what could a pragmatic yet principled reform of the international refugee law regime could look like.

The law and policy are stated as of November 2024.
15 December 2024

Abbreviations

ARSIWA	2001 Articles on the Responsibility of States for Internationally Wrongful Acts
CBDR	Common but differentiated responsibilities
CBDRRC	Common but differentiated responsibilities and respective capabilities
CEAS	Common European Asylum System
CIREFCA	Conferencia Internacional sobre los Refugiados Centroamericanos (International Conference on Central American Refugees)
COP	Conference of the Parties to the United Nations Convention on Climate Change
CPA	Comprehensive Plan of Action
ECOWAS	Economic Community of West African States
ECtHR	European Court of Human Rights
EU	European Union
ExCom	UNHCR Executive Committee
GATT	General Agreement on Tariffs and Trade
ICESCR	International Covenant on Economic Social Cultural Rights
ICJ	International Court of Justice
ILC	International Law Commission
INDC	Intended Nationally Determined Contribution
IOM	International Organisation on Migration
ITLOS	International Tribunal for the Law of the Sea
MEAS	
NDC	Nationally Determined Contribution
NIEO	New International Economic Order
OAU	Organisation of African Unity
OECD	Organisation for Economic Cooperation and Development
OSPAR	1992 Oslo and Paris Conventions for the Protection of North-East Antlantic
STC	Safe Third Country
TWAIL	Third World Approaches to International law
UN	United Nations
UNCED	United Nations Conference on Environment and Development
UNCHR	United Nations High Commissioner for Refugees
UNCLOS	United Nations Convention on the Law of the Sea
UNCTAD	United Nations Conference on Trade and Development
UNFCCC	United Nations Framework Convention on Climate Change
UNGA	United Nations General Assembly

US	United States
VCLT	Vienna Convention on the Law of Treaties
WTO	World Trade Organization

Cases

International Court of Justice

Application of the Convention on the Prevention and Punishment of the Crime of Genocide (*The Gambia v. Myanmar*) (Order of 23 January 2020) [2020] ICJ Rep 3
Armed Activities on the Territory of the Congo (*DRC v. Uganda*) (*Judgment*) [2005] ICJ Rep 168
Case Concerning Application of the Convention on the Prevention and Punishment of the Crime of Genocide (*Bosnia and Herzegovina v. Serbia and Montenegro*) [1996] ICJ Rep 595
Case Concerning Armed Activities on the Territory of the Congo (*Democratic Republic of the Congo v. Uganda*) [2005] ICJ Rep 168
Case Concerning East Timor (*Portugal v. Australia*) [1995] ICJ Rep 90
Case Concerning the Barcelona Traction, Light and Power Company, Limited (*Belgium v. Spain*) [1970] ICJ Rep 3
Legal Consequences of the Construction of a Wall in the Occupied Palestinian Territory (Advisory Opinion) [2004] ICJ Rep 136
Legality of the Threat or Use of Nuclear Weapons (Advisory Opinion) [1996] ICJ Rep 226
Questions relating to the Obligation to Prosecute or Extradite (*Belgium v. Senegal*) [2012] ICJ Rep 422
Reservations to the Convention on the Prevention and Punishment of the Crime of Genocide (Advisory Opinion) [1951] ICJ Rep 15

Permanent Court of Arbitration

Dispute between Argentina and Chile concerning the Beagle Channel (18 February 1977) Volume XXI Reports of International Arbitral Awards
Dispute Concerning Access to Information Under Article 9 of the OSPAR Convention Ireland v. United Kingdom (2 July 2003) Volume XXIII Reports of International Arbitral Awards

International Tribunal of the Law of the Sea

Responsibilities and Obligations of States Sponsoring Persons and Entities with Respect to Activities in the Area, (Advisory Opinion) (Order of 1 February 2011)

Court of Justice of the European Union

NS v United Kingdom and M.E v Ireland Joined Cases C-411/10 and C-493/10 GC 21 December 2011

Slovak Republic and Hungary v Council of the European Union Joined Cases C-643/15 and C-647/15 GC 6 September 2017

Commission v Poland Hungary and the Czech Republic Joined Cases C-715/17, C-718/17, C-719/17 2 April 2020

European Court of Human Rights

Hirsi Jamaa and Others v Italy, App No 277665/09 GC (23 February 2012)

Soering v United Kingdom, Application No 5856/72 (15 March 1978)

National Courts

Australia

Plaintiff M70/2011 and Plaintiff M106/2011 v Minister for Immigration and Citizenship [2011] HCA 32 (31 August 2011)

Canada

Canadian Council for Refugees, Canadian Council of Churches, Amnesty International, and John Doe v. Her Majesty the Queen [2007] F.C.J. No. 1583, 2007 FC 1262.

Canadian Council for Refugees v. Canada (Citizenship and Immigration) [2024] 2023 SCC 17

Singh v Canada (Minister of Employment and Immigration) [1985] 1 S.C.R. 177

Greece

Greek Council of State (Plenary) Decision 2348/2017

Papua New Guinea

Namah v Pato (Minister for Foreign Affairs and Immigration)

United Kingdom

R (on the application of AAA (Syria) and others) v Secretary of State for the Home Department [2023] UK SC 42

Select Treaties and Other Instruments

League of Nations Instruments

Arrangements Related to the Issue of Identity Certificates to Russian and Armenian Refugees, 12 May 1926 84 League of Nations Treaty Series No. 2004.

Convention of 28 October, 1933 Relating to the International Status of Refugees League of Nations, Treaty Series Vol. CLIX No. 3663.

Provisional Arrangements Concerning the Status of Refugees coming from Germany 1936 171 League of Nations Treaty Series No. 3952.

Treaties

General Agreement on Tariffs and Trade (GATT) 1948

Convention Relating to the Status of Refugees (adopted 28 July 1951, entered into force 22 April 1954) 189 UNTS 137

Protocol Relating to the Status of Refugees (adopted 31 January 1967, entered into force 4 October 1967) 606 UNTS 267

Vienna Convention on the Law of Treaties (22 May 1969) UNTS 331

OAU Convention Regulating The Specific Aspects of Refugee Problems in Africa 1969 UNTS 1469

United Nations Convention on the Law of the Sea (adopted Montego Bay, 10 December 1982 and entered into force 16 November 1994) 1833 UNTS 397.

International Covenant on Economic, Social and Cultural Rights (ICESCR) (Adopted in 16 December 1966, entered into force 3 January 1976) UNTS Vol 993.

General Agreement on Tariffs and Trade (GATT) Decision of 28 November 1979 (L/4903) Differential and More Favourable Treatment, Reciprocity and Fuller Participation of Developing Countries'

Convention Against Torture and Other Cruel, Inhuman and Degrading Treatment or Punishment (1984) UNTSE 1465, 85

Montreal Protocol on Substances that Deplete the Ozone Layer (adopted 16 September 1987, entered into force 1 January 1989) UNTS 1522

Vienna Convention on the Protection of the Ozone Layer (adopted 22 March 1985, entered into force 22 September 1988) UNTS 1513

Basel Convention on the Control of Transboundary Movements of Hazardous Wastes and their Disposal, (adopted in 1989 and it came into force in 1992) UNTS 1673

Convention on Biological Diversity (5 June 1992, entered into force 29 December 1993) UNTS 1760 69

GATT Multilateral Trade Negotiations (the Uruguay Round) Marrakesh Agreement Establishing the Multilateral Trade Organization (World Trade Organization) 15 December 1993

United Nations Framework Convention on Climate Change (adopted May 1992, entered into force March 1994) UNTS 1771 107

Kyoto Protocol to the United Nations Framework Convention on Climate Change (adopted 11 December 1997, entered into force 16 February 2005) UNTS 2303 162

Optional Protocol to the Convention against Torture and Other Cruel, Inhuman or Degrading Treatment or Punishment (18 December 2002, entered into force 22 June 2006) UNTS 2375 237

Select UN Documents

UN General Assembly Resolutions and Declarations

Universal Declaration of Human Rights of 10 December 1948

Refugees and Stateless Persons, UN GA Resolution 319 A (IV) of 3 December 1949

UN Secretary General: Ad Hoc Committee on Statelessness and Related Problems, 'Status of Refugees and Stateless Persons: Memorandum by the Secretary-General, 3 January 1950, UN Doc E/AC.32/2.

UNGA Declaration on Principles of International Law Concerning Friendly Relations and Cooperation among States in Accordance with the Charter of the United Nations (1970)

UNGA Declaration on the Establishment of New International Economic Order (S-VI) A/Res/S-63201 (May 1974)

UNGA Resolution Programme of Action on the Establishment of a New International Economic Order 3202 (S-VI). (May 1974)

UNGA Resolution Charter of Economic Rights and Duties of States A/Res/29/3281 (December 1974)

UNGA Meeting on Refugees and Displaced Persons in South-East Asia, Convened by the Secretary-General of the United Nations at Geneva, on 20 and 21 July 1979, and subsequent developments: Report of the Secretary-General, A/34/627 7 (November 1979)

UNGA Procedure for the Establishment of a Firm and Lasting Peace in Central America (Esquipulas II) A/42/521 Annex (31 August 1987)

UNGA Resolution International Conference on Indo-Chinese Refugees A/RES/44/138 (December 1989)

UNGA Resolution Transforming our world: the 2030 Agenda for Sustainable Development A/RES/70/1(21 October 2015)

UNGA New York Declaration for Refugees and Migrants A/RES/71/1 (October 2016)

UNGA Report of the United Nations High Commissioner for Refugees to the UNGA (73 Session No 12) Part II Global Compact on Refugees A/73/12 (August 2018)

Other UN Documents (Reports and Conferences)

Report of the United Nations Conference on the Human Environment, Stockholm Declaration on the Human Environment A/CONF48./14/Rev.1(Stockholm 5-16 June 1972)

United Nations Conference of Plenipotentiaries on the Status of Refugees and Stateless Persons, Final Act of the United Nations Conference of Plenipotentiaries on the Status of Refugees and Stateless Persons, A/CONF.2/108/Rev.1 (July 1951)

UN Committee on Economic, Social and Cultural Rights CESCR General Comment No. 3 The Nature of States Parties' Obligations (Art. 2, Para. 9, of the Covenant) Document E/1991/23 (4 December 1990)

UNGA Report of the Special Rapporteur on torture and other cruel, inhuman or degrading treatment or punishment, Juan E. Méndez – Addendum – Observations on communications transmitted to Governments and replies received by Juan E. Méndez Twenty-eighth session A/HRC/28/68/Add.1 (March 2015)

International Maritime Organisation

IMO Resolution MSC.167(78) (adopted on 20 May 2004) MSC 78/26/Add.2 Guidelines on the Treatment of Persons Rescued at Sea.

International Law Commission

Draft Articles on Responsibility of States for Internationally Wrongful Acts, Report of the ILC on the Work of its 53rd Session, A/56/10 (2001)

UNHCR Documents

Statute of the Office of the United Nations High Commissioner for Refugees of 14 December 1950

UNHCR, Global Consultations on International Protection/Third Track: Asylum Processes (Fair and Efficient Asylum Procedures), EC/GC/01/12 (31 May 2001)

UNHCR, Global Consultations on International Protection 'Mechanisms of International Cooperation to Share Responsibilities and Burdens in Mass Influx Situations', 1st Meeting, EC/GC/01/7 (19 February 2001)

Challenges to the 1951 Convention in its 50th Anniversary Year: Statement by Ms. Erika Feller, Director, Department of International Protection, UNHCR, at the Seminar on "International Protection within one single asylum procedure", Norrkoping, Sweden, 23–24 April 2001

UNHCR (2002), Summary Conclusions on the Concept of the 'Effective Protection' in the Context of Secondary Movements of Refugees and Asylum Seekers (Lisbon Expert Roundtable, 9–10 December 2002)

UNHCR Bilateral and/or Multilateral Arrangements for Processing Claims for International Protection and Finding Durable Solutions for Refugees (Position paper, 20 April 2016)

UNHCR Conclusions adopted by the Executive Committee on the International Protection of Refugees, 1975–2009 (Conclusions No 1–109), December 2009

UNHCR Intervention before the European Court of Human Rights in the Case of Hirsi and Others v. Italy Application No. 27765/09 (March 2010)

UNHCR Expert Meeting on International Cooperation to Share Burdens and Responsibilities: Summary Conclusions (Amman, 28 June, 2011)

UNHCR Handbook and Guidelines on Procedures and Criteria for Determining Refugee Status under the 1951 Convention and the 1967 Protocol Relating to the Status of Refugees, HCR/1P/4/ENG/REV.3 (December 2011)

UNHCR Resettlement Handbook (2011)

UNHCR, UNHCR monitoring visit to the Republic of Nauru 7 to 9 October 2013 (November 2013)

UNHCR, Guidance Note on bilateral and/or multilateral transfer arrangements of asylum-seekers (May 2013)

UNHCR Guterres A, 'Closing Remarks at the Session of the 66th Executive Committee of the High Commissioner's Programme' speech delivered on the 5th October 2015

66th Meeting of the Standing Committee of the Executive Committee of the High Commissioner's Programme, Agenda item 2: International Protection Statement by Volker Türk, Assistant High Commissioner for Protection (21-24 June 2016)

Zero Draft of the Global Compact on Responsibility Sharing for Refugees, (UNHCR 30 June 2016)

UNHCR Position on Returns to Libya (Update II) September 2018

UNHCR Global Trends Forced Displacement 2024

UNHCR Position on the Designations of Libya as a Safe Third Country and as a Place of Safety for the Purpose of Disembarkation Following Rescue at Sea (September 2020)

UNHCR Global Appeal 2020-2021

UNHCR Executive Committee Conclusions

ExCom No. 15 'Refugees Without an Asylum Country' (1979)

ExCom No. 11 (XXX) 'General Conclusion on the International Protection' (1978)

ExCom No. 15 (XXX) 'Refugees Without an Asylum Country' (1979)
ExCom No. 22 (XXXII) 'Protection of Asylum -Seekers in Situations of Large -Scale Influx' (1981)
ExCom No. 23 (XXXII) 'Problems Related to the Rescue of Asylum-Seekers in Distress at Sea' (1981)
ExCom No. 58 (XL) 'Problem of Refugees and Asylum- Seekers Who Move in an Irregular Manner from a Country in Which They Had Already Found Protection' (1989)
ExCom No. 99 (LV) 'General Conclusion on International Protection' (2004)
ExCom No. 100 (LV) 'General Conclusion on International Cooperation and Burden and Responsibility Sharing in Mass Influx Situations' (2004)
ExCom No. 108 (LIX) 'General Conclusion on International Protection' (2008)
ExCom No. 109 (LXI) 'Conclusion on Protracted Refugee Situations' (2009)
ExCom No. 11, 22, 52, 77, 79, 80, 85, 89, 100, 102. UN High Commissioner for Refugees (UNHCR), 'A Thematic Compilation of Executive Committee Conclusions', 7th edition (June 2014)

Decisions of the Conference of the Parties to the UNFCCC (COP Decisions)

Decision 1/CP.1 'The Berlin Mandate: Review of the Adequacy of Article 4, paragraph 2 (a) and (b), of the Convention, including proposals related to a protocol and decisions on follow-up' (6 June 1995) FCCC/CP/1995/7 Add. 1, 4 Berlin Mandate
Decision 2/CP.1 'Review of First Communications from the Parties Included in Annex I to the Convention' (6 June 1995) Add.1,7
Decision 2/CP.3, 'Methodological Issues Related to the Kyoto Protocol' (25 March 1998) FCCC/CP/1997/7/Add. 1, 31
Decision 24/CP.7, 'Procedures and Mechanisms Relating to Compliance under the Kyoto Protocol; (21 January 2002) FCCC/CP//2001/12 Add.3
Decision 1/CP.1, 'Bali Action Plan' (14 March 2008) FCCC/CP/2007/6 Add.1,3
Decision 2/CP.15, 'Copenhagen Accord' (30 March 2010) FCCC/CP/2009/11 Add. 1
Decision 1/CP.16, 'The Cancun Agreements: Outcome of the work of the Ad Hoc Working Group on Long-term Cooperative Action under the Convention (15 March 2011) FCCC/CP/2010/7/Add.1 2
Decision 1/CP.17 'Establishment of an Ad Hoc Working Group on the Durban Platform for Enhanced Action' (11 December 2011) FCCC/CP/2011/9/ Add. 1, 2
Decision 1/CP.20, 'Lima Call for Climate Action' (2 February 2015) FCCC/CP/2014/10 Add.1, 2.

Decision 1/CP/.21 'Adoption of the Paris Agreement' (entered into force 29 January 2016) FCCC/CP/2015/10/Add.1, Annex. (Paris Agreement)

Decision 1/CP. 22 'Aggregate Effect of the Intended Nationally Determined Contributions: an Update' FCCC/CP/2016/2

Conference of the Parties serving as the meeting of the Parties to the Paris Agreement

Decision 18/CMA.1 'Modalities, Procedures and Guidelines for the Transparency Framework for Action and Support Referred to in Article 13 of the Paris Agreement' FCCC/PA/CMA/2018/3/Add.2

Decision of decision 1/CP.21, 19/CMA.1 Matters Relating to Article 14 of the

Paris Agreement and paragraphs 99–101' FCCC/PA/CMA/2018/3/Add.2

Decision 20/CMA.1 'Modalities and Procedures for the Effective Operation of the Committee to Facilitate Implementation and Promote Compliance Referred to in Article 15, paragraph 2, of the Paris Agreement. FCCC/PA/CMA/2018/3/Add.2

Regional Instruments

EU

Legislation

Treaty on European Union (Consolidated version 2016)

Treaty on the Functioning of the European Union (Consolidated version 2016)

Charter of Fundamental Rights of the European Union (2012) OJ C 326/391

Regulations

Regulation (EU) No 604/2013 of the European Parliament and of the Council of 26 June 2013 Establishing the Criteria and Mechanisms for Determining the Member State Responsible for Examining an Application for International Protection lodged in one of the Member States by a third-country national or a stateless person (recast) 2013 L.180/31

Commission Proposal for a Regulation of the European Parliament and of the Council Establishing the Criteria and Mechanisms for Determining the Member State responsible for Examining an Application for International Protection lodged in one of the Member States by a third-country national or a stateless person (recast), COM (2016). Dublin IV.

Commission announces New Migration Partnership Framework: Reinforced Cooperation with Third Countries to Better Manage Migration, European Commission, Press Release, 7 June 2016. Migration Partnership Framework, A New Approach to Better Manage Migration.

Council of the European Union

Council Resolution of 30 November 1992 on a Harmonized Approach to Questions Concerning Host Third Countries ("London Resolution"), 30 November 1992

Council Decision (EU) 2015/1523 of 14 September 2015 establishing provisional measures in the area of international protection for the benefit of Italy and of Greece L 239/80

Council Decision (EU) 2015/1601 of 22 September 2015 establishing provisional measures in the area of international protection for the benefit of Italy and Greece L 248/80

Council of the European Union Press Release, "EU–Turkey statement, 18 March 2016." (March 18, 2016)

Bilateral Agreements

Accordo tra la Repubblica Italiana e la Gran Giamahiria Araba Libica Popolare Socialista per la Collaborazione nella Lotta al Terrorismo, alla Criminalità Organizzata, al Traffico Illegale di Stupefacenti e Sostanze Psicotrope e All'Immigrazione Clandestina (Rome, 13 Dec 2000).

2017 Memorandum d'intesa sulla cooperazione nel campo dello sviluppo, del contrasto all'immigrazione illegale, al traffico di esseri umani, al contrabbando e sul rafforzamento della sicurezza delle frontiere tra Io Stato della Libia e la sul rafforzamento della sicurezza delle frontiere tra Io Stato della Libia e la Repubblica Italiana. (May 2 2017)

Italy–Albania

Australia and the Pacific

2012 Memorandum of Understanding between the Republic of Nauru and the Commonwealth of Australia, relating to the transfer to and assessment of persons in Nauru, and related issues

2012 Memorandum of Understanding between the Government of the Independent State of Papua New Guinea and the Government of Australia, relating to the transfer to, and assessment and settlement in, Papua New Guinea of certain persons, and related issues

North America

Agreement Between the Government of the United States of America and the Government of Canada for Cooperation in the Examination of Refugee Status Claims from Nationals of Third Countries (December 5, 2002). (US -Canada Safe Third Country Agreement)

National Legislation

198A of the Migration Act, as inserted by the Migration Amendment (Excision from the Migration Zone) (Consequential Provisions) Act 2001

Migration Amendment Act (Urgent Medical Treatment) Bill 2018

US

US Senate Resolution 98, 25 July 1997 105th Cong., 143 Congress Records. S8138-39 (Byrd-Hagel Resolution).

Central America

1984 Cartagena Declaration on Refugees, adopted by the Colloquium on the International Protection of Refugees in Central America, Mexico and Panama, held at Cartagena, Colombia from 19–22 November 1984

CIREFCA, Declaration and Concerted Plan of Action in Favour of Central American Refugees, Returnees and Displaced Persons, (30 May 1989), CIREFCA 89/13/Rev.1,

Mexico Declaration and Plan of Action to Strengthen the International Protection of Refugees in Latin America Mexico City, (16 November 2004)

Brazil Declaration on "A Framework for Cooperation and Regional Solidarity to Strengthen the International Protection of Refugees, Displaced and Stateless Persons in Latin America and the Caribbean" (Brasilia, 3 December 2014)

PART 1

The Responsibility Sharing Gap

CHAPTER 1

Introduction

1 The Responsibility Sharing Gap of the Refugee Convention

The international refugee law regime is predicated upon the idea that states have a collective responsibility to protect refugees.[1] Since the establishment of the United Nations (UN) in 1945, shortly after the Second World War, the management of refugees acquired salience and the refugee problem was recognised by the General Assembly as international in scope and nature.[2] The brutal excesses of a war that left Europe with millions of refugees led to the establishment of a temporary, at the time, UN body, the United Nations High Commissioner for Refugees (UNHCR).[3] It was not too long after the international community came to realize that the refugee problem was not going to be a temporary one.[4]

The international law regime on refugee protection consists of two main legal instruments: the 1951 Convention Relating to the Status of Refugees and its 1967 Protocol Relating to the Status of Refugees (together, the Refugee Convention), which removed the geographical and temporal limitations of the Convention.[5] These two are further supplemented by a series of soft law instruments, regional refugee and human rights instruments[6] and, together

---

1 Agnès Hurwitz 'Norm Making in International Refugee Law' (2012) 106 American Society of International Law Proceedings 430, 431.

2 UNGA Res (8) I (1946) Question of refugees GAOR First Session.

3 UNGA Res 428 (V) of 1950 Statute of the Office of the United Nations High Commissioner for Refugees. (UNHCR Statute).

4 Laura Barnett 'Global Governance and The Evolution of the International Refugee Regime' New Issues in Refugee Research (2002) Working Paper No. 54, 6.

5 The term 'refugee' is used as defined in Article 1A (2) of the 1951 Convention Relating to the Status of Refugees (adopted 28 July 1951, entered into force 22 April 1954) 189 UNTS 137. (Refugee Convention). Protocol Relating to the Status of Refugees (adopted 31 January 1967, entered into force 4 October 1967) 606 UNTS 267 (Protocol). Hereafter in this book, the Refugee Convention.

6 Supranational refugee law instruments include the Organisation of African Unity Convention Regulating the Specific Aspects of Refugee Problems in Africa (adopted 14 September 1969, entered into force 20 June 1974) UNTS 14691, (OAU Convention). The 1984 Declaration Cartagena Declaration on Refugees adopted by the Colloquium on the International Protection of Refugees in Central America, Mexico and Panama held at Cartagena, Colombia from 19–22 November 1984. (Cartagena Declaration).

 | DOI:10.1163/9789004547711_002

with the Office of the UNHCR, complete the architecture of the so-called international refugee law regime.

On one hand, the international refugee law regime has been praised for its enduring relevance throughout the years. It has indeed been a unique protection framework for individuals around the world fleeing persecution and has managed to stay current when new causes of flight have been added to the complex nature of forced displacement.[7] On the other hand, it has also been heavily criticised for lacking a framework on responsibility sharing.[8] Goodwin-Gill and McAdam refer to it as a 'responsibility deficit' of the Refugee Convention,[9] while Hathaway sees it as an implementation or operational gap.[10] Scholarship from International Relations (IR) on forced migration has also grappled with the challenge of responsibility sharing, framed within the wider cooperation challenge between the Global North and the Global South.[11]

The collective responsibility to protect refugees that the very regime is predicated upon is not met with a concomitant legal obligation whereby states are required to relieve overwhelmed asylum states and provide assistance and solutions to refugees in the territories of other states.[12] This is to a certain extent because the Refugee Convention is built on the concept of territorial asylum, and the enjoyment of the Convention rights and standards

7 Jane McAdam, 'The Enduring Relevance of the 1951 Refugee Convention' (2017) 29 International Journal of Refugee Law Editorial 1 https://doi.org/10.1093/ijrl/eex017; Volker Türk, Madeline Garlick, 'From Burdens and Responsibilities to Opportunities: The Comprehensive Refugee Response Framework and a Global Compact on Refugees' (2016) 28 International Journal of Refugee Law 656, 673 https://doi.org/10.1093/ijrl/eew043.

8 James C Hathaway, 'The Global Co-Op Out on Refugees' (2018) 30 International Journal of Refugee Law 591, https://doi.org/10.1093/ijrl/eey062.

9 Guy S Goodwin-Gill, 'The Movements of People Between States in the 21st Century: An Agenda for Urgent Institutional Change' (2016) 28 International Journal of Refugee Law 679, 688, https://doi.org/10.1093/ijrl/eew040; McAdam 'The Enduring Relevance of the 1951 Refugee Convention' (n7) 1.

10 James C Hathaway and Alexander Neve, 'Making International Refugee Law Relevant Again', (1997) 10 Harvard Human Rights Journal 115, 141; Hathaway, 'The Global Co-Op Out' (n 8) 591.

11 Astri Surhke, 'Burden Sharing During Refugee Emergencies: The Logic of Collective versus National Action' (1998) 11 Journal of Refugee Studies 396 https://doi.org/10.1093/jrs/11.4.396; Terje Einarsen 'Mass Flight The Case of International Asylum' (1995) 7 International Journal of Refugee Law 551, https://doi.org/10.1093/ijrl/7.4.551; Asha Hans, Astri Surhke, 'Responsibility Sharing' in James Hathaway (ed) *Reconceiving International Refugee Law* (Martinus Nijhoff Publishers 1997) 83.

12 Alexander Betts, *Protection by Persuasion, International Cooperation in the Refugee Regime* (Cornell University Press 2009) 2, 3.

of treatment requires at minimum that the refugee has come under the state's jurisdiction, whether territorial or extraterritorial.[13] The absence of a legal obligation has placed responsibility sharing in the sphere of voluntarism, while geography and proximity[14] are in reality the determinant factors for assigning responsibility for refugees rather than actual capacity.[15] David Owen has eloquently put this:

> It is worth recalling that the lack of fair apportionment of refugee protection is a key contributor to the reluctance of states to admit refugees for whom, in virtue of the principle of non-refoulement, they thereby bear sole responsibility for what often amounts to indefinite protection.[16]

Adding to this, Northern states have engaged in externalisation practices that seek to externalise international protection obligations and confine the *locus* of refugee protection predominantly within the Global South.[17] Such externalisation takes the form of multilateral or bilateral agreements whereby states of the Global North circumvent their refugee law obligations by contracting out or externalising part of their asylum functions to partner states in the Global South.[18]

2 Contextualising the Responsibility Sharing Gap

Key facts and figures contextualise some of the implications of the responsibility sharing gap for refugees. Arguably, the most cited percentage is the one published every year by the UNHCR on the total number of refugees and the

---

13 James C Hathaway, *The Rights of Refugees under International Law* (Cambridge University Press 2021) 183–184.

14 Mathew J Gibney, *The Ethics and Politics of Asylum Liberal Democracy and the Response to Refugees* (Cambridge University 2004) 240; Betts, *Protection by Persuasion* (n 12) 34.

15 Hathaway, 'The Global Cop-Out on Refugees' (n 8) 597.

16 David Owen, 'Refugees and Responsibilities of Justice' (2018) 11 Global Justice: Theory Practice Rhetoric 23.

17 Matthew J Gibney, 'Refugees and Justice Between States' (2015) 14 European Journal of Political Theory 448, https://doi.org/10.1177/1474885115585325

18 David Cantor, Nikolas-Feith Tan, Mariana Gkliati, Elizabeth Mavropoulou, Katherine Allinson, Sreetapa Chakrabarty, Maja Grundler, Lynn Hillary, Emilie McDonnell, Riona Moodley, Stephen Phillips, Annick Pijnenburg, Adel Reyhani, Sophia Soares, Natasha Yacoub, 'Externalisation, Access to Territorial Asylum, and International Law' (2022) 34 International Journal of Refugee Law 120 https://doi.org/10.1093/ijrl/eeac023.

large percentage hosted by developing countries. Although statistics do not always reflect the qualitative differences between refugee situations – and can cause 'statistics fatigue' – the fact that 75% of the world's refugees in 2023 is hosted by low and middle income countries in the regions confirms that geographic proximity to refugee-producing countries determines legal responsibility.[19] Of the 75%, 21% is hosted by Least Developed Countries (LDCs) as defined by the World Bank's classification.[20] The percentage hosted by LDCs corresponds to 7.7 million refugees.[21] Resettlement as a contribution to protection and responsibility sharing and a solution to refugeehood has fared the past two years, with numbers of refugees resettled reaching pre-pandemic levels.[22] Yet, resettlement opportunities met only the needs of a fraction of the total number of refugees still in need of resettlement.[23]

The absence of an obligation of responsibility sharing is also evident in the financial contributions to international protection through the financing of UNHCR. UNHCR's budget is primarily, if not exclusively, financed by developed and high-income countries, with the United States, the EU, Germany, Japan, Sweden and France ranking as top donors.[24] In spite of the earmarked character of many of these contributions, the financing of UNHCR's activities is a concrete contribution by Western states to responsibility sharing. In 2023, UNHCR flagged the alarming level of its funding that covers only 32% of its global budget, underscoring that the decrease of financial contributions not only has severe operational implications but also exacerbates existing inequalities between donor and host states, with the latter facing additional strains.[25] The hosting of refugees carries with it important social and eco-

19 UNHCR 'Global Trends Forced Displacement Report 2023 2 <https://www.unhcr.org/global-trends-report-2023> accessed 17 October 2024.

20 Defined by the United Nations as low-income countries confronting severe structural impediments to sustainable development. They are highly vulnerable to economic and environmental shocks and have low levels of human assets <https://www.un.org/development/desa/dpad/least-developed-country-category.html> accessed 17 October 2024.

21 UNHCR Global Trends Forced Displacement Report 2023 (n 19) 21.

22 UNHCR Global Trends Forced Displacement Report 2022 <https://www.unhcr.org/global-trends-report-2022> accessed 17 October 2024.

23 Only 8% of the refugees gets to be resettled, UNHCR Global Trends Forced Displacement 2023 (n 19) 42.

24 UNHCR Global Funding Overview <https://reporting.unhcr.org/dashboards/contributions> accessed 17 October 2024.

25 UNHCR, 'A threat to life dignity and hope, The Implications of Underfunding of UNHCR's Activities in 2023' (UNHCR 2023) 5 https://www.unhcr.org/media/underfunded-report-2023 accessed 17 October 2024.

nomic capital for Southern host countries, which adds to the developing countries' existing developmental challenges.

The above statistics are illustrative of the inherent inequalities in refugee protection responsibilities because of the current *ad hoc* and voluntary responsibility sharing system. The voluntary nature of financing refugee assistance programmes or admitting refugees for resettlement or other complementary pathways has created what Betts has described as a 'North-South impasse'.[26] Southern states assume the *de facto* responsibility to protect refugees while Northern states have no legal obligation to contribute to responsibility sharing and relieve the host states.

3 Responsibility Sharing in the *Travaux Preparatoires* of the Refugee Convention

The negotiating history of the Refugee Convention suggests that states at the time viewed responsibility sharing as a matter of domestic policy that consequently had no place in a treaty on the rights and duties of states with respect to refugees in their territories.[27] Nonetheless, the drafters had envisaged that some states, at times, would be disproportionately affected by refugee flows more than others, due to their geographic proximity to refugee producing regions.[28] The then Secretary General and the French delegation sought to remedy this imbalance in responsibilities that would arise in situations of large numbers of refugees by suggesting a provision on responsibility sharing in the operative part of the draft Convention that would correct the resulting unfairness. Draft Article 3, proposed by the Secretary General, read:

> [T]he High Contracting Parties shall to the fullest possible extent relieve the burden assumed by initial reception countries (…). They shall do so,

26 Betts, *Protection By Persua*sion (n 12) 13. Alexander Betts, Cathryn Costello, Natascha Zaun, 'A Fair Share; Refugees and Responsibility Sharing' (The Migration Studies Delegation) Report (Delmi 2017:10) <https://www.rsc.ox.ac.uk/publications/a-fair-share-refugees-and-responsibility-sharing> accessed 17 October 2024.

27 UNHCR, *The Refugee Convention 1951: The Travaux Preparatoires Analysed with a Commentary by Dr. Paul Weis* (1990) 15 <https://www.unhcr.org/uk/media/refugee-convention-1951-travaux-preparatoires-analysed-commentary-dr-paul-weis> accessed 17 October 2024.

28 Ibid.

> inter alia, by agreeing to receive a certain number of refugees in their territories.[29]

In the commentary that followed the draft provision, the rationale was fleshed out further:

> Owing to their geographical position and liberal traditions, some States are destined to become the initial reception countries for refugees. It is but just that other countries should not allow these to bear the whole burden and by agreeing to admit a certain number of refugees to their territory should assume their equitable share.[30]

Interestingly, the Secretary General added:

> Clearly no binding and precise obligations can be imposed on Governments – for example by specifying the extent to which they must agree to receive refugees on their territory. It is for this reason that the Article includes the deliberately vague form of words: 'a certain number of refugees'.[31]

The provision was not welcomed by the negotiating parties, which made clear that the Refugee Convention would only be limited to the rights and the duties of states *vis-à-vis* the refugees in their territories.[32] France insisted that the words 'international cooperation' should remain in the Preamble of the Convention, as it eventually did, because 'the protection of refugees', when a state is faced with a mass influx, 'becomes a problem of assistance and if there is no international cooperation, the refugee problem cannot be solved'.[33] Yet again, the French delegate was cautious to stress that the factual acknowledgement of the challenge the refugee problem places upon certain countries could not translate into a concomitant legal obligation to

29 UN Secretary General: *Ad Hoc Committee on Statelessness and Related Problems, 'Status of Refugees and Stateless Persons*: Memorandum by the Secretary-General (3 January 1950) UN Doc E/AC.32/2, Chapter II Admission, Article 3 para (2).

30 Ibid.

31 UN Secretary General: *Ad Hoc Committee on Statelessness and Related Problems, 'Status of Refugees and Stateless Persons:* Memorandum by the Secretary-General (3 January 1950) UN Doc E/AC.32/2 Chapter II Admission, Article 3 para (2) and following commentary.

32 Weiss, *Travaux Préparatoires & Commentary* (n 27) 15.

33 Weiss, *Travaux Préparatoires & Commentary* (n 27) 30.

provide such assistance.[34] China openly objected to the proposed provision that 'it was not in the position to accept refugees from other countries'.[35] The Canadian representative submitted that the distribution of refugees should not even be in the Preamble, as the draft Convention provides for legal obligations towards refugees and thus 'an acceptance of a decision on high policy was therefore unsuited to form part of a preamble to a convention conferring specified rights on specified categories of refugees'.[36] The U.S. representative agreed with France that there should in principle be some sort of international cooperation for overwhelmed asylum countries; however, such a provision should not be included in the preamble of a legally binding instrument.[37]

These extracts from the *Travaux Preparatoires* of the Refugee Convention illustrate the perennial reluctance to bring responsibility sharing within international law and the divergent views on what responsibility sharing entails that are representative of today's debates.

4 Terminology and Definitional Challenges in the Discourse of International Cooperation for Refugees

Defining terms is an important starting point for a productive discussion of most issues.[38] In the context of international cooperation for refugees, there are various terms that are used interchangeably by states, UNHCR, academics and policy makers often without defined content.[39] The terms 'international cooperation', 'solidarity', 'burden sharing' and 'responsibility sharing' are not

---

34 France's advocacy on the inclusion of a refugee redistribution clause in times of crisis had as a purpose to safeguard its own liberal asylum policies at the time and the smooth application of the Convention in practice. Due to its geographical position, France had been historically a haven for many refugees at the time. *Travaux Preparatoires & Commentary,* by Dr. Paul Weis, 19.

35 Weiss, *Travaux Préparatoires & Commentary* (n 27), 18.

36 Ibid.

37 Ibid, 26.

38 Benjamin Cook, 'Method in its Madness: The Endowment Effect in an Analysis of Refugee Burden Sharing and a Proposed Refugee Market' (2004) 19 Georgetown Immigration Law Journal 333, 335.

39 Claire Inder, 'The Origins of "Burden Sharing" in the Contemporary Refugee Protection Regime' (2017) 29 International Journal of Refugee Law 523, 554, https://doi.org/10.1093/ijrl/eex047; Suhrke 'Burden Sharing during Refugee Emergencies' (n 11) 399; Alexander Betts, Jean-Francois Durieux, 'Convention Plus as a Norm Setting Exercise' (2007) 20 Journal of Refugee Studies 509, 533, https://doi:10.1093/jrs/fem010.

employed by the various actors under a shared conceptual understanding. International refugee law does not define any of these terms. The fact that there is varied terminology is indicative of the complexity and the lack of consensus on what responsibility sharing entails. Hence, clarifying the various terms is a necessary analytical step.

A significant part of the debate surrounding these terms revolves around the linguistic connotations of each term rather than what counts as responsibility sharing. 'Burden sharing' for instance has been criticised for the negative and prejudicial connotation of the word 'burden' in the context of refugees.[40] Some commentators however have stressed that the term 'burden sharing' is terminologically more appropriate as it is the one used by states. Noll wrote back in 1997, that despite the negative connotation of the word 'burden', which implies that refugee protection is necessarily burdensome, 'burden sharing' is preferred, since '[o]ther, better terminological alternatives, have failed to gain entry into the language used by the actors of international law'.[41] Likewise, Inder, in a study on refugee burden sharing through the *Travaux Préparatoires* of the 1951 Refugee Convention, opted for 'burden sharing' in order to avoid further terminological confusion.[42]

The drafters of the 1951 Convention did not refer to a principle of 'burden sharing' explicitly but referred to 'international cooperation' and 'solidarity'. The Refugee Convention's Preamble recognises as a matter of fact that 'the grant of asylum may place an unduly heavy burden on certain countries' and calls upon states to cooperate and relieve such burdens.[43] The so-called principle of equitable or fair burden sharing only began to emerge in UNHCR's Executive Committee Conclusions and crystallized in the 1970s with the onset of the Indo-Chinese exodus.[44]

'Responsibility sharing', on the other hand, entered the discourse only in the 1990s.[45] Some commentators saw this shift in terminology as 'ill-advised'

40 Türk and Garlick, 'From Burdens and Responsibilities to Opportunities: The Comprehensive Refugee Response Framework and a Global Compact on Refugees' (n 7) 664.

41 Gregor Noll, '"Prisoners Dilemma" in Fortress Europe: On the Prospects for Equitable Burden Sharing in the European Union' (1997) 40 German Yearbook of International Law 405, footnote 2.

42 Inder, 'The Origins of "Burden Sharing" in the Contemporary Refugee Protection Regime' (n 39) 530.

43 Refugee Convention, Preamble, Recital 4.

44 UNHCR Executive Committee Conclusion No 15 (1979) 'Refugees Without an Asylum Country' para (f) 'the principle of equitable burden sharing'.

45 Türk and Garlick, 'From Burdens and Responsibilities to Opportunities: The Comprehensive Refugee Response Framework and a Global Compact on Refugees' (n 7) 664.

and responsible for 'obfuscating a better understanding of the normative content of burden sharing in practice'.[46] UNHCR, one of the biggest proponents of the term 'responsibility sharing', deemed the inclusion of this term in the broader context of international cooperation for refugees strategic. In one of its meetings during the Global Consultations on International Protection in 2001, UNHCR noted that '[t]he inclusion of "responsibility" along with "burden" sharing reflects a more positive image of refugees and a stronger framework for international cooperation [...]'.[47]

Türk and Garlick have explained why 'responsibility sharing' is the more appropriate term. Such wording contains an inherently positive value, '[a]s it casts refugees in a more favourable light as potential contributors and assets for their host societies and as the holder of rights that create correlating responsibilities for states'. Further, '"responsibility" can be seen to imply legal obligations and a requirement to take positive actions'.[48]

While UNHCR makes use of all the above terms, it has nonetheless flagged the risk that extensive analysis on terminology, considering the definitional imprecision,[49] if given too much linguistic attention, can eventually distract from substantive efforts on international cooperation in practice. In a meeting in Jordan, UNHCR commented:

> [I]t was felt that lengthy discussions on terminology (especially on the merits of "burden" versus "responsibility") at the expense of making concrete progress on enhancing international cooperation in practice needs to be avoided.[50]

States too have their terminological preferences, which are illustrative of their wider stance towards refugees. Ireland's Ambassador to the UN at the time of the negotiation and adoption of the New York Declaration on Migrants and

---

46 Inder, 'The Origins of "Burden Sharing" in the Contemporary Refugee Protection Regime' (n 39) 530.

47 UNHCR, Global Consultations on International Protection 'Mechanisms of International Cooperation to Share Responsibilities and Burdens in Mass Influx Situations', 1st Meeting, EC/GC/01/7 (19 February 2001), para 1.

48 Türk and Garlick, 'From Burdens and Responsibilities to Opportunities: The Comprehensive Refugee Response Framework and a Global Compact on Refugees' (n 7) 665.

49 Benjamin Cook, 'Method in its Madness, The Endowment Effect in an Analysis of Refugee Burden Sharing and a Proposed Refugee Market' (2004) 19 Georgetown Immigration Law Journal 334, 338.

50 UNHCR 'International Cooperation to Share the Burdens and Responsibilities: Summary Conclusions' (Expert Meeting, Amman, Jordan, 27–28 June 2011) Summary Conclusions Part A.

Refugees and the Global Compacts offered his insights from the negotiating experience.

> The concept of responsibility sharing is acceptable in effect to the Global North, it is not acceptable to states such as Russia, China, Egypt and other developing countries, they insist on burden sharing.[51]

Canada has even made use of the arguably more generous and symbolic term 'opportunity sharing'.[52] In practice, states and UNHCR – the latter so as to appeal to the former – make use of one single term 'responsibility and burden sharing' before various fora,[53] often for reasons of political and rhetorical expediency.[54] It is for this reason that the Global Compact on Refugees makes use of all terms. As one of its guiding principles, the Global Compact states:

> The global compact emanates from fundamental principles of humanity and international solidarity and seeks to operationalize the principles of burden- and responsibility-sharing to better protect and assist refugees and support host countries and communities.[55]

Regarding the term 'international cooperation', no widely accepted definition exists. Although variously used and deeply embedded within the UN Charter and the quest for multilateralism as means to resolve common problems and protect human rights,[56] its scope remains undefined.[57] Wolfrum, in his

---

51 David Donoghue, Closing Keynote Address at Annual Kaldor Conference 'The Global Compacts on Refugees and Migration', November 2017, at 8:14 <https://www.youtube.com/watch?v=bCwEMmqNQHM> accessed 17 October 2024.

52 Antonio Guterres, 'Closing Remarks at the Session of the 66th Executive Committee of the High Commissioner's Programme' speech delivered on the 9th October 2015 <https://www.unhcr.org/en-au/excom/speeches/562f4a5415/closing%20remarks-%2066th-session-executive-committee-high-commissioners-programme.html> accessed 17 October 2024.

53 Rebecca Dowd and Jane McAdam, 'International Cooperation and Responsibility Sharing to Protect Refugees: What, Why and How?' (2017) 66 International and Comparative Law Quarterly 863, 871 doi:10.1017/S0020589317000343.

54 Inder, 'The Origins of 'Burden Sharing' in the Contemporary Refugee Protection Regime' (n 39) 530.

55 UNGA Report of the United Nations High Commissioner on Refugees, Part II Global Compact on Refugees (2 August 2018) RES A/73/12, paragraph (5).

56 UN Charter, Article 1 para (3).

57 'The term cooperation has never been defined by an international treaty or a resolution of an international organization'. Rüdiger Wolfrum, 'Cooperation, International law of'

authoritative article on the Law of International Cooperation, defined international cooperation as 'the voluntary coordinated action of two or more states under a legal regime to accomplish a specific objective by joint action'.[58]

Given the vast spectrum of activities than can arguably fall within the scope of international cooperation and given its 'inherently opaque' nature,[59] a single universal definition could prove difficult to agree upon. Some conceptual clarity in the refugee context can be offered if international cooperation is seen as a broader concept, with responsibility or burden sharing as its objective, as arguably there is international cooperation that results in shifting rather than sharing responsibilities.[60]

This study adopts the term responsibility sharing for two reasons. Firstly, because even in terms of semantics, responsibility sharing casts refugees with a positive value and serves as a reminder of their human dignity. Secondly, responsibility sharing is a more assertive term and denotes most emphatically that refugee protection is a collective responsibility of the international community and not just the responsibility of the host states.

5 Defining Responsibility Sharing

What complicates further the challenge of filling the responsibility sharing gap is the lack of agreement and clarity on its content. In practice, responsibility sharing takes two main forms, financial sharing and physical or people sharing.[61]

Financial responsibility sharing entails the financing of refugee protection associated costs so that the rights of refugees guaranteed by the Refugee Con-

Max Plank Encyclopaedia of Public International Law <http://opil.ouplaw.com/view/10.1093/law:epil/9780199231690/law-9780199231690-e1427>.

58 Ibid.

59 Rebecca Dowd, Jane McAdam 'International Cooperation and Responsibility Sharing to Combat Climate Change: Lessons for International Refugee Law' (2017) 18 Melbourne Journal of International Law 180, 216.

60 Betts, Costello, Zaun 'A Fair Share; Refugees and Responsibility Sharing' (n 26) 20.

61 Hathaway, 'The Global Co-Op Out on Refugees' (n 8) 3. Noll identifies a third form of responsibility sharing in the context of the European Union the asylum policy harmonisation. Gregor Noll, 'Risky games? A theoretical Approach to Burden Sharing in the Asylum Field' (2003) 16 Journal of Refugee Studies 236. See also Hurwitz, *The Collective Responsibilities of States to Protect Refugees* (n 1) 147–56; Alexander Betts, 'International Cooperation in the Global Refugee Regime' Global Economic Governance Programme Working Paper (GEG 2008/44) (November 2008) 5 <https://www.geg.ox.ac.uk/sites/default/files/Betts_GEG%20WP%202008_44.pdf> accessed 17 October 2024.

vention are met in host countries. Financial sharing is primarily facilitated through voluntary donations of countries to UNHCR's humanitarian assistance programmes.[62] Under financial responsibility sharing comes the provision of refugee targeted development aid through bilateral or multilateral channels, technical assistance or capacity building in host countries.[63]

Physical or people sharing as it sometimes appears, refers to refugee relocation between states either for resettlement or through other pathways. Refugee sharing between states has been the least popular form of sharing as since the negotiation of the Refugee Convention states see it as a matter within their *domaine réservé*.

The Global Compact on Refugees broadened the scope of responsibility sharing significantly, further obfuscating a common conceptual understanding. Contributions to responsibility sharing can be made towards preventing displacement such as addressing root causes, technical assistance and capacity-building, information sharing and generally 'any other action that States and other actors have elected to take, for example, at the policy level through policies and practices to promote refugee inclusion or launching a new initiative'.[64] This has not only hindered analytical clarity but also broadened the scope of refugee responsibility sharing to matters going beyond the provision of international protection and solutions.

The root causes strategy that has been conventionally hailed as the appropriate response to refugees predominantly coming from the Global South has been challenged.[65] This strategy has been conceptually facilitated by the proc-

---

62 There have been regions specific mechanisms of financial responsibility sharing within regional asylum frameworks. In the EU for example, there has been the European Refugee Fund, an intra-EU financial compensation mechanism for refugee receiving frontline Member States. The European Refugee Fund was succeeded by the Asylum, Migration and Integration Fund (AMIF), which cannot however, be considered as a pure refugee responsibility sharing tool as its objectives cover all aspects of migration management at EU level. Regulation (EU) 2021/1147 of the European Parliament and of the Council of 7 July 2021 establishing the Asylum, Migration and Integration Fund.

63 UNGA Report of the United Nations High Commissioner on Refugees, Part II Global Compact on Refugees (2 August 2018) RES A/73/12. (Global Compact on Refugees); Global Compact on Refugees para 32.

64 Global Compact on Refuges, Part III.B serves as such non-exhaustive list of responsibility sharing tokens against areas of support. See also Explanatory text on the Global Compact on Refugees pledges dashboard. https://globalcompactrefugees.org/pledges-contributions/what-are-pledges.

65 BS Chimni, 'The Geopolitics of Refugee Protection A View from the South' (1998) 11 Journal of Refugee Studies 350, 351–352 https://doi.org/10.1093/jrs/11.4.350-a; Hurwitz, *The Collective Responsibility of States to Protect Refugees* (n 1) 154.

lamation of 'the right to remain', which has had the consequence of deemphasizing the right to seek asylum.[66] The fact that the Global Compact on Refugees has reduced the right to asylum in a footnote is illustrative of this dominant approach.[67] The right to remain, precisely because it is conditioned upon some sort of intervention to prevent flight in the first place, ultimately negates the palliative nature of refugee protection.[68] What is more, such contributions do not correct the resulting unfair distribution of refugee-related responsibilities between states.

This study adopts a conception of responsibility sharing that is considerably narrower than the one found in the Global Compact on Refugees. Most scholarly proposals that advocate for legal commitments to responsibility sharing also put forward a narrower conception of sharing that is predominantly limited to the financing of refugee protection costs through humanitarian or development aid and to refugee relocation through resettlement and other admission pathways.[69] This is because only these two forms of sharing have the potential to redistribute refugee-related responsibilities more equitably between states. What is more, this narrower conception of responsibility sharing better aligns with the palliative nature of refugee protection and the humanitarian scope of the 1951 Convention. As a result, contributions towards policy harmonisation, political support in countries of origin, addressing root causes, exchange of personnel, research and expertise between states should fall outside the scope of the responsibility sharing taking place under the Refugee Convention.

6 The Global Compact on Refugees: Reframing Refugee Protection as a Common but Differentiated Responsibility

Interest in formalising responsibility sharing under a framework that allocates a fair share of responsibilities between states has ebbed and flowed every time

66 Hathaway, Neve 'Making International Refugee Law Relevant Again' (n 10) 133.

67 Global Compact on Refugees, para 5 footnote 5.

68 Hathaway, Neve, 'Making International Refugee Law Relevant Again' (n 10) 140; Chimni, 'The Geopolitics of Refugee Studies' (n 10) 351–352.

69 Hathaway, Neve 'Making International Refugee Law Relevant Again' (n 10) 115; Peter Schuck, 'Refugee Burden Sharing: A Modest Proposal' (1997) 22 Yale Journal of International Law 243; Model International Mobility Convention International Convention on the Rights and Duties of All Persons Moving from One State to Another and of the States they Leave, Transit or Enter by the Model International Mobility Commission (2018) 56 Columbia Journal of Transnational Law 342.

a mass influx of refugees has challenged the dynamics and put pressure on frontline states, making the protection of refugees conditioned upon assistance. The Syrian refugee exodus and the large-scale arrivals of migrants and refugees from Africa to European shores in 2015–2016 led the international community to the negotiating table to respond to the challenge of forced displacement as well as migration in a concerted way. While in the past, the international community's response had been *ad hoc*, the momentum in 2016 was such that an instrument vesting responsibility sharing under a formal structure had to be concluded.[70]

The New York Declaration for Refugees and Migrants adopted in 2016 sought to identify ways to balance inequities in the way refugee responsibilities are shared and to meet the increasing assistance needs of Southern host states.[71] The adoption of the Declaration was hailed as a key moment in the recent history of global refugee protection,[72] negotiated and endorsed by 196 States, setting, *inter alia*, the direction for global refugee policy in relation to responsibility sharing.

The Global Compact on Refugees followed and was adopted in 2018. Interestingly, the Compact was originally intended to be concluded as the 'Global Compact on Responsibility Sharing for Refugees', but in order to secure the widest consensus and adoption, the term 'responsibility sharing' was dropped from the title.[73] Although non-binding,[74] the Compact establishes certain political commitments with an objective to achieve 'a more equitable and predictable burden and responsibility sharing with host countries and communities'.[75]

---

70 On ad hoc responses to responsibility sharing challenges, see discussion in Chapter 4.

71 New York Declaration for Refugees and Migrants UN Doc A/RES/71/1 (3 October 2016).

72 UN Summit for Refugees and Migrants 19 September 2016 <https://refugeesmigrants.un.org/summit> accessed 17 October 2024.

73 See Zero Draft of the Global Compact on Responsibility Sharing for Refugees, 30 June 2016, http://www.unhcr.org/events/conferences/578369114/zero-draft-global-compact-responsibility-sharing-refugees.html. The Compact was adopted with two objections by the United States and Hungary and two abstentions by Eritrea and Libya. Filippo Grandi, 'The Global Compact on Refugees: A Historic Achievement' (2019) 57 International Migration UN IOM, 23.

74 Global Compact on Refugees, para 4.

75 Global Compacts on Refugees, para 4 and 15. Gilbert also argues that the non-legally binding nature of the Compact does not entail the absence of commitments for refugees, even if political. Geoff Gilbert, 'Not Bound but Committed: Operationalising the Global Compact on Refugees' (2019) 59 International Migration IOM 27, 29 https://doi.org/10.1111/imig.12632.

Building on the New York Declaration, the Global Compact on Refugees framed refugee responsibility sharing within the logic of a 'common but differentiated' responsibility. The Compact reinstates the common responsibility to protect refugees, whose predicament is acknowledged as 'the common concern of humankind',[76] while envisaging a bottom-up differentiation where states determine their contributions to international protection on the basis of 'their national realities, capacities and levels of development, and respecting national policies and priorities'.[77]

It is said that the Compact's language draws from the international environmental law principle of 'common but differentiated responsibilities and respective capabilities' (CBDRRC), which framed responsibility sharing for environmental protection, with its most popular application the treaty regime on climate change.[78] Some scholarly commentary that followed the adoption of the Declaration and the Compact noted this reframing, while others looked at international environmental law to distil the essence and contours of this principle.[79] That said, scholarly proposals that advocate for the principle of CBDRRC to international refugee law have not engaged with the fairness *problematique* it carries.[80]

While it was the first time in UN refugee policy that refugee protection was reframed as a common but differentiated responsibility, it was not the first time refugee law scholars engaged with the principle of international environmental law. Hathaway and Neve were the first to explicitly advocate for a 'common but differentiated responsibility' framework to guide a fair allocation of responsibility sharing contributions.[81] A logic of differentiated protec-

76 Global Compact on Refugees, para 1.

77 Global Compact on Refugees, para 1 and 4.

78 Common but differentiated responsibilities and respective capabilities was first formulated as Principle 7 in the 1992 Rio Declaration on Environment and Development. Report of the United Nations Conference on the Environment and Development, Annex I Rio Declaration on Environment and Development, UNGA A/CONF.151/26 (Vol. I) (August 1992). See further discussion in Chapter 6.

79 See McAdam, 'International Cooperation and Responsibility Sharing to Protect Refugees: What, Why and How' (n 53) 885; Dowd, McAdam, 'International Cooperation and Responsibility Sharing to Combat Climate Change: Lessons from International Climate Change Law' (n 59) 180; Patrick Wall, 'A New Link in the Chain: Could a Framework Convention for Refugee Responsibility Sharing Fulfil the Promise of the 1967 Protocol?' (2017) 2 International Journal of Refugee Law 201 https://doi.org/10.1093/ijrl/eex025.

80 Here it is emphasized that the comment is addressed to legal scholarship as there are major scholarly accounts on justice and refugee protection from other fields such as ethics, political science and international relations.

81 Hathaway, Neve, 'Making International Refugee Law Relevant Again' (n 10) 118.

tion responsibilities based on states' capacities can be found in the predetermined quotas proposed by Grahl-Madsen in his 1960s Plan to correct the then disproportionate refugee distribution at regional level,[82] in Schuck's predetermined quotas against national wealth[83] and in Gibney's integrative capabilities principle.[84] What these proposals have in common is that they seek to redistribute asylum-related responsibilities against objective capacities and correct the resulting unfairness.

This explicit reframing of refugee protection as a common but differentiated responsibility within the Refugee Compact is however significant, as it represents yet another evidence on the community interest nature of refugee protection that this book advances.[85] It is also important because the Compact brought the discourse on the fairness of the international refugee regime back into the spotlight.[86] Whether borrowing from international environmental law's language was intentional or just a result of negotiations towards a flexible yet tangible responsibility sharing arrangement is not known. What is known, and what this book advances, is that the principle of CBDRRC is the doctrinal expression of the practice of differential treatment in international environmental law. The practice of differential treatment is today structurally embedded within multilateral treaties and it has been the legal device for accommodating existing inequalities within multilateral legal regimes on resource and burden allocation. What is more, it is today part and parcel of international cooperation and responsibility sharing at UN level and as such it was high time it crept into refugee law and policy.[87]

To conclude, despite the laudable efforts to reframe and operationalise responsibilitysharing under new modalities, the Global Compact on Refugees cannot fill the responsibilitysharing gap left by the Refugee Convention. The gap will remain for as long as there is a 'disjuncture' between the institutional obligation of the international community to protect refugees and the legal obligations on the part of individual states.[88] The only way to sync the two is

82 Atle Grahl-Madsen, 'Further Development of International Refugee Law' (1965) 35 Nordic Journal of International Law, 172.

83 Schuck, 'Refugee Burden Sharing: A Modest Proposal' (n 69) 277.

84 Matthew J Gibney, 'Refugees and Justice Between States' (2015) 14 European Journal of Political Theory 448, 456 https://doi.org/10.1177/1474885115585332.

85 See Chapter 2.

86 David Cantor, 'Fairness Failure and the Refugee Regime' (2019) International Journal of Refugee Law 627 https://doi.org/10.1093/ijrl/eey069.

87 See Chapter 5.

88 Guy Goodwin Gill, Jane McAdam, Emma Dunlop, *The Refugee in International Law* (Oxford University Press 2021) 51. See further discussion in Chapter 2.

by making the necessary 'structural adjustment'[89] to the international refugee law regime. Against this premise, the book advances a detailed proposal on why a Protocol on Refugee Responsibility Sharing is necessary and how such Protocol could strike the necessary balance between principle and pragmatism.

7 Legal Positivism and the Study of International Refugee Law

The way in which international law scholars theorise international law lays bare, 'the set of assumptions each international lawyer has on what the world is like, and more specifically, what international law is like'.[90] Traditionally, refugee law scholarship, like general international law scholarship, has been dominated by the jurisprudence of legal positivism.[91] Under legal positivism, international refugee law is a self-contained regime of rules, objectively identified and applied by states and international organisations.[92] In fact, legal positivism combined with a human rights approach to refugee law – denoting that the focus is on sources, and the content of rules and their enforceability[93] – has been the dominant approach to the study of refugee law; at least the kind of scholarship undertaken by the majority of refugee lawyers.[94] Under the human rights paradigm, international human rights law reinforces refugee protection by providing a rights-based framework, thus giving full meaning to the 'right to seek and enjoy asylum' in international law.[95]

89 Marjoleine Zeick, 'Doomed to Fail from the Outset? UNHCR's Convention Plus Initiative Revisited' (2009) 21 International Journal of Refugee Law 387, 413 https://doi.org/10.1093/ijrl/eep011.

90 Jan Klabbers *International Law* (Cambridge University Press 2017, second edition) 3.

91 Chimni, 'The Geopolitics of Refugee Studies, a View from the South' (n 64) 352.

92 Hélène Lambert, 'International Refugee Law: Dominant and Emerging Approaches' in D Armstrong (ed) *Routledge Handbook of International Law* (London Routledge 2009) 344.

93 Ibid.

94 Legal positivism remains the dominant approach in the practice of international law taken by international lawyers. Robert Cryer, Tamara Harvey, Bal Sohki-Bulley, Alexandra Bohm, *Research Methodologies in European and International Law* (Hart Publishing 2011) 38.

95 Lambert, 'International Refugee Law: Dominant and Emerging Approaches' (n 91) 348. The right to seek and enjoy asylum is provided in Article 14 of the 1948 Universal Declaration of Human Rights. Universal Declaration of Human Rights (adopted 10 December 1948 UNGA Res 217 A(III).

Unsurprisingly, the positivist tradition to refugee law has not gone unchallenged by scholars from critical legal studies.[96] Amongst the critics, Chimni, a proponent of the Third World Approaches (TWAIL) school of thought, has criticised legal positivism for its 'over reliance on the sources of law to validate a claim' and its state-centred focus, 'which eschews any engagement with politics'.[97] TWAIL scholars contend that international law has developed to serve a 'neo-liberal western vision of the world' and, therefore, it is 'playing a crucial role in helping legitimize and sustain the unequal structures and processes'.[98] Specifically in the refugee context, it has also failed to articulate a more comprehensive and humane response to the contemporary refugee problem through dialogue with the Third World.[99] What is more, it has been argued that the positivist tradition to refugee law has been complicit to the justification of externalisation and asylum restriction policies.[100]

7.1 *Enlightened Legal Positivism: International Law as Protecting Community Interests and Promoting Global Justice*

Positivism, like any other epistemological method, has undergone considerable development since the 19th century, when it first emerged and established itself as the dominant jurisprudential school. To use a vivid quote, legal positivism is no longer equated with 'old fashioned, conservative, continental European nineteenth century views – naïve ideas of dead white males on the objectivity of law and morals'.[101] International legal positivism has, over the years, softened across a spectrum. Softer versions of legal positivism espouse a more progressive view of the role of international law in the quest for

96 The term 'critical legal studies' is used here rather loosely. I do not distinguish between the various schools of critical studies, namely 'post modernism', 'new stream' and 'Critical' scholarship. For a detailed appraisal of the critical legal studies in international law, See Anne Marie Slaughter, Steven Ratner, 'Symposium on Method in International Law, Appraising the Methods of International Law, A Prospectus for the Readers' (1999) 93 The American Journal of International Law 291; Andreas L Paulus, 'International Law After Postmodernism: Towards Renewal or Decline of International Law? (2001) 14 Leiden Journal of International Law 727 https://doi.org/10.1017/S092215650100036X.

97 Chimni, 'The Geopolitics of Refugee Studies: A View from the South' (n 64) 353.

98 Ibid., 369.

99 Ibid.

100 Ibid. See also Antony Angie, 'Rethinking International Law: A TWAIL Retrospective' European Journal of International Law 76.

101 Bruno Simma, Andrea Paulus, 'The Responsibility of Individuals for Human Rights Abuses in Internal Conflicts: A Positivist's View' (1999) 93 American Journal of International Law 302, 308 https://doi.org/10.2307/2997991.

global justice, whilst eschewing some of the deficiencies of the classic legal positivism highlighted by its very critics.

In the scholarship of Bruno Simma and Andreas Paulus, one comes across a normative version of legal positivism, which reflects the thesis that international law is not and cannot be independent of the political and social context in which it operates.[102] Simma argues that there exists an international community of states with shared values and interests, and that community 'comprises not only of states, but in the last instance of all human beings'.[103] For Simma, the emergence of community interests at the time had 'begun to change the nature of international law profoundly'.[104] This thesis, which was developed at the turn of the millennium, reflects a cosmopolitan thinking in international law, even if covertly under the veil of legal positivism.[105] Even those who subscribe to conventional legal positivist understandings of law as a system of rules strictly regulating the relationship between states, nonetheless cannot rebut that, in regulating these interstate relationships, international law directly protects human rights,[106] the environment, the deep ocean seabed and its resources,[107] cultural heritage[108] and biodiversity,[109] all widely acknowledged expressions of community interests.[110]

Simma developed an empirical approach to the identification and generation of community interests rooted in state consent. Community interests are

---

102 Ibid.

103 Bruno Simma, 'From Bilateralism to Community Interest in International Law' in *Collected Courses of The Hague Academy of International Law* (Hague Academy of International Law 1994) 234.

104 Ibid. Emphasis added.

105 Steven Ratner, 'From Enlightened Positivism to Cosmopolitan Justice Obstacles and Opportunities' in Fastenrath G, Khan P, Von Schorlemer V (eds) *From Bilateralism to Community Interest: Essays in Honour of Bruno Simma* (Oxford University Press 2011) 162.

106 One example is the International Covenant on Civil and Political Rights (adopted 16 December 1966, entered into force 23 March 1976) 999 UNTS 171 (ICCPR).

107 *Responsibilities and Obligations of States Sponsoring Persons and Entities with Respect to Activities in the Area* (Advisory Opinion) [1 February 2011] ITLOS Reports 2011, para. 180.

108 UNESCO Convention Concerning the Protection of the World Cultural and Natural Heritage (adopted 16 November 1972, entered into force 16 November 1972) 1972 ILM 1358.

109 Convention on International Trade in Endangered Species of Wild Fauna and Flora (adopted 3 March 1973, entered into force 1 July 1975) 1973 12 ILM 1085.

110 Simma 'From Bilateralism to Community Interest' (n 103) 236–243; Santiago Villapaldo, 'The Legal Dimension of the International Community: How Community Interests Are Protected in International Law' (2010) 21 European Journal of International Law 387, 394 https://doi.org/10.1093/ejil/chq038; Eyal Benvenisti, Georg Nolte, 'Introduction' in Eyal Benvenisti, Georg Nolte (eds) *Community Interests Across International Law* (Oxford University Press 2018), 4.

reflected in the 'consensus according to which respect for certain fundamental values is not to be left at the free disposition of States individually or inter se but is recognised and sanctioned by international law as a matter of concern to all States'.[111] What qualifies as community interest therefore stems from international law itself and from the agendas and work of the various UN bodies and conferences. Similar to Simma, Wolfrum suggests that the qualification of community interests is a *quasi*-legislative decision of the international community, one that is firstly 'factually well-founded and secondly accepted in a legitimizing process'.[112] For example, the concern for human rights in the UN Charter[113] and the near-universal participation in UN human rights treaties are compelling evidence of the community interest nature of human rights.[114] Besson, too, identifies legitimacy expressed through state consent as one crucial condition towards the identification of community interests in international law.[115]

The widespread or, in certain cases, near-universal consent that a particular matter reflects a community interest is usually found in treaties codifying collective obligations (owed to all parties to the treaty) or obligations owed to the international community as a whole (*obligations erga omnes*).[116] Community interests are also reflected in regimes that provide for 'non-directed' responsibilities like those arising from 'common concern' or 'common heritage' principles predominantly found in the international law of the sea and

---

111 Simma, 'From Bilateralism to Community Interest in International law' (n 103) 236–237.

112 Rüdiger Wolfrum, 'Identifying Community Interests in International Law: Common Spaces and Beyond' in Benvenisti, Nolte, *Community Interests Across International Law* (n 109) 20.

113 United Nations Charter 1945 XV UNCIO 335, amendments in 557 UNTS 143, 638 UNTS 308 and 892 UNTS 119 Article 1 (3). (United Nations Charter).

114 Wolfrum, 'Identifying Community Interests in International Law: Common Spaces and Beyond' (n 112) 29; Sarah Thin, 'In Search of Community: Towards a Definition of Community Interest', in Gentian Zyberi (ed.), *Protecting Community Interests through International Law (Intersentia 2021)* 11, 29.

115 Samantha Besson 'Community Interests in International Law; Whose Interests are they and How Should We Best Identify Them?' in Benvenisti, Nolte, *Community Interests Across International Law* (n 109) 48.

116 *Barcelona Traction, Light and Power Company, Limited (Belgium v. Spain) (Judgment)* [1970] ICJ Rep 3, para 33. On obligations *erga omnnes and erga omnes partes*, see Maurizio Ragazzi, The Concept of International Obligations Erga Omnes (CUP 1997); Christian Tomuschat and Jean Marc Thouvenin (eds), The Fundamental Rules of the International Legal Order: Jus Cogens and Obligations Erga Omnes (Martinus Nijhoff 2006); Christian J Tams, Enforcing Obligations *Erga Omnes* in International Law (CUP 2005); Christian J Tams, 'Individual States as Guardians of Community Interests, in *From Bilateralism to Community Interest Essays in Honour of Bruno Simma* (n 102) 379.

international environmental law.[117] The specific means to the protection of a community interest further depend on how it is normatively articulated and implemented in multilateral treaties and customary international law.[118] What is important to note is that community interests are not manifested only in areas beyond national territories and jurisdiction where, in theory, all states have an interest in their protection or use – such as the deep seabed or outer space – but are equally advanced within seemingly territorial activities, such as the protection of biodiversity and human rights.[119] Human rights treaties, for example, are today widely accepted as codifying obligations that are owed to the international community of states or in the case of regional human rights treaties to all parties.

The characterisation of treaty obligations as *erga omnes* or *erga omnes partes* is not only a methodological outlook but has distinct legal consequences regarding state responsibility in international law. As the ICJ famously put it in its *obiter dicta* in *Barcelona Traction Case* and as confirmed in subsequent cases before it, good faith implementation and compliance with such obligations is the concern of all states and hence all states have a legal interest in their protection and a concomitant legal right to invoke responsibility under the rules of state responsibility in cases of breach.[120]

The Court has recognised and pronounced the *erga omnes* nature of the prohibition and punishment of genocide,[121] the 'principles and rules concerning the basic rights of the human person, including protection from slavery

117 Tams (n 116) 379.

118 For a discussion on how international organisations formulate and promote community interests, See Jan Klabbers, 'What Role for International Organizations in the Promotion of Community Interests? Reflection on the Ideology of Functionalism' in Benvenisti, Nolte, *Community Interests Across International Law* (n 110) 86.

119 Wolfrum, 'Identifying Community Interests in International Law: Common Spaces and Beyond' (n 111) 20.

120 *Barcelona Traction,* para 33; See also indicatively *East Timor* (*Portugal v. Australia*), *Judgment, I.C.J. Reports 1995,* p. 90 para. 29; *Legality of the Threat or Use of Nuclear Weapons, Advisory Opinion, I.C.J. Reports 1996,* p. 226, para. 83; *Application of the Convention on the Prevention and Punishment of the Crime of Genocide* (*Bosnia and Herzegovina v. Serbia and Montenegro*),*Preliminary Objections, Judgment, I.C.J. Reports 1996,* p. 595 paras. 31–32; *Application of the Convention on the Prevention and Punishment of the Crime of Genocide* (*The Gambia v. Myanmar*) (Order of 23 January 2020) ICJ Rep 3, para 41. Regarding legal standing for serious breaches of international law see ILC Draft Articles on State Responsibility with Commentaries, vol II (Part Two) Yearbook of the International Law Commission 2001; (ARSIWA) Article 48 1 (b).

121 *Questions relating to the Obligation to Prosecute or Extradite* (*Belgium v. Senegal*), *Judgment, I.C.J. Reports 2012, p. 422,* para 69.

and racial discrimination'[122] and certain rules of international humanitarian law.[123] It thus becomes apparent that community interest obligations are primarily but not exclusively found in primary rules of international law that are widely recognised to have attained the status of customary international law or even *jus cogens*.[124] *Jus cogens* norms in particular represent the doctrinal expression of 'the core of community obligations in international law'.[125] As the International Law Commission noted in its codification of the law of state responsibility, treaties that set general standards of protection of a group of people transcend the bilateral interests of states as they have been concluded to foster 'a common interest over and above any interests of the states concerned individually'.[126] Hence, as collective obligations, their breach may give rise to any state party to the Convention to invoke the responsibility of another State.[127]

7.2 *Refugee Protection as a Community Interest and the Quest for Fairness: The Case for a Methodology*

International refugee law has not but marginally been studied from a community interests perspective.[128] Kritzman Amir did inquire into the potential community interest of international refugee law and found that the international refugee regime today goes beyond 'a set of consent-based norms' and the perennial quest for fair responsibility sharing is evidence of the community interest nature of refugee protection that requires 'a community to

122 *Barcelona Traction*, para 44; *Reservations to the Convention on Genocide, Advisory Opinion ICJ. Reports 1951, p.15*, p. 23.

123 *Legal Consequences of the Construction of a Wall in the Occupied Palestinian Territory (Advisory Opinion)* [2004] *ICJ Rep 136*, para. 155; *Armed Activities on the Territory of the Congo (DRC v. Uganda) (Judgment)* [2005] *ICJ Rep 168* and in particular Separate Opinion of Judge Simma, para. 37.

124 The International Law Commission Report on Peremptory Norms of General International Law includes the following norms: (a) The prohibition of aggression; (b) The prohibition of genocide; (c) The prohibition of crimes against humanity; (d) The basic rules of international humanitarian law; (e) The prohibition of racial discrimination and apartheid; (f) The prohibition of slavery; (g) The prohibition of torture; (h) The right of self-determination. See UNGA res A/74/10 (20 August 2019) Annex to the Draft Conclusions on Peremptory Norms of General International Law (Jus Cogens) 208 (Draft Conclusions on Peremptory Norms of General International Law).

125 George Nolte, 'The International Law Commission and Community Interests', in Benvenisti and Nolte (n 109), 104.

126 ARSIWA with Commentaries, Article 48 1 (a) para 7.

127 Ibid.

128 Tally Kritzman-Amir, 'Community Interests in International Migration and Refuge law' in Benvenisti and Nolte *Community Interests Across International Law* (n 110) 341, 356.

solve'.[129] Goodwin-Gill and McAdam have recognised in the law and practice of the Security Council related to refugees, forced displacement and international crimes, that there exist 'certain elements in an emerging community interest'.[130]

This book adopts an enlightened positivist methodology to the study of international cooperation and responsibility sharing for refugees. From the vantage point of enlightened positivism, the book puts forward two claims. Firstly, the protection of refugees is a community interest of international law. This is confirmed by the existence of refugees as a distinct legal category of individuals in international law for whom states have enacted a dedicated treaty regime with widespread ratification and participation. The international consensus on the community interest nature of refugee protection is further evidenced by the near-universal participation to the Refugee Convention and Protocol and in UNHCR's international protection mandate and its role as the institutional trustee of the community interest.[131] According to the International Law Commission, treaty obligations established by a group of states in the protection of some wider common, collective interest, are collective obligations in the sense that they transcend the parties' bilateral relations.[132] The Refugee Convention falls within this category of treaties laying down a regime of 'collective obligations' that sets the standards of treatment and rights owed to refugees, by which in the case of breach, any state party has a right to invoke the responsibility of another state.[133]

Secondly, questions of fairness between states are not only integral to the debate on how to share refugee protection responsibilities more equitably between states but normatively permeate international law, the role of which is to contribute, albeit modestly to global justice. As a result, the global refugee law regime does not operate in isolation and cannot insulate itself from broader questions of global justice.[134] What this chapter illustrated is that in the absence of a responsibility sharing framework that corrects the consequences of geography, the international refugee law regime exacerbates existing inequalities undermining fairness between states. To this end, the *de lege ferenda* proposal on a Protocol on Refugee Responsibility Sharing engages with the discourse on fairness and its role in international law and demon-

129 Ibid. 355.
130 Goodwin-Gill, McAdam, Dunlop, *The Refugee in International Law* (n 88) 5.
131 See Chapter 2.
132 ARSIWA with Commentaries, Article 48 1 (a) para 7.
133 Ibid.
134 Gibney, 'Refugees and Justice between States' (n 84) 359.

strates how fairness considerations can be accommodated within a legally binding instrument on responsibility sharing.

The parallel study of the principle of CBDRRC in environmental and climate change law is instrumental and also part of the methodology. Firstly, it serves to gain a well-rounded understanding of the origins, potential and limitations of the principle as an expression of fairness in multilateral law-making. Secondly, and borrowing from Thomas Franck, international environmental law is a field where 'much institutional and normative creativity has taken place', illustrative of the broader 'fairness *problematique* in contemporary international law'.[135] The proposed Protocol on Refugee Responsibility Sharing draws inspiration from the international legal regime on climate change and specifically from the Paris Agreement on Climate Change as an example of a model treaty on responsibilitysharing.

8 The Structure of the Book

The book is structured in two Parts and eight Chapters. **Chapter 1** introduces the responsibility sharing gap of the Refugee Convention, the scholarly debate on responsibilitysharing and the methodology of enlightened legal positivism to the study of refugee law. **Chapter 2** makes the case for the community interest nature of refugee protection and through a doctrinal analysis it traces the origins and legal foundations of international cooperation and responsibility sharing in international refugee law. The chapter also includes a cursory reading of the main regional refugee instruments and their approaches to responsibility sharing. The regional refugee systems in Africa, Latin America and the EU illustrate how responsibility sharing for refugee protection has been institutionalised in various legal and non-legal structures.

Chapter 3 looks at how states have implemented the duty to cooperate towards fair responsibility by critically looking into some of the most questionable practices of international cooperation on migration and asylum management. It argues that these arrangements are examples of international cooperation that go against the Refugee Convention, not only because they constitute a bad faith implementation of the duty to cooperate, which is tantamount to responsibility shifting, but also because they have resulted in refugee rights violations at states' borders and refugee containment in the Global South.

135 Thomas Franck *Fairness in International Law and Institutions,* (Oxford University Press 1995) 355. Footnote omitted.

Chapter 4 discusses instances of international cooperation that have made a positive contribution to refugee protection and have sought to redistribute responsibilities between states in cases of mass influx. The Comprehensive Plan of Action for Indo-Chinese Refugees (CPA) and the International Conference on Central American Refugees (CIREFCA) were two overall successful instances of responsibility sharing in the practice of states from which one can draw elements of best practice that can have universal application. The chapter also discusses the UN Convention Plus Initiative as a multilateral process not entirely dissimilar to the Global Compact on Refugees before concluding with an analysis of the current modalities and processes of responsibility sharing envisaged in the Compact.

Part 2 is dedicated to the *de lege ferenda* proposal on a Protocol on Responsibility Sharing. Chapters 5 and 6 accommodate a parallel study of international environmental law. **Chapter 5** traces the practice of differential treatment as an application of fairness in international law. The chapter argues that elements of differentiation, either at the level of treaty obligations or treaty implementation, permeate international law and that differential treatment has been the legal device for accommodating existing inequalities within multilateral legal regimes on resource and burden allocation. This is illustrated by the discussion of differential practice in international trade law, international law of the sea, international human rights law and international environmental law where CBDRRC was explicitly articulated as a guiding principle.

Chapter 6 zooms further into international environmental law and studies the unique trajectory of the CBDRRC principle in the international legal regime on climate change. As one of the most progressive responsibility sharing regimes in international law, it serves as a case study on how vexed matters of fairness and differentiation have been structurally integrated within a multilateral treaty through the principle of CBDRRC. The chapter focuses on the Paris Agreement and the operationalisation of the CBDRRC thereunder as it illustrates the art of the possible for a protocol on refugee responsibility sharing that would optimise fair sharing and codify a light package of responsibility sharing obligations.

Chapter 7 puts forward a *de lege ferenda* proposal for a Protocol on Responsibility Sharing that would complement the Refugee Convention and the 1976 Protocol and fill in the responsibility sharing gap. The proposal builds on previous reform proposals and draws from certain elements and processes set in motion by the Global Compact on Refugees. Under the proposed Protocol, responsibility sharing would be structured against a minimal package of common but differentiated legal obligations. In adapting the CBDRRC to international refugee law, the enquiry engages with the fairness *problematique* inherent to the principle and explores the role of fairness in the international refugee law regime. Drawing inspiration from international climate change law instruments, questions of legal design are explored in detail. The proposed Protocol offers a modest solution on how vexed matters of fairness, differentiation in resources and capacities and prescriptiveness of the obligations can be accommodated within a single legal architecture.

Chapter 8 summarises the thread of the argument and offers concluding remarks. It reinstates the need for legal development as one means towards a more equitable and fair sharing of refugee responsibilities between states. It also responds to anticipated criticisms relating to the proposal's feasibility in the current political climate and explains why it is possible to find the 'sweet spot' between principle and pragmatism.

CHAPTER 2

The Legal Framework on International Cooperation and Responsibility Sharing on Refugees

1 Refugee Protection as a Community Interest

1.1 *The 1951 Refugee Convention*

The international community has historically treated refugee protection as a community interest. The existence of refugees as a distinct legal category of individuals in international law is the first such evidence. Even before the establishment of the UN, under the auspices of the League of Nations in the 1920s, various group-based categories were recognised by the international community as refugees and, as such, in need of international protection and assistance by the international community, which was facilitated through the conclusion of interstate arrangements on the various categories of interest.[1]

Initially established to provide legal and political protection to Russian refugees only, the Nansen International Office for Refugees, in the years that followed, extended its mandate to include Armenians, Assyrians, refugees from the Greco-Turkish wars and, later, the Jews fleeing Germany.[2] In 1943, the Allies established the United Nations Relief and Rehabilitation Administration to provide relief to those displaced by the war and to assist with repatriation for those who wanted it.[3] In 1946, with still many unable or unwilling to return, the UN General Assembly created the International Refugee Organisation (IRO), a temporary specialised agency to deal with the refugee problem created by the Second World War – a problem proclaimed in IRO's constitution to be 'international in scope and character'.[4] The community interest

1 Guy Goodwin Gill, Jane McAdam, Emma Dunlop, *The Refugee in International Law* (Oxford University Press 2021) 16.

2 Arrangement relating to the Legal Status of Russian and Armenian Refugees (signed 30 June 1928) 2004 LNTS 48; Convention Relating to the International Status of Refugees (signed 28 October 1933) 3663 LNTS; Provisional Arrangement Concerning the Status of Refugees Coming from Germany (signed 4 July 1936) 3952 LNTS 77.

3 On UNRRA work, See George Woodbridge, *UNRRA: The History of the United Nations Relief and Rehabilitation Administration* (Columbia University Press 1950 3 Vols).

4 1946 Constitution of the International Refugee Organisation 18 UNTS 3; UNGA res 62/1 (I–II) Refugees and displaced persons (15 December 1946) Preamble.

 | DOI:10.1163/9789004547711_003

nature of refugee protection was further confirmed in the post-IRO era and during the negotiations of the Refugee Convention.

Beyond the universal refugee definition,[5] the 1951 Convention entrusts the asylum state to provide a set of civil, social and economic rights to refugees, gradually accruing over time as the bond with the asylum state gets stronger.[6] The Refugee Convention and the Protocol have today been signed and ratified by 146 and 147 states accordingly out of 196 UN Members. This arguably widespread participation to the treaty reflects the legislative decision of the international community that the protection of refugees is a collective responsibility,[7] and the Refugee Convention is the treaty regime whereby the community interest is normatively articulated and implemented. The case for the community interest nature of refugee protection is also supported by the *ratio legis* of the Refugee Convention. The claim to asylum as surrogacy protection[8] is the claim to a collective protection system 'through the host community as a mere consequence of exclusion by the home community'.[9] The international community intervenes and restores the severance of the bond between the individual and the state through the state of asylum, ensuring his safety and dignity; the 'right to have rights'.[10]

1.2 *UNHCR as the Institutional Trustee of the Community Interest*

The case for the community interest nature of refugee protection is strengthened by the very existence of a UN special agency tasked with protection. States establish international organisations that are tasked with specific community interests acting either as platforms for the promotion and cooperation of the interest they represent or are explicitly mandated to protect the interest through the adoption of quasi-legal resolutions and related instru-

5 The 1967 Protocol contains the same definition which removed the geographical and temporal limitation of the Refugee Convention, thereby making the definition universal.

6 On the gradual attachment to the asylum state and the accrual of refugee rights, see James C Hathaway, *The Rights of Refugees in International Law* (Cambridge University Press 2021) 176–218.

7 Rüdiger Wolfrum, 'Identifying Community Interests in International Law: Common Spaces and Beyond' in Eyal Benvenisti, Georg Nolte, 'Introduction' in Eyal Benvenisti, Georg Nolte (eds) *Community Interests Across International Law* (Oxford University Press 2018) 22.

8 On the nature of international protection as surrogate and on the challenges the notion of surrogacy presents, See discussion in Goodwin-Gill, McAdam, Dunlop, *The Refugee in International Law* (n 1) 8–9.

9 Gregor Noll, *Negotiating Asylum: The EU Acquis, Extraterritorial Protection and the Common Market of Deflection* (Brill 2000) 75.

10 Hannah Arendt, *The Origins of Totalitarianism* (Penguin Classics 2017) 156.

ments.[11] A primary example of this is the Security Council of the UN, mandated to maintain international peace and security, the primary community interest of the organisation. The UN General Assembly is an UN organ with quasi-legislative powers that has issued various resolutions elevating certain matters of concern to community interests.[12] While non-legally binding, UN General Assembly resolutions have normative significance as evidence of state practice and collective *opinio juris* of the member states.

UNHCR is a unique case of a UN agency that has assumed the institutional responsibility for refugee protection on behalf of the community of states.[13] In the words of the UNHCR Executive Committee, '[i]nternational protection provides the basic *raison d'être* for the creation of UNHCR. It is this international protection role, which gives UNHCR its distinctive position among the agencies of the United Nations'.[14] UNHCR has today an indefinite refugee protection mandate *rationae temporis* – 'until the refugee problem is solved'.[15]

In addition, the institutional responsibilities of UNHCR have expanded over the years through UNGA Resolutions and UNHCR's Executive Committee Conclusions. With regard to its protection mandate, UNHCR today has extensive operational and in-country presence. It works with a large majority of states, including with large refugee host states that have not signed the Convention, most notably through the admission and reception of refugees and the undertaking of refugee status determination and legal representation.[16] Further,

11 Jan Klabbers, 'What Role for International Organizations in the Promotion of Community Interests? Reflection on the Ideology of Functionalism' in Benvenisti, Nolte *Community Interests Across International Law* (n 7) 92–93.

12 Isabel Feichtner, 'Community Interests' Max Plank Encyclopaedia of Public International Law (7 February 2009) <https://opil.ouplaw.com/view/10.1093/law:epil/9780199231690/law-9780199231690-e1677?rskey=pFa3v5&result=1&prd=MPIL> accessed 17 October 2024; Wolfrum, 'Identifying Community Interests in International Law: Common Spaces and Beyond (n7) 22.

13 Goodwin Gill, McAdam, Dunlop, *The Refugee in International law* (n 1) 50.

14 UNHCR Note on International Solidarity and Refugee Protection EC/SCP/50 (1988), para 16.

15 The interest of the international community, as reflected in UNHCR's work towards certain categories of individuals, has since 1945 expanded beyond refugees and today includes the internally displaced, stateless and the forcibly displaced as a result of climate change.

16 Guy Goodwin-Gill, 'The Office of the United Nation High Commissioner for Refugees and the Sources of International Refugee Law' (2020) 69 International and comparative Law Quarterly 1, 6; Walter Kälin, 'Supervising the 1951 Convention on the Status of Refugees: Article 35 and Beyond' in Erika Feller, Volker Türk, Frances Nicholson *Refugee Protection in International Law: Global Consultations on International Protection* (Cambridge University Press 2003) 620; Tally Kritzman Amir, 'Community Interests in International

UNHCR also intervenes for the benefit of refugees in the litigation of refugee rights at domestic, regional and international level through the submission of *amicus curiae*.[17]

UNHCR is, therefore, by virtue of its mandate and operational presence, quite unlike any other UN agency: the institutional trustee of the community interest, the 'custodian of refugee protection'.[18] Against this background, international cooperation and responsibility sharing are essential for the effective protection of the community interest and for the fair and effective operation of the international refugee law regime.

2 The Duty of States to Cooperate in the Contemporary International Refugee Law Regime

2.1 *Refugees and the UN Charter*

A general duty of states to pursue multilateralism and cooperate in areas of common concern is firmly rooted in the UN Charter. The Charter, concluded in 1946, five years before the conclusion of the Refugee Convention, is the primary source on multilateralism, harmonisation and international cooperation between states.[19] The UN Charter, the closest the international community has ever come to 'a written constitutional document',[20] was the first instrument of universal state participation that explicitly acknowledged that the maintenance of international peace and security, the self-determination of peoples, the solution of international problems of an economic, social, cultural, or humanitarian character and respect for human rights and freedoms without discrimination are the interests of the international community of states and of their peoples,[21] as represented in the UN membership.[22] Enlight-

Migration and Refugee Law' in Benvenisti and Nolte *Community Interests Across International Law* (n 7) 341, 352.

17 UNHCR submits routine amicus curiae and intervenes in judicial proceedings. Goodwin-Gill notes that the 1951 Convention is one of the most litigated treaties at the domestic level. Goodwin-Gill, 'The Office of the United Nation High Commissioner for Refugees and the Sources of International Refugee Law' (n 16) 11; See also Geoff Gilbert, 'UNHCR and Courts: Amicus curiae (…) sed curia amica est?' (2016) 28 International Journal of Refugee Law, 623–636.

18 Gilbert refers to UNHCR as the 'custodian of international refugee protection'. Ibid.

19 *Charter of the United Nations* 24 October 1945, 1 UNTS XVI. Article 1(4). (UN Charter)

20 Bruno Simma, Andreas L Paulus, 'The International Community Facing the Challenge of Globalization' (1998) 9 European Journal of International Law 266, 274.

21 UN Charter, Preamble.

22 UN Charter, Article 1 (1), (2), (3), (4).

ened positivists such as Simma and Paulus treat the UN Charter as the primary source of community interests manifesting of Kantian cosmopolitan elements:

> The UN has an important impact on the shaping of common values, be it in the General Assembly or in convoking international conferences on a vast array of topics, which bring together non-governmental actors as well as governments. With its human rights regime, the UN also provides an institutional framework for the 'Kantian' elements in the interstate system.[23]

A positive duty of states to cooperate in the resolution of common challenges is expressed in the provision of Article 1 paragraph 3 of the UN Charter. The provision prescribes that, among the purposes of the Charter, is to 'achieve international cooperation in solving international problems of an economic, social, cultural or humanitarian character'.[24] Such is the necessity of international cooperation to resolve common challenges that the Charter has a dedicated chapter on International Economic and Social Cooperation.[25]

Article 56 explicitly prescribes its Members 'to pledge themselves to take joint and separate action in cooperation with the Organization' for the achievement of the purposes set forth in Article 55.[26] UN member states have a legal duty to cooperate with the UN as an international organisation, as well as among themselves, in a constructive way and in compliance with the good faith duty of implementation of the Charter's provisions.[27] A good faith implementation of the duty to cooperate under the UN Charter arguably then precludes the development of obstructive policies, namely policies that go against the intended objective.[28] The Charter requires that joint action shall be taken, *inter alia*, for the higher standards of living, full employment and conditions for social progress and development; for solutions of international economic, social, health and related problems; and for universal respect

---

23 Ibid.

24 UN Charter, Article 1 (3).

25 Ibid., Articles 55–60.

26 Ibid., Article 56.

27 *Vienna Convention on the Law of Treaties* (adopted 23 May 1969) 1155 UNTS 331 (VCLT) Article 26.

28 Bruno Simma, Daniel-Erasmus Khan, Georg Nolte, Andreas Paulus, Nikolai Wessendorf (eds) *Charter of the United Nations: A Commentary* Vol II (Oxford University Press 2012)., 'Chapter IX: International Economic and Social Co-operation', Article 56, at 942.

for and observance of human rights and fundamental freedoms without distinction as to race, sex and religion.[29]

A combined reading of the Charter provisions suggests that the management of the refugee problem is also a 'humanitarian, social and economic' challenge that relies on international cooperation by UN member states.[30] A plausible interpretation of the Charter's provisions for refugee-related matters is that each Member state, irrespective whether it is a party or not to the Refugee Convention, must respect and protect the rights and fundamental freedoms of refugees without discrimination and cooperate in good faith in resolving the refugee problem. This is as far as the Charter goes in establishing a positive duty of states to cooperate in matters pertaining to refugee protection. The formulation of Article 55 is made in programmatic terms as it 'describes purposes and not substantive obligations to be achieved by means of cooperation'.[31] It sets the general direction of the institution towards the realisation of the fundamental community interests and principles of the UN leaving their further elaboration and implementation in subsequent treaty regimes.[32]

The general positive duty to cooperate is further reaffirmed in the UN General Assembly Declaration of Friendly Relations and Co-operation among States.[33] The Declaration states that 'the principles embodied in this Declaration constitute basic principles of international law' that guide states' international conduct in their mutual relations.[34] Although the Declarations of the General Assembly are non-legally binding, this Resolution is the most authoritative statement made by the General Assembly on the UN Charter – and thus it can be said that it is endowed with added normativity, if not constitutional status similar to the Charter.[35]

29 UN Charter, Article 55 (a), (b), (c). Ibid, 922.

30 UN Charter, Articles 55, 56.

31 Simma, Erasmus Khan, Nolte, Paulus, Wessendorf *UN Charter Commentary* (n 28) Article 56, at 943.

32 Rüdiger Wolfrum, 'Cooperation, International Law of', *Max Plank Encyclopaedia of Public International Law*, (April 2010) <https://opil.ouplaw.com/view/10.1093/law:epil/9780199231690/law-9780199231690-e1427?rskey=y4DCTt&result=1&prd=MPIL> accessed 17 October 2024; Tally Kritzman-Amir, 'Not in My Backyard, On the Morality of Responsibility Sharing in Refugee Law' (2009) 34 Brooklyn Journal of International Law 355, 376.

33 UNGA *Declaration on Principles of International Law Concerning Friendly Relations and Cooperation among States in Accordance with the Charter of the United Nations*, 4 October 1970, UNGA A/RES/2625(XXV).

34 Ibid, 3.

35 Ronald St. J McDonald, 'The Charter of the United Nations as a World Constitution' in Michael N Schmitt (ed), 'International Law Across the Spectrum of Conflict Essays in

2.2 *International Cooperation and Responsibility Sharing under the 1951 Refugee Convention*

While the drafters did not codify a responsibility sharing obligation in the Refugee Convention, they however recognised the necessity of responsibility sharing in the management of the refugee problem in the Preamble|:[36]

> The grant of asylum may place unduly heavy burdens on certain countries and that a satisfactory solution of a problem of which the United Nations has recognized the international scope and nature cannot therefore be achieved without international cooperation.[37]

The Preamble calls for international cooperation as means to ease pressure upon refugee-hosting states and to find solutions to the refugee problem. A more indirect call for cooperation that has received considerably less attention in commentary is found in recital 5 of the Preamble that calls contracting states 'to do everything in their power to prevent the refugee problem from becoming a cause of tension' given its social and economic dimensions.[38]

The Preamble of a treaty, while non-binding, has normative significance; it guides the interpretation of the treaty's substantive provisions reflecting its object and purpose.[39] Pursuant to a textual interpretation, per Article 31 of the Vienna Convention on the Law of Treaties, 'a treaty shall be interpreted in good faith in accordance with the ordinary meaning to be given to the terms of the treaty in their context and in the light of its object and purpose'.[40] The Preamble of a treaty is reflective of the drafter's purposes and considerations,[41] but it may be additionally relevant for the treaty's in-

---

Honour of Professor L.C. Green On the Occasion of his Eightieth Birthday' (2000) 75 International Law Studies 263, 280.

36 See discussion of the *Travaux Preparatoires* of the Refugee Convention in Chapter 1, pp. 7–9.

37 Refugee Convention, Preamble recital 4.

38 Refugee Convention, Preamble paragraph 5.

39 VCLT, Article 31 (2). See also Volker Türk, Madeline Garlick, 'From Burdens and Responsibilities to Opportunities: The Comprehensive Refugee Response Framework and a Global Compact on Refugees' (2016) 28 International Journal of Refugee Law 656, 659 https://doi.org/10.1093/ijrl/eew043.

40 VCLT, Article 31.

41 Makane Moïse Mbengue *'Preamble'* Max Plank Encyclopaedia of Public International Law <https://opil.ouplaw.com/display/10.1093/law:epil/9780199231690/law-9780199231690-e1456?prd=EPIL> accessed 14 October 2024.

terpretation shedding further light on its object and purpose.[42] Feller argues that the Preamble to the Refugee Convention explicitly relies upon international cooperation in order to fulfil the very aim of the Convention, namely to ensure that refugees 'enjoy the widest possible exercise of fundamental rights and freedoms'.[43] It can therefore be said that the Preamble recognises the 'functional necessity'[44] of responsibility sharing to the effective implementation of the Convention.

Most commentators stop at the Preamble of the Refugee Convention when tracing the foundations of international cooperation and responsibility sharing. A careful reading of the Convention however suggests that the doctrinal enquiry ought to go further in describing the content of the duty to cooperate in refugee matters. Article 35 paragraph 1 is significant and has not received much scholarly attention. The provision codifies an obligation for the parties to cooperate with UNHCR, or any other agency that may succeed it in the future, in both the exercise of its protection and supervisory mandates.[45] Paragraph 2 of the same provision requires parties to cooperate with the High Commissioner in its reporting to the UN Economic Social Council. The same duty is reiterated verbatim in Article II (1) (2) of the 1967 Protocol. The contours of the duty to cooperate with the UNHCR in the exercise of its protection and supervisory mandate are further reinstated in the High Commissioner's Statute. States, including those that have not signed the Refugee Convention are called to cooperate, *inter alia*, by:

> admitting refugees to their territories, not excluding those in the most destitute categories, assisting the High Commissioner in his efforts to promote the voluntary repatriation of refugees; promoting the assimilation of refugees, especially by facilitating their naturalization.[46]

---

42 Dispute between Argentina and Chile concerning the Beagle Channel, Volume XXI Reports of International Arbitral (18 February 1977) 53, 89, para 19.

43 Challenges to the 1951 Convention in its 50th Anniversary Year: Statement by Ms. Erika Feller, Director, Department of International Protection, UNHCR, at the Seminar on 'International Protection within one single asylum procedure' (April 2001) <https://www.unhcr.org/admin/dipstatements/429d74282/challenges-1951-convention-its-50th-anniversary-year-statement-ms-erika.html.> accessed 17 October 2024.

44 JPL Fonteyne, 'Burden-Sharing: An Analysis of the Nature and Function of International Solidarity in Cases of Mass Influx of Refugees' (1980) Australian Yearbook of International Law 162, 175.

45 Refugee Convention, Article 35 (1).

46 UNHCR Statute, Article 8 (d).

Article 35 (1) of the Refugee Convention and Article II (1) (2) of the 1967 Protocol codify a treaty obligation on the part of states parties that links the good faith application of the Convention to UNHCR's functional responsibilities, 'irrespective of their legal basis'.[47] Kallin notes that the duty of Article 35 has a 'highly dynamic and evolutive character' that requires states to cooperate with UNHCR throughout time.[48] This reading is significant to the extent that it clarifies the scope of the duty to cooperate in refugee protection towards responsibility sharing and the finding of durable solutions as intrinsic components of UNHCR's protection mandate.[49]

In his Commentary of the Refugee Convention, Grahl-Madsen noted that the Convention itself falls within the scope of Article 55 of the UN Charter, which promotes international cooperation for the solution of social and economic problems.[50] More specifically, Article 35 of the Refugee Convention and Article II of the 1967 Additional Protocol, according to Grahl-Madsen, give effect 'to the obligation, which member states have entered into by virtue of Article 56 of the UN Charter', bringing within the community interests of the UN the material provisions of the Refugee Convention.[51]

The UN General Assembly Declaration on Territorial Asylum emphasised the importance of responsibility sharing in the effective operation of the international refugee law regime.[52] Adopted 16 years after the conclusion of the Refugee Convention, the Declaration emphasised the right to asylum and, *inter alia*, reinstated the functional necessity of international cooperation and responsibility sharing by calling states to take appropriate measures to lighten the burden of overwhelmed asylum states in a spirit of solidarity.[53]

To conclude, the combined reading of the UN Charter and the Refugee Convention suggests that there is a legal duty of states to cooperate in refugee protection with one another and with UNHCR in the exercise of its responsibilities. Although these duties of cooperation do not concretise into a concomitant legal obligation of responsibility sharing on the part of each party individually, the combined reading of the above sources suggests that there is at least a normative requirement for responsibility sharing in times and in cases

47 Atle Grahl-Madsen, 'Commentary of the Refugee Convention 1951 Articles 2–11, 13–37' (1963) republished by UNHCR Division of International Protection (October 1997) 254.

48 Kälin, 'Supervising the 1951 Convention on the Status of Refugees: Article 35 and Beyond' (n 16) 617.

49 Ibid., 621.

50 Grahl-Madsen, 'Commentary of the Refugee Convention 1951' (n 47) 149.

51 Ibid.

52 UNGA Declaration on Territorial Asylum (1967) UNTS 189 (2545)

53 Ibid., Article 2.

where the state of asylum is overwhelmed. The above reading additionally suggests that there are certain legal parameters on international cooperation for refugees. International cooperation that aims by design or results in responsibility shifting or which obstructs access to asylum and refugee rights would be prohibitive as going against a good-faith application of the Refugee Convention and against the principle of responsibility sharing.

3 International Cooperation and Responsibility Sharing before the UNHCR

As discussed above, in addition to its international protection mandate, UNHCR is the guardian of the Refugee Convention and has an important supervisory role in its application and implementation.[54] Such expansion of institutional responsibility as reflected in UNHCR's mandate has not however followed with the concomitant expansion of the individual legal obligations of states *vis-a-vis* refugees and refugee host states.[55] This is where a 'disjuncture', as it has been described, exists between the institutional obligation of the international community to protect refugees and the absence of a responsibility sharing obligation on the part of individual states.[56]

UNHCR has played a unique normative role to the development of international refugee law through its Executive Committee, including with respect to responsibility sharing. Established by ECOSOC in 1958, the Executive Committee has, over the years, issued various conclusions on matters of international protection,[57] ranging from interpretative guidelines on the application of treaty provisions to the development of legal standards applicable to refugees.[58] The Executive Committee resolutions, such as the Notes and Guidelines on International Protection, complement the international refugee regime, contributing to the process of refugee law's formation, interpretation

54 UNHCR Statute, para 8(a).

55 Goodwin Gill, McAdam Dunlop, *The Refugee in International Law* (n 1) 50.

56 Ibid., 51.

57 ECOSOC Res. 672 (XXV) (30 April 1958) further to UNGA res. 1166(XII), 'International assistance to refugees within the mandate of the United Nations High Commissioner for Refugees' (26 November 1957). See indicatively only UNHCR Executive Committee Conclusions: No. 11, 22, 52, 77, 79, 80, 85, 89, 100, 102. UNHCR, *A Thematic Compilation of Executive Committee Conclusions* (UNHCR 7th edition June 2014).

58 On UNHCR's standard setting role, See Goodwin-Gill, 'The Office of the United Nation High Commissioner for Refugees and the Sources of International Refugee Law' (n 16) 2–9.

and direction.[59] Despite their soft law character, the conclusions of the Executive Committee are widely accepted to have normative weight as standard-setting exercises.[60] Crucial in assessing the normative weight of UNHCR Executive Committee Conclusions is the Committee's membership. The Committee includes states that are not parties to the Refugee Convention or states that are 'specially affected' by the refugee problem having a very strong vested interest in its solution.[61] Lebanon, Jordan and Pakistan, for example, have been major refugee hosts and members of the Executive Committee of UNHCR but not signatories to the Refugee Convention. Turkey, a member of the UNHCR Executive Committee and one of the largest refugee hosts, maintains a geographical limitation on who qualifies for refugee status. This broader membership of the Executive Committee can be said to reflect the *opinio juris* of a greater majority of states on the normative development of the international refugee law regime.[62]

In the absence of a permanent structure for responsibility sharing under the Refugee Convention framework, UNHCR has in practice become the multilateral forum where international cooperation and responsibility sharing for refugees has primarily taken place. At the same time, the Executive Committee of UNHCR has on numerous occasions affirmed and stressed the quintessential importance and functional necessity of responsibility sharing in refugee matters, in particular in cases of mass influx of refugees.[63] As early as 1981, the UNHCR, in its Executive Committee Conclusion No. 22 on the Protection of Asylum Seekers in Situations of Large-Scale Influx, stated:

> A mass influx may place unduly heavy burdens on certain countries; a satisfactory solution of a problem, international in scope and nature, cannot be achieved without international cooperation. States shall, within the framework of international solidarity and burden sharing,

---

59 Goodwin-Gill, McAdam, Dunlop, *The Refugee in International Law* (n 1) 489–491.

60 Corine Lewis, 'UNHCR's Contribution to the Development of International Refugee Law: Its Foundations and Evolution' (2005) 17 International Journal of Refugee Law 67 https://doi.org/10.1093/ijrl/eei004.

61 Ibid.

62 By the end of June 2024, there were 110 ExCom members states <https://reporting.unhcr.org/excom-members-and-parties-conventions> accessed 17 October 2024; Maja Janmyr 'Non-signatory States and the international refugee regime' (2021) 67 Forced Migration Review 39, 41.

63 It shall be noted that no definition of a mass influx situation exists however in international law.

> take all necessary measures to assist at their request, States which have admitted asylum seekers in mass influx.[64]

The Executive Committee, in Conclusion No. 100, emphasised the global dimension of refugee protection in the context of mass influx and called states to cooperate in a spirit of solidarity and responsibility sharing to address refugee situations.[65]

To conclude, the reading of relevant UNHCR's Executive Committee Conclusions represents the collective *opinio juris* that responsibility sharing has crystallised into a well-established principle of the international refugee law regime and that, especially in cases of mass influx, international cooperation should result in responsibility sharing.

4 Regional Approaches to Responsibility Sharing

The challenge of responsibility sharing is better illustrated in regional refugee protection regimes.[66] While the focus of this study is on international cooperation and responsibility sharing at the UN level, a cursory look into regional asylum frameworks offers insights into how states have institutionalised responsibility sharing in legal and non-legal ways, reflective of each

---

64 UNHCR Executive Committee Conclusion No. 22 'The Protection of Asylum-Seekers in Situations of Large-Scale Influx' (1981) Executive Committee, 32nd session. Contained in United Nations General Assembly Document No. 12A (A/36/12/Add.1).

65 UNHCR, Conclusion on International Cooperation and Burden and Responsibility Sharing in Mass Influx Situations, Conclusion on International Cooperation and Burden and Responsibility Sharing in Mass Influx Situations No. 100 (LV) – 2004 Executive Committee 55th session. Contained in United Nations General Assembly Document A/AC.96/1003.

66 The discussion of the regional refugee instruments is by no means comprehensive. There are several scholarly accounts on regional asylum instruments in the context of Latin America, Africa and the European Union. See indicatively David J Cantor, Nicolás Rodriguez Serna (eds) 'The New Refugees: Organised Crime and Displacement in Latin America' (ILAS Publications, University of London 2016); Liliana Jubilut, *Refugee Protection in Brazil and Latin America – Selected Essays* (*Transnational London Press 2018*); Marina Sharpe, *The Regional Law of Refugee Protection in Africa* (OUP 2018); Tamara Wood, *'The 1969 OAU Convention Governing the Specific Aspects of Refugee Problems in Africa'*, in Satvinder Juss (*ed*), *Research Handbook on Refugees* (*Edward Elgar Publishing, 2019*). George Okoth-Obbo, 'Thirty Years On: A Legal Review of the 1969 OAU Convention Governing the Specific Aspects of Refugee Problems in Africa' (2000) 8 African Yearbook of International Law 3.

region's history and tradition on asylum. The regional asylum frameworks for Africa,[67] Latin America and the EU discussed here complement the international refugee law regime.[68]

4.1 *The 1969 OAU Convention Governing the Specific Aspects of Refugee Problems in Africa*

The 1969 OAU Convention Governing the Specific Aspects of Refugee Problems in Africa is a rather progressive regional instrument on refugee protection. This is due to the 'African refugee' definition that goes beyond that of Article 1 A (2) of the Convention, reflecting the continent's history.[69] It is also a progressive instrument regarding its distinct approach to responsibility sharing. The OAU Convention explicitly posits that refugee protection is the 'joint responsibility of all the African Union's member states'[70] and codifies a certain responsibility sharing obligation within the operative part of the Convention.

Article II, paragraph 4, stipulates:

> [w]here a Member State finds difficulty in continuing to grant asylum to refugees, such Member State may appeal directly to other Member States and through the OAU, and such other Member States shall in the spirit of African solidarity and international co-operation take appropriate measures to lighten the burden of the Member State granting asylum.[71]

---

67 'The present Convention shall be the effective regional complement of the 1951 United Nations Convention on the Status of Refugees in Africa. OAU Convention, Article VIII para 2.

68 This has been explicitly acknowledged in the context of Latin America. See 2004 Mexico Declaration and Plan of Action to Strengthen the International Protection of Refugees in Latin America, Mexico City, (16 November 2004) and 2014 Brazil Declaration on 'A Framework for Cooperation and Regional Solidarity to Strengthen the International Protection of Refugees, Displaced and Stateless Persons in Latin America and the Caribbean', Brasilia, (3 December 2014).

69 The 1969 OAU refugee definition covers "every person who, owing to external aggression, occupation, foreign domination or events seriously disturbing public order in either part or the whole of his country of origin or nationality compelled to leave his place of habitual residence in order to seek refuge in another place outside his country of origin or nationality. OAU Convention, Article I (2).

70 Guy Martin, 'International Solidarity and Co-Operation in Assistance to African Refugees: Burden-Sharing or Burden-Shifting (1995) 7 International Journal of Refugee Law 250, 259.

71 Bill Rutinwa 'The end of asylum? The changing nature of refugee policies in Africa' (2002) 21 Refugee Survey Quarterly 12, 18.

Despite this 'positivisation' of an inter-African responsibility sharing obligation within a regional treaty on asylum, the provision, rather than codifying an individual obligation of responsibility sharing on the part of the parties, incorporates a mechanism. Commentators have, however, noted that measures of assistance under this responsibility sharing mechanism have rarely been taken in practice.[72] The majority of African states have failed to establish the necessary institutional arrangements for responsibility sharing that would effectively implement Article II (4).[73] In fact, only four African states have enacted national legislation to incorporate the provision of Article II (4) of the OAU Convention as an obligation in their respective national asylum laws.[74]

African states host a large proportion of the world's refugees, and at the regional as well as in some sub-regional partnerships, the African values of solidarity and good neighbourliness vest a generally open-door policy towards African citizens and refugees.[75] The legal anchor of Africa's open-door policy to refugees has always been premised, however, upon assistance both from within and outside the region.[76] UNHCR, during a regional intergovernmental conference in Benin in 2004, acknowledged that refugee protection challenges in Africa stem from the limited capacities of host States, as well as the absence of meaningful responsibility sharing from the international community.[77] Commentators have noted that the failure might not be the continent's fault alone, as assistance from the Global North is a necessary condition for operationalising responsibility sharing and providing international protection within a region still struggling to realise the right to development.[78]

72 Marina Sharpe, 'The Global Compact on Refugees and Conflict Prevention in Africa: "Root Causes" and Yet Another Divide' (2018) 30 International Journal of Refugee Law 707, 708 https://doi.org/10.1093/rsq/21.1_and_2.12.

73 Tamara Wood, 'The 1969 OAU Convention Governing the Specific Aspects of Refugee Problems in Africa', (n 66) 24.

74 David J Cantor, Farai Chikwanha, 'Reconsidering African Refugee Law' (2019) 31 International Journal of Refugee Law 182, 212 https://doi.org/10.1093/ijrl/eez032.

75 See 1993 Revised Treaty of Economic Community of West African States (ECOWAS), Article 4(b), Article 4(e) and Treaty Establishing the East African Community (30 November 1999) (entered into force 7 July 2000) Article 124 (4).

76 Rutinwa 'The End of Asylum? The changing nature of refugee policies in Africa' (n 71)18.

77 José Riera, Demian Casey (eds), 'Refugees in Africa: The Challenges of Protection and Solutions Regional Parliamentary Conference on Refugees in Africa'(Cotonou Benin 1–3 June 2004) UNHCR in association with the Inter-Parliamentary Union and the ICRC, 34 <https://www.refworld.org/pdfid/427224a44.pdf> accessed 17 October 2024.

78 Rutinwa 'The End of Asylum? The changing nature of refugee policies in Africa' (n 71) 34.

What becomes apparent when looking at the African approach to responsibility sharing is that, although a South-South responsibility sharing structure exists at OAU level within the OAU Convention as well as in certain subregional economic partnerships, such structures and the existence of common values alone are not sufficient and are further dependent on international development assistance.

4.2 *Latin America: The Cartagena Framework*

The Latin American framework offers another distinct South-South approach to responsibility sharing, reflecting what has been described as a 'common but differentiated' responsibility for refugees coming from countries in the region.[79]

The earliest key regional instrument for refugee protection in Latin America was the Cartagena Declaration of 1984.[80] Even though Latin American states joined the international refugee regime at a later stage, they already had longstanding experience with political asylum.[81] The Cartagena Declaration also expanded the refugee definition to reflect the political realities of the region. Causes of persecution include 'generalized violence, foreign aggression, internal conflicts and massive human rights violations or other circumstances which have seriously disturbed public order'.[82] More importantly, the Cartagena Declaration links refugee protection in the region with the search for durable solutions.[83]

The Latin American refugee protection framework reflects the so-called 'Cartagena Spirit' – a spirit of regional solidarity reflected in generous asylum polices and in ideas of a joint responsibility for refugees.[84] This regional framework has progressively developed over the years under a series of soft law instruments and processes. The characterisation 'soft', in this context, refers to the form, namely the non-binding nature of the various instruments.

---

79 David Cantor, 'Responsibility-sharing in the refugee field: lessons from Latin America' (2018) Policy Brief: Pisa Observatory on European Migration Law 3.

80 Cartagena Declaration on Refugees, adopted by the Colloquium on the International Protection of Refugees in Central America, Mexico and Panama, Cartagena de Indias, Colombia, 22 November 1984.

81 Cantor, 'Responsibility-sharing in the refugee field: lessons from Latin America' (n 79) 1.

82 Cartagena Declaration, Conclusion 3 para III.

83 Ibid.

84 Stefania E Barichello, 'Responsibility Sharing in Latin America', in Satvinder Juss (ed) *Research Handbook of International Refugee Law* (Edward Elgar 2019) 111.

The Mexico Declaration and Plan of Action[85] was adopted in 2004 – by 20 Latin American states in commemoration of the 20 years since the adoption of the Cartagena Declaration – and established a new guiding framework reflecting commitments to regional solidarity and responsibility sharing.[86] Like the Cartagena Declaration, the Mexico Plan of Action linked refugee protection with the search for durable solutions.[87] In 2014, 30 years since the Cartagena Declaration, the Latin American states and the states of the Caribbean concluded another instrument, the Brazil Declaration and Plan of Action.[88] The 2014 Brazil Declaration integrated the previous lessons learned and renewed the commitments of states to existing programmes on regional protection and solutions. The Declaration premises refugee protection in the region as a 'common but differentiated responsibility', foreseeing different roles for states of origin, transit and destination.[89]

Latin America as a region has historically treated responsibility sharing on the basis of bilateral agreements between the countries of origin and the host countries. As a result of the region's tradition and culture, responsibility sharing takes place within the broader practice on informal instruments and policies.[90] According to commentators, the informal nature of Latin America's responsibility sharing arrangements has worked well for refugees in the region and Latin American states have meaningfully participated in regional responsibility sharing.[91] Latin America's approach to asylum and responsibility sharing can be contrasted by the EU's formal and harmonised asylum legislation that has yet, however, to optimise a fair sharing of responsibilities between Member States, as the next section discusses.

4.3 *Responsibility Sharing in the Common European Asylum System (CEAS): From Dublin to the New Pact on Asylum and Migration*

The Common European Asylum System (CEAS) is the regional refugee and asylum management system at EU level. The CEAS is a rather complex and

---

85 Mexico Declaration and Plan of Action to Strengthen International Protection of Refugees in Latin America.

86 Tristan Harley, 'Regional Cooperation and Refugee Protection in Latin America: A 'South-South' Approach' (2014) 26 International Journal of Refugee Law 22 https://doi.org/10.1093/ijrl/eeu004.

87 Mexico Declaration and Plan of Action, Chapter 3, Solidarity Cities Programme for Self Sufficiency and Local Integration, Solidarity Resettlement Programme.

88 Brazil Declaration.

89 Cantor, 'Responsibility-sharing in the refugee field: lessons from Latin America' (n 79) pp. 3–5.

90 Ibid., 2.

91 Barichello, 'Responsibility Sharing in Latin America' (n 84) 118.

sophisticated asylum framework put in place since the 1990s and comprises of a series of legislative, responsibility allocation and practical cooperation components.

One of the pillars of the CEAS is solidarity and fair responsibility sharing between Member states of the EU. The CEAS takes a distinct approach to responsibility sharing compared to the ones seen in Africa and Latin America. Despite the EU's advanced levels of integration and harmonisation of legislation, the EU asylum system also suffers from a responsibility sharing deficit by design.[92] While the management of asylum in the region is conceptually understood and posited as a common responsibility, Member States have struggled to agree on and design a responsibility sharing mechanism that optimises fair sharing.

The CEAS is rooted in primary EU law and, in particular, Articles 78 and 80 of the Treaty on the Functioning of the European Union (TFEU).[93] Article 80 of the TFEU reads:

> [T]he policies of the Union set out in this Chapter and their implementation shall be governed by the principle of solidarity and fair sharing of responsibility, including its financial implications, between the Member States. Whenever necessary, the acts of the Union adopted pursuant to this Chapter shall contain appropriate measures to give effect to this principle.[94]

The strong formulation of Article 80 of the TFEU suggests that the provision of asylum to third-country nationals is the common responsibility of the EU, as an institution as well as of its Member States.[95] Article 80 of the TFEU has been criticised for being overtly vague in its legal construction so that it can hardly impose any subsequent legal obligations of fair sharing upon Member

92 Elizabeth Mavropoulou, Evangelia (Lilian) Tsourdi, 'Solidarity as Normative Rationale for Differential Treatment: Common but Differentiated Responsibilities from International Environmental to EU Asylum Law?' in Maarten den Heijer, Harmen van der Wilt *Global Solidarity and Common But Differentiated Responsibilities* (2020) 51 Netherlands Yearbook of International Law 311, 328.

93 Consolidated versions of the Treaty on European Union and the Treaty on the Functioning of the European Union (TFEU) [2016] OJ C202/1.

94 Consolidated versions of the Treaty on European Union and the Treaty on Functioning of the European Union (TFEU) [2016] OJ C202/1. TFEU.

95 Evangelia (Lilian) Tsourdi, 'Solidarity at Work? The Prevalence of Emergency Driven Solidarity in the Administrative Governance of the Common European Asylum System' (2017) 24 Maastricht Journal of European and Comparative Law 667, 674 https://doi.org/10.1177/1023263X17742801.

States.[96] Commentators argue that the provision is couched in mandatory terms within the treaty and therefore imposes at least an obligation of result on the part of Member States, as well as the EU, to achieve a fair sharing of asylum-related responsibilities.[97] Those who object to such an interpretation of the provision as establishing an obligation of result do not nonetheless disregard the otherwise normative requirement of fair sharing entailed thereunder.[98]

Despite the arguably structural character of the principle of solidarity and fair sharing of responsibility under Article 80 of the TFEU, solidarity measures in practice have been largely emergency-driven and *ad hoc*, consisting of mostly exceptional responses, such as emergency funding to frontline Member States faced with a sudden mass influx or emergency relocations.[99] The CEAS fair sharing deficit is the result of the responsibility allocation system underpinned by the so-called Dublin III Regulation.[100] Although the Dublin Regulation was never meant to be a responsibility sharing instrument, it has *de facto* functioned as one by assigning protection responsibility to the Member state of first entry.[101] The implementation of the first-country-of-entry rule

96 Gregor Noll, 'Failure by Design? On the Constitution of EU Solidarity', Odysseus Network Searching for Solidarity in the EU Asylum and Border Policies, A Collection of Short Papers following the Odysseus Network's First Annual Policy Conference (26–27 February 2016) 3 <http://odysseus-network.eu/wp-content/uploads/2015/09/Searching-for-Solidarity-Short-Papers.pdf.> accessed 17 October 2034; Eleni Karageorgiou,'The law and practice of solidarity in the Common European Asylum System: Article 80 TFEU and its Added Value' 2016 European Policy Analysis, 5.

97 Tsourdi, 'Solidarity at Work? The Prevalence of Emergency Driven Solidarity in the Administrative Governance of the Common European Asylum System' (n 95) 673.

98 Esin Küçük, 'The Principle of Solidarity and Fairness in Sharing Responsibility: More than Window Dressing?'(2016) 22 European Law Journal 449 https://doi.org/10.1111/eulj.12185.

99 Tsourdi, Solidarity at Work? The Prevalence of Emergency-Driven Solidarity in the Administrative Governance of the Common European Asylum System (n 95) 675; Mavropoulou, Tsourdi, 'Solidarity as Normative Rationale for Differential Treatment: Common but Differentiated Responsibilities from International Environmental to EU Asylum Law?' (n 92) 344.

100 Regulation (EU) No 604/2013 of the European Parliament and of the Council of 26 June 2013 establishing the criteria and mechanisms for determining the Member State responsible for examining an application for international protection lodged in one of the Member States by a third-country national or a stateless person (recast), OJ L 180/31 of 29 June 2013 (Dublin III Regulation).

101 E.g. the Member State that issued a residence document or a visa. See Dublin III Regulation, Art. 12. Sheila Maas, Elena Jurado, Mathieu Capdevila, Maylis Labayle, Laura Hayward, 'Evaluation of the Dublin III Regulation DG Migration and Home Affairs

under Dublin has, as a result, unilaterally shifted responsibility for asylum towards the EU's frontline Member States.[102] The Mediterranean South, comprising of Italy, Greece and Spain has shouldered a somewhat arbitrary responsibility for the majority of asylum seekers because of their geographic location and the responsibility allocation rule under Dublin. The first-country–of-entry rule has been criticised for preserving inequalities in the sharing of asylum responsibilities between Member states and for legitimizing the practice of burden-shifting.[103]

The unfairness and unsustainability of the Dublin regime were starkly manifested during the so-called refugee crisis in 2015–2016, when the Council of the EU had to take emergency solidarity measures. Two emergency Relocation Decisions were put in place in 2015 as relief measures to Greece and Italy, respectively, which witnessed increasingly large-scale arrivals of third-country nationals from Turkey and Libya. The two Council Decisions ordered the relocation of 160,000 asylum seekers from Italy and Greece over the course of two years.[104] The first Council Decision ordered the relocation of 24,000 asylum seekers from Italy and 16,000 from Greece,[105] and the second ordered the relocation of 120,000 asylum seekers in total.[106] The second Relocation Decision also included a sophisticated distribution formula that allocated a quota of asylum seekers between Member States on the basis of population size, GDP, unemployment rate as well as on previous efforts of Member States in resettlement.[107] The Relocation Decisions however proved hard to enforce. Despite the efforts of the Commission to distribute asylum seekers against

---

Final Report' (4 December 2015) 4 <https://home-affairs.ec.europa.eu/system/files/2020-09/evaluation_of_the_dublin_iii_regulation_en.pdf> accessed 17 October 2024.

102 Paul McDonough, Magdalena Kmak, and Joanne van Selm 'Sharing Responsibility for Refugee Protection in Europe: Dublin Reconsidered' European Council on Refugees and Exiles (ECRE), (March 2008), 13 <https://ecre.org/wp-content/uploads/2016/07/ECRE-Sharing-Responsibility-for-Refugee-Protection-in-Europe-Dublin-Reconsidered_March-2008.pdf> accessed 17 October 2024.

103 Eiko Thielemann, 'Why Refugee Burden-Sharing Initiatives Fail: Public Goods, Free-Riding and Symbolic Solidarity in the EU' (2018) 56 Journal of Security and Migration Studies 63, 79.

104 Council Decision (EU) 2015/1523 of 14 September 2015 establishing provisional measures in the area of international protection for the benefit of Italy and of Greece (L.239/80); Council Decision (EU) 2015/1601 of 22 September 2015 establishing provisional measures in the area of international protection for the benefit of Italy and Greece (L.248/80).

105 Council Decision (EU) 2015/1523, Article 4.

106 Ibid.

107 The distributive key is found in the Annex of Commission Recommendation (EU) 2015/914 of 8 June 2015 on a European Resettlement Scheme.

an idea of differentiation in accordance with integrated relative capabilities, Member States pledged and relocated only a small percentage of their allocated shares.[108] Some Member States, like Hungary, Poland and Austria, did not relocate any asylum seekers.[109]

A series of new legislative measures were introduced by the EU Commission in 2020 and adopted by Parliament in May 2024 under the Asylum and Migration Pact.[110] Among other things, the Pact sought to restructure solidarity and responsibility sharing in a more permanent manner. The new Asylum and Migration Management Regulation (AMMR) replaces the Dublin Regulation but retains, with minor tweaks, the allocation criteria of Dublin III, including the 'first-entry criterion', which is in fact now extended to include persons disembarked after Search and Rescue (SAR) at sea operations.[111]

The AMMR introduces a permanent but extremely complex solidarity and fair sharing mechanism that is activated under various circumstances.[112] Although an extensive analysis of the operation and the intricacies

108 Elspeth Guild, Cathryn Costello, Violeta Moreno Lax, 'Study on Implementation of the 2015 Council Decisions establishing provisional measures in the area of international protection for the benefit of Italy and of Greece' Study for the LIBE Committee (March 2017) 27 <https://www.europarl.europa.eu/RegData/etudes/STUD/2017/583132/IPOL_STU(2017)583132_EN.pdf> accessed 17 October 2024.

109 European Commission 'Relocation and Resettlement: Commission calls on all Member States to deliver and meet obligations' Press Release (16 May 2017) <https://ec.europa.eu/commission/presscorner/detail/en/ip_17_1302> accessed 17 October 2024.

110 The EU Asylum and Migration Pact consists of the following Regulations and Directives: Directive (EU) 2024/1346 of the European Parliament and of the Council of 14 May 2024 laying down standards for the reception of applicants for international protection; Regulation (EU) 2024/1347 of the European Parliament and of the Council of 14 May 2024 on standards for the qualification of third-country nationals or stateless persons as beneficiaries of international protection; Regulation (EU) 2024/1348 of the European Parliament and of the Council of 14 May 2024 establishing a common procedure for international protection in the Union; Regulation (EU) 2024/1349 of the European Parliament and of the Council of 14 May 2024 establishing a return border procedure; Regulation (EU) 2024/1350 of the European Parliament and of the Council of 14 May 2024 establishing a Union Resettlement and Humanitarian Admission Framework' Regulation (EU) 2024/1351 of the European Parliament and of the Council of 14 May 2024 on asylum and migration management (AMMR); Regulation (EU) 2024/1356 of the European Parliament and of the Council of 14 May 2024 introducing the screening of third-country nationals at the external borders; and Regulation (EU) 2024/1359 of the European Parliament and of the Council of 14 May 2024 addressing situations of crisis and force majeure in the field of migration and asylum.

111 AMMR, Article 21.

112 See Regulation (EU) 2024/1359 (crisis and force majeure Regulation), Article 4.

of the new solidarity mechanism of the AMMR go beyond the scope of this study,[113] a few observations are warranted, given the potential impact of this regional approach to responsibility sharing on responsibility sharing at the UN level.

On a closer look, the solidarity mechanism under the AMMR consists of a series of processes that are not too dissimilar from responsibility sharing efforts at the UN level, particularly the pledging exercise before the Global Refugee Forums that take place every four years. Once the AMMR comes into effect in 2026, there will be an annual pledging exercise by the Member States of the EU before a High-Level Solidarity Forum. The solidarity pledges will be made against the Commission's proposal on the annual projected needs of EU Member states facing migratory pressure.[114] Following the pledging exercise, the Council, through an implementing act, will set out the various contributions to a Solidarity Pool that can then be used by states facing migratory pressure or a significant mandatory situation.[115] While participation in responsibility sharing through annual pledges to the Solidarity Pool becomes mandatory for Member States, replacing the previous *ad hoc* nature, the types of contributions are left to be determined by states. A Member state can pledge relocations of asylum seekers, financial contributions, including financing capacity in third countries, or alternative solidarity measures such as capacity building or technical cooperation.[116] Evidently, financing third countries goes beyond intra-EU solidarity and falls within the broader EU migration management framework and cooperation with third countries. The pledges should reflect a fair share calculated on the basis of a reference key that combines the total population size (50%) and GDP (50%) as per the latest Eurostat data.[117] In addition, Member States, which find themselves in 'migratory pressures' and 'significant migratory situations', as determined by

113 For an extensive commentary of the solidarity mechanism under the AMMR See, ECRE Comment on the Regulation of the European Parliament and of the Council on Asylum and Migration Management Amending Regulations EU 2021/1147 and EU 2021/1060 and Repealing (EU) No 604/2013 (May 2024) <https://ecre.org/wp-content/uploads/2024/05/ECRE_Comments_Asylum-and-Migration-Management-Regulation.pdf> accessed 17 October 2024; Tsourdi, Mavropolou 'Solidarity as Normative Rationale for Differential Treatment: Common but Differentiated Responsibilities from International Environmental to EU Asylum Law?' (n 92) 334–337.

114 AMMR, Article 11.

115 AMMR PART IV, Articles 56, 57, 61 and 62.

116 AMMR Part IV, Article 56 (2).

117 AMMR, Article 66.

the Commission or as self-identified,[118] can request a partial or full deduction of their pledged contributions for the year.[119]

The Solidarity Mechanism ascribes to what has been described as a conception of 'flexible and half compulsory *à-la-carte* solidarity',[120] whereby states can choose the type of solidarity contributions they are willing to make. Commentators have voiced various concerns over the design and the complex operationalisation of the new solidarity and responsibility sharing framework.[121] While the new mechanism reflects a logic of differentiated contributions in what is conceived as a common EU responsibility – essentially an idea of common but differentiated responsibilities based on capabilities – this differentiation in the regional setting is merely serving political expediency by endorsing certain states' reluctance to engage with refugee protection, offering them the possibility to opt out of relocations.[122] If one adds to the assessment the dominant externalisation impetus of EU migration policy whereby a disproportionate focus of the EU and its Member States is directed instead at externalising protection obligations to third States and containing asylum seekers outside the EU's territory, it is unlikely that the new framework will improve access to asylum or achieve fair responsibility sharing. Be that as it may, it is however commendable that responsibility sharing comes within permanent governance structures, even if imperfect.

5 Conclusions: The Disjuncture in Legal Obligations

This chapter has argued that refugee protection is a well-established community interest of international law. This is confirmed by the existence of refugees as a distinct legal category of individuals in international law for whom states have enacted a dedicated treaty regime in their protection with widespread ratification and participation. Seen from the perspective of community interests, the Refugee Convention transcends the bilateral relations of states

118 AMMR, Article 11.

119 AMMR, Article 61 and 62 covering the two scenarios accordingly.

120 Francesco Maiani, 'A "Fresh Start" or One More Clunker? Dublin and Solidarity in the New Pact', EU Immigration and Asylum Law and Policy (Odysseus Network 20 October 2020) <http://eumigrationlawblog.eu/a-fresh-start-or-one-more-clunker-dublin-and-solidarity-in-the-new-pact/> accessed 17 October 2024.

121 Mavropolou, Tsourdi, 'Solidarity as Normative Rationale for Differential Treatment: Common but Differentiated Responsibilities from International Environmental to EU Asylum Law?' (n 92) 334–335.

122 Ibid.

prescribing universal standards of treatment and rights for refugees. The community interest nature of refugee protection is further reflected in the existence of a specialised UN agency that has been tasked with the institutional responsibility for the protection of refugees. Quite unlike any other UN agency, UNHCR acts as the trustee of the community interest.

Effective protection of the community interest and ultimately the management and solution to the global refugee problem requires international cooperation and responsibility sharing. An enlightened positivist reading of the UN Charter, the 1951 Convention and other relevant sources suggests that there is a well-established duty of international cooperation in refugee protection matters and a normative requirement that such cooperation results in responsibility sharing. By the same token, international cooperation that is designed or results in responsibility shifting goes against a good faith implementation of the duty to cooperate towards responsibility sharing under the Refugee Convention.

Within the regional refugee law instruments too, one comes across various degrees of institutionalisation of international cooperation and responsibility sharing with some more positivized than others. While the EU's example is most illustrative of the responsibility sharing challenge at regional level mirroring some of deficiencies of responsibility sharing at UN level, all three regional systems conceptualise the protection of refugees as a common responsibility and represent regional expressions of the community interest.

In the absence of an obligation of responsibility sharing on the part of individual states, there exists a certain disjuncture between the institutional obligation of the international community to protect the refugees and find solutions as reflected in the Refugee Convention and UNHCR's mandate and the subsequent individual legal obligations of states. The disjuncture is clearly illustrated by the responsibility sharing gap and the absence of any obligation of assistance to host states. Even in the Global Compact era, the nature of responsibility sharing at the UN level remains voluntary and *ad hoc*. The only way to correct this disjuncture and fill in the responsibility sharing gap is to sync the institutional obligation of the international community to protect refugees with a concomitant legal obligation of responsibility sharing under a second protocol to the Refugee Convention.

CHAPTER 3

Externalisation and Responsibility Shifting in the Practice of States

As the previous chapter argued, the Refugee Convention requires states to cooperate to protect refugees and refrain from international cooperation that intentionally seeks to externalise and shift refugee responsibilities into other states as well as constrain refugee movement and rights. This chapter looks at how states have implemented the duty to cooperate towards fair responsibility, by critically analysing some of the most questionable safe third-country agreements on migration and asylum management. The examples of international cooperation discussed here are the EU–Turkey Statement, the bilateral agreement between Italy and Libya, Australia's offshore processing agreements with Papua New Guinea and Nauru and the US-Canada Safe Third Country Agreement. This chapter argues that these safe third-country arrangements are examples of international cooperation that go against the Refugee Convention not only because they constitute a bad faith implementation of the duty to cooperate, tantamount to responsibility shifting, but also because they have resulted in refugee rights violations at states' borders and refugee containment in the Global South.

1 Tracing the Origins of Externalisation of Asylum and Migration Control

The longstanding preference of the Global North to finance refugee protection in the Global South rather than host refugees can be well captured by the externalisation paradigm. Externalisation in the asylum and migration field has been defined as the process of outsourcing core state functions such as border control and/or asylum processing onto third states so that they take place, in part or in whole, outside its territory.[1]

1 This is one of the definitions that exist in academic commentary. David Cantor, Nikolas Feith Tan, Mariana Gkliati, Elizabeth Mavropoulou, Kathryn Allinson, Sreetapa Chakrabarty, Maja Grundler, Lynn Hillary, Emilie McDonnell, Riona Moodley, Stephen Phillips, Annick Pijnenburg, Adel-Naim Reyhani, Sophia Soares and Natasha Yacoub, 'Externalisa-

 | DOI:10.1163/9789004547711_004

While international law does not explicitly prohibit externalisation in the sense that there is no rule that, in principle, prohibits the outsourcing of governmental functions like defence, security, border control and asylum functions to another state or non-state actor, this is qualified by the requirement that externalisation measures are consistent with states' international legal obligations. One such international legal obligation that places limits on externalisation is the duty to cooperate in refugee protection matters under the Refugee Convention. A good faith implementation of this duty would suggest that multilateral or bilateral agreements on border control and asylum management that tend to shift responsibilities onto other states and restrict access to asylum are prohibited.[2]

As early as the 1980s, refugee law policies developed by the Global North sought to contain the *locus* of refugee protection predominantly within countries of the Global South.[3] These externalisation measures, coined by Hathaway in the 1990s as *non-entrée*,[4] have been defined as comprising of efforts by powerful states 'to prevent refugees from ever reaching their jurisdiction, at which point they become entitled to the benefit of protection from *non-refoulement* and other rights set forth in the Refugee Convention'.[5] Measures of non-arrival seek to prevent access to the territory through migration control like, for example, maritime interceptions, while measures of non-admission seek to retroactively exclude refugees who have already arrived at the territory from the 'procedural door'.[6]

A typology of *non-entrée* measures put forward by Hathaway and Gammeltoft-Hansen is helpful to the overall picture. *Non-entrée* measures can be unilateral, bilateral and multilateral. They range from carrier sanctions, visa controls and international zones, to more sophisticated cooperation-based measures, such as interception on the high seas, deployment of immigration

---

tion, Access to Territorial Asylum, and International Law' (2022) 34 International Journal of Refugee Law 120 https://doi.org/10.1093/ijrl/eeac023.

2 This is also the position taken by UNHCR. See UNHCR Note on the Externalization of International Protection (28 May 2021) para 4.

3 James C Hathaway, *Reconceiving International Refugee Law* (Martinus Nijhoff 1997) xxi.

4 James C Hathaway, 'The Emerging Politics of Non-Entrée' (1992) 91 Refugees 40.

5 James C Hathaway and Thomas Gammeltoft-Hansen 'Non-Refoulement in a World of Cooperative Deterrence' (2015) 53 Columbia Journal of Transnational Law 235, 244.

6 Thomas Gammeltoft-Hansen, Nikolas Feith Tan, 'The End of the Deterrence Paradigm? Future Directions for Global Refugee Policy' (2018) 5 Journal on Migration and Human Security 28, 34 https://doi.org/10.1177/233150241700500103; Jens Vedsted-Hansen, 'Europe's Response to the Arrival of Asylum Seekers: Refugee Protection and Immigration Control' UNHCR New Issues in Refugee Research, Working Paper No. 6 (May 1999), 4.

officials, joint or shared law enforcement and offshore processing arrangements.[7] Such externalisation measures can be said to serve a very specific objective of the Northern countries:

> Non-entrée allows wealthier states to insist upon the importance of refugee protection as a matter of international legal obligation, knowing full well that they themselves will largely be spared its burdens. It enables a pattern of minimalist engagement under which the formal commitment to refugee law can be proclaimed as a matter of principle without risk that the wealthier world will actually be compelled to live up to that regime's burdens and responsibilities to any serious extent.[8]

These practices have created, what Gibney describes as a *'cordon sanitaire'* around the world's richest countries, keeping most of the world's refugees confined to the South.[9] Historically, the rise of externalisation has been attributed to the demise of what Hathaway explains as an interest-convergence between receiving states and refugees existing until then.[10] The acute need for labour, post-World War II, which had made the stock of European refugees and their cultural assimilation at the time a domestic interest for some developed countries, gradually disappeared.[11] Later, the strong Cold War sentiment had refugees fleeing the Soviet Union, being welcomed in the West.[12] The African decolonisation process that resulted in large scale refugee movements in the 1960s and 1970s[13] was seen as putting an end to the pattern of generous admission policies at the time and gave rise to restrictive ones in the 1990s.[14]

Today, with migration being portrayed as the 'global celery that nobody desires',[15] states of the Global North, particularly but not exclusively, have

7 Hathaway, Gammeltoft-Hansen 'Non-Refoulement in a World of Cooperative Deterrence (n 5) 242.

8 Ibid.

9 Matthew J Gibney, 'Refugees and Justice Between States' (2015) 14 European Journal of Political Theory 448, 452 https://doi.org/10.1177/1474885115585325.

10 Hathaway, *Reconceiving International Refugee Law* (n 3) xviii.

11 Ibid., xix.

12 Asha Hans, Astri Surhke, 'Responsibility Sharing' in James Hathaway (ed) *Reconceiving International Refugee Law* (Martinus Nijhoff Publishers 1997) 87.

13 Ibid., 88.

14 Hathaway, *Reconceiving International Refugee* (n 3) xix.

15 Yuval Noah Harari, *21st Lessons for the 21st Century* (Vintage 2019) 23.

become even more reluctant to admit large numbers of refugees in their territories and have doubled down on border control budgets.[16]

2 Protection Elsewhere and the Notion of Safe Third Country

International cooperation in the asylum field has been dominated by an underlying logic of 'protection elsewhere', which has been further facilitated through the legal construct of the Safe Third Country (STC).[17] The proliferation of STC agreements over the last 40 years has been attributed by some commentators to the responsibility sharing gap of the Refugee Convention, which has offered a fertile ground for such developments.[18]

The STC notion is essentially a departure from the rule of territorial asylum through the use of legal fictions, illustrated in rules such as the 'first country of asylum', the 'safe host country' and the 'safe third country'.[19] Despite their conceptual differences, they are all premised on the availability of protection in another country.[20] The term STC is used here as an umbrella concept that encloses the underlying basis of these various rules, which ac-

16 In a Report issued in 2014, Amnesty International claimed that the EU allocated 1,820 million for activities, equipment and technological infrastructure focusing on control of the external borders of the Schengen area, and only 17%,(EU 700 million) were allocated to support asylum procedures, reception services and the resettlement and integration of refugees. Amnesty International, 'The Human Cost of Fortress Europe, Human Rights Violations Against Migrants and Refugees at Europe's Borders' (9 July 2014), 9 <https://www.amnesty.org/en/documents/eur05/001/2014/en/> accessed 17 October 2024.

17 Rosemary Byrne, Andrew Schacknove 'The Safe Country Notion in European Asylum Law' (1996) Harvard Human Rights Journal 185.

18 Isabel Swerissen, 'Shared Responsibility in International Refugee Law' Expert Seminar Report 'Shared Responsibility in International Refugee Law' (Amsterdam, 2011) published March 2012, 6 <http://www.sharesproject.nl/> accessed 17 October 2024; Julian M Lehmann 'Outsourcing Protection and the Transnational Relevance of Protection Elsewhere, The Case of UNHCR' in Thomas Gammeltoft-Hansen and Jens Vedsted-Hansen (eds) *Human Rights and the Dark Side of Globalisation* (Routledge Studies in Human Rights 2017) 333.

19 Thomas Gammeltoft-Hansen 'The Extraterritorialisation of Asylum and the Advent of "Protection Lite' Danish Institute of International Studies Working Paper No. 2007/2, 15. <https://www.econstor.eu/bitstream/10419/84510/1/DIIS2007-02.pdf> accessed 17 October 2024.

20 UNHCR Executive Committee 'Problem of Refugees and Asylum-Seekers Who Move in an Irregular Manner from a Country in Which They Had Already Found Protection' No. 58 (XL) – 1989.

cording to Legomsky, occupy in actual practice, two points of the same continuum.[21]

The STC has been the legal device upon which various regional arrangements on asylum and refugee protection have been structured.[22] The idea originated in Europe around the 1990s,[23] in response to the then perceived forum shopping and irregular movement of asylum seekers.[24] As a legal device, it serves a twofold function in law; a procedural one – as a rule of admissibility of an asylum claim – and a substantive one – as an exclusion clause from refugee status during the merits phase.[25] The STC notion has also been used in the context of maritime interceptions[26] and in the context of forcible transfers of asylum seekers to third countries.[27] According to Shacknove and Byrne, the STC concept has normative implications, to the extent that it 'stresses the random geographic proximity of host States to the country of origin, runs counter to the intended universal scope of the Refugee Convention (…) and undermines the principle of burden sharing'.[28]

As a matter of international law, the legality of STC agreements is deeply contested. To begin with, the notion of STC is not explicitly anchored in

---

21 Stephen H Legomsky, 'Secondary Refugee Movements and the Return of Asylum Seekers to Third Countries: The Meaning of Effective Protection' (2003) 15 International Journal of Refugee Law 567, 570 <https://doi.org/10.1093/ijrl/15.4.567> accessed 17 October 2024.

22 María-Teresa Gil-Bazo, 'The Safe Third Country Concept in International Agreements on Refugee Protection. Assessing State Practice' (2015) 33 Netherlands Quarterly of Human Rights 42, 43.

23 European Union Council of the European Union, Council Resolution of 30 November 1992 on a Harmonized Approach to Questions Concerning Host Third Countries ("London Resolution") 30 November 1992.

24 Violeta Moreno-Lax, 'The Legality of the "Safe Third Country" Notion Contested: Insights from the Law of Treaties in Guy S Goodwin-Gill and Philippe Weckel (eds), *Migration & Refugee Protection in the 21st Century: Legal Aspects*. The Hague Academy of International Law Centre for Research (Martinus Nijhoff 2015) 665.

25 Ibid.

26 *Hirsi Jamma and Others v Italy*, App No 277665/09 ECtHR Grand Chamber (23 Feb 2012).

27 The UK Rwanda deal was a bilateral agreement premised on safe third country, whereby all asylum seekers who arrived in the UK illegally would have their claims deemed inadmissible and would be forcibly transferred to Rwanda. Agreement Between the Government of the United Kingdom of Great Britain and Northern Ireland and the Government of the Republic of Rwanda for the Provision of an Asylum Partnership to Strengthen Shared International Commitments on the Protection of Refugees and Migrants (5 December 2023) <https://assets.publishing.service.gov.uk/media/656f51d30f12ef07a53e0295/UK-Rwanda_MEDP_-_English_-_Formatted__5_Dec_23__-_UK_VERSION.pdf> accessed 17 October 2024.

28 Byrnie, Shacknove 'The Safe Country Notion in European Asylum Law' (n 17) 227.

international refugee law. The Refugee Convention does not explicitly authorise the transfer of refugees from one state party to another. Crucially, it does not prohibit it either. The legality of STC arrangements has been based on Article 31 paragraph (1) of the Refugee Convention. An asylum seeker who comes from a country in which they were safe from persecution – rather than coming *directly* from a territory where their life or freedom was threatened – can be transferred back to the transit state or a third country for the purpose of claiming international protection. Under this reading, the non-penalisation for illegal entry or presence rule enshrined in Article 31 (1) is only from asylum seekers coming directly from unsafe countries.[29] This rather restrictive reading has been questioned by some commentators on the basis that international law does not impose a duty on the part of refugees to seek asylum in the first state they find themselves.[30] In fact, there is sufficient support in international law that some limited choice can be legitimately exercised, in particular where family members already reside in one country.[31] Be that as it may, the safety of a country for the purposes of transferring an asylum seeker, and ultimately the legality of such transfer, is a question of fact and is determined by the actual situation in the third country on the ground and the risk of ill-treatment to that particular individual.[32]

3 Safe Third Country Agreements

3.1 *The EU's Migration Management Arrangements with Third Countries*

In the peak of the so called refugee crisis in 2015–2016, the EU launched the New Migration Partnership Framework with regional countries outside

29 Ibid., 186.

30 UNHCR Guidance Note on bilateral and/or multilateral transfer arrangements of asylum-seekers, (May 2013) para 3 (i).

31 EXCOM Conclusion No. 15 (XXX) 1979, para. (h) (iii), (iv).

32 *Soering v the UK* (Application no. 14038/88) 7 July 1989; House of Lords, European Union Committee 11th Report of Session 2003–04 'Handling EU asylum claims: new approaches examined Report with Evidence House of Lords' para 66; This view was recently confirmed by the UK Supreme Court in the context of UK Rwanda agreement and the blanket designation through legislation of Rwanda as safe third country. *R (on the application of AAA (Syria) and others) v Secretary of State for the Home Department* [2023] UK SC 42.

the EU.[33] Against a background of 'containment strategy,'[34] coupled with the logic of protection elsewhere, the EU in 2016 concluded the EU–Turkey Statement[35] and re-established its cooperation with Libya through Italy's bilateral cooperation agreement with the former.[36] Libya and Turkey are not, however, the only partners in the region with which the EU, or individual Member States, have entered into migration and asylum management arrangements.[37] The EU's external dimension of migration management has an extensive network of partner states. More recently, the EU has concluded questionable deals that include measures on migration management and border control with Tunisia,[38] Egypt,[39] Lebanon[40] and Mauritania.[41] These agreements have been already criticised for their evident externalisation objectives, their informality and their restrictive human rights policies.[42] The Italy–Libya and EU–Turkey are two examples of questionable cooperative arrangements covering the Central and Eastern Mediterranean migratory routes that illustrate how the EU and its member states

---

33 Commission announces New Migration Partnership Framework: reinforced cooperation with third countries to better manage migration, European Commission, (Press Release, 7 June 2016).

34 Mariagiulia Giuffré, 'From Turkey to Libya, the EU Migration Partnership from Bad to Worse' Eurojus (20 March 2017).

35 'EU–Turkey Statement' Council of the European Union Press Release (March 18, 2016).

36 Malta Declaration by the members of the European Council on the external aspects of migration: addressing the Central Mediterranean route (February 3, 2017).

37 Elizabeth Collet, Aliya Ahad, 'EU Migration Partnerships: A Work in Progress Report' (2017) European Migration Policy Institute) <https://www.migrationpolicy.org/research/eu-migration-partnerships-work-progress> accessed 17 October 2024.

38 Memorandum of Understanding on a Strategic and Global Partnership between the European Union and Tunisia <https://ec.europa.eu/commission/presscorner/detail/en/IP_23_3887> accessed 17 October 2024.

39 Joint Declaration on the Strategic and Comprehensive Partnership between The Arab Republic Of Egypt and the European Union (March 2024) <https://neighbourhood-enlargement.ec.europa.eu/news/joint-declaration-strategic-and-comprehensive-partnership-between-arab-republic-egypt-and-european-2024-03-17_en> accessed 17 October 2024.

40 President von der Leyen reaffirms EU's strong support for Lebanon and its people and announces a €1 billion package of EU funding (May 2024) <https://neighbourhood-enlargement.ec.europa.eu/news/president-von-der-leyen-reaffirms-eus-strong-support-lebanon-and-its-people-and-announces-eu1-2024-05-02_en> accessed 17 October 2024

41 The European Commission launches new migration partnership with Mauritania (March 2024) <https://ec.europa.eu/commission/presscorner/detail/en/ip_24_1335> accessed 17 October 2024.

42 See contributions in E Kassoti, N Idriz (eds) *The Informalisation of the EU's External Action in the Field of Migration and Asylum* (T.M.C. Asser Press 2022).

outsource border control and shift asylum responsibilities onto third countries in the region.

3.1.1 Italy–Libya

Europe's cooperation with Libya has attracted widespread criticism for its objective to shift responsibility migration control and generally prevent migrants and refugees from arriving at European borders.[43] The Central Mediterranean Route has been described by IOM and continues to be the world's deadliest sea migration route.[44]

Libya has had a long-standing cooperation history with the EU and particularly with Italy in the context of combatting illegal migration.[45] With Italy being the first point of entry via the Central Mediterranean route, Italy's bilateral cooperation with Libya stretches long back in the Gaddafi years. Following the fall of the Gaddafi regime in 2011, Italy resumed cooperation with Libya despite the dire human rights situation that emerged in the country. In 2017, Italy concluded a new Memorandum of Understanding (MoU) with Libya's Government of National Accord.[46]

The purpose of the cooperation under the MoU has been, among others, to combat illegal immigration and human trafficking.[47] Under the MoU, Italy funds, with the help of EU funding, the establishment of reception centres in Libya,[48] while the EU has been training and equipping Libyan Coast Guard officials with assets so that they engage in what has been reported as

43 Amnesty International, 'Libya: Shameful EU Policies Fuel Surge in Detention of Migrants and Refugees' (16 May 2018) <https://www.amnesty.org/en/latest/news/2018/05/libya-shameful-eu-policies-fuel-surge-in-detention-of-migrants-and-refugees/> accessed 17 October 2024.

44 IOM 'Mediterranean Shipwreck Sounds Alarm for Lifesaving Action' (19 December 2023) <https://www.iom.int/news/mediterranean-shipwreck-sounds-alarm-lifesaving-action> accessed 17 October 2024.

45 For an overview on Libya's and Italy's bilateral cooperation history, See Mariagiulia Giuffré, 'State Responsibility Beyond Borders: What Legal Basis for Italy's Push-backs to Libya? (2012) 24 International Journal of Refugee Law 692, 701–703 https://doi.org/10.1093/ijrl/ees05.

46 2017 *Memorandum d'intesa sulla cooperazione nel campo dello sviluppo, del contrasto all'immigrazione illegale, al traffico di esseri umani, al contrabbando e sul rafforzamento della sicurezza delle frontiere tra Io Stato della Libia e la Repubblica Italiana.* (May 2 2017) <https://www.governo.it/sites/governo.it/files/Libia.pdf> assessed 17 October 2024. (Italy–Libya Memorandum of Understanding).

47 Italy–Libya Memorandum of Understanding, Article 1 (b).

48 Italy–Libya Memorandum of Understanding, Article 2.

systematic 'pull-back' operations of migrants and refugees.[49] Italy and the EU treat Libya as a safe country. UNHCR's position on Libya has been the same since 2011, when the High Commissioner intervened in the proceedings of *Hirsi* before the European Court of Human Rights.[50] The landmark case of Hirsi was about the interception and collective expulsion by the Italian authorities of 24 Eritrean and Somali refugees from Libya, without the opportunity to apply for asylum or to obtain an effective remedy. The Strasbourg Court asserted that Italy did exercise extraterritorial jurisdiction and had effective control over the intercepted, who faced a serious risk of *refoulment* in Libya.[51] As a result, it found Italy in violation of Article 3, Article 4, Protocol No. 4 and Article 13 of the European Convention on Human Rights. UNHCR intervened in the proceedings with the following statement:

> The lack of an asylum system in Libya means that there are not sufficient safeguards to ensure that persons in need of international protection will be recognized as such and accorded legal status and associated entitlements that could ensure their rights, including to protection against *refoulement,* are not violated. The risk of chain refoulement denying international protection, especially to Eritrea, cannot be excluded.[52]

In 2018, following investigations and reports from Amnesty International and Human Rights Watch, UNHCR restated that it does not consider it appropriate for states to apply in practice a designation of Libya as 'safe third country'.[53] The High Commissioner stressed in a statement that Libya is not even to be considered 'a place of safety' for disembarkation of rescued individuals, irrespective of status pursuant to the IMO Guidelines on the Treatment of Persons Rescued at Sea.[54] The Statement reads:

---

49 See discussion in Violeta Moreno-Lax, Mariagiullia Giuffré, 'The Raise of Consensual Containment: From 'Contactless Control' to 'Contactless Responsibility' for Forced Migration Flows' in Satvinder Juss (ed), *Research Handbook on International Refugee Law* (Elgar 2009) 89–92.

50 UNHCR intervention before the European Court of Human Rights in the case of *Hirsi and Others v Italy* Application no. 27765/09 (March 2010) <https://www.refworld.org/docid/4b97778d2.html> accessed 17 October 2024.

51 *Hirsi and Others v Italy* para 136.

52 UNHCR Intervention in *Hirsi* (n 50),10.

53 UNHCR Position on Returns to Libya (Update II) (2018) para 15 <https://www.refworld.org/pdfid/5b8d02314.pdf> accessed 17 October 2024.

54 A 'Place of safety', as defined in the IMO Guidelines, para 6.17 (and as referred to in the Annex to the 1979 SAR Convention, paragraph 1.3.2) 'is a location where rescue operations are considered to terminate. It is also a place where the survivors' safety of life is no

> In light of the volatile security situation in general and the particular protection risks for third-country nationals (including detention in sub-standard conditions, and reports of serious abuses against asylum-seekers, refugees and migrants) UNHCR does not consider that Libya meets the criteria for being designated as a place of safety for the purpose of disembarkation following rescue at sea.[55]

As a response to the international civil society outcry on the human rights violations committed against migrants and refugees in Libya, UNHCR signed a Memorandum of Understanding with Rwanda and the African Union in September 2019 for purposes of evacuating refugees from Libya's detention centres.[56] According to UNHCR, the rescued individuals have been given 'asylum-seeker status' in Rwanda and while their cases are being assessed, further solutions are pursued, 'including resettlement, voluntary return to countries of previous asylum, voluntary return to countries of origin, where safe to do so, and local integration in Rwanda'.[57]

Despite numerous reports from the UN and human rights organisations on systematic pullbacks of migrants and refugees by the Libyan Coast Guard and Libyan militia[58] who end up facing torture and ill-treatment in detention centres,[59] the EU and Italy consider Libya safe and continue to outsource border control functions aimed at containing migratory movement. The coop-

---

longer threatened and where their basic human needs (such as food, shelter and medical needs) can be met. The need to avoid disembarkation in territories where the lives and freedoms of those alleging a well-founded fear of persecution would be threatened is a consideration in the case of asylum-seekers and refugees recovered at sea'. Resolution MSC.167(78) (adopted on 20 May 2004) MSC 78/26/Add.2 Guidelines on the Treatment of Persons Rescued at Sea.

55 UNHCR Position on Returns to Libya (n 53) para 40–42.

56 Joint Statement: Government of Rwanda, UNHCR and African Union agree to evacuate refugees out of Libya (Press Release 2019) <https://www.unhcr.org/uk/news/news-releases/joint-statement-government-rwanda-unhcr-and-african-union-agree-evacuate> accessed 17 October 2024.

57 UNHCR Third group of refugees evacuated to Rwanda from Libya with UNHCR support Press Release (25 November 2019) <https://www.unhcr.org/uk/news/news-releases/third-group-refugees-evacuated-rwanda-libya-unhcr-support> accessed 17 October 2024.

58 A UN Report on Independent Fact-Finding Mission on Libya in 2022 found that migrants and refugees faced murder, enforced disappearance, torture, enslavement, sexual violence, rape, and other inhumane acts'. Report of the Independent Fact-Finding Mission on Libya (A/HRC/50/63) (27 June 2022) <https://reliefweb.int/report/libya/report-independent-fact-finding-mission-libya-ahrc5063-advance-unedited-version-enar ≥ accessed 17 October 2024.

59 Ibid.

eration of Italy and the EU with Libya in its current form is a clear example of prohibitive cooperative action under the Refugee Convention, not only because of its evident responsibility shifting objectives but also because it has led to systematic violations of migrants' and refugees' rights, raising issues of complicity on the part of Italy and the EU under the law of state responsibility.[60]

3.1.2 EU–Turkey Statement

The EU–Turkey Statement signed in March 2016 and communicated at the time as press release[61] is another example of a legally dubious cooperation-based arrangement serving externalisation and responsibility shifting objectives.[62] Despite its informal character,[63] Turkey, under the Statement, is designated as a safe third country for the return of all irregular migrants and asylum seekers, whose asylum applications have been declared inadmissible by Greece and who entered Greece irregularly through the maritime border with Turkey. The rationale for returns to Turkey has been the STC notion that functions as an admissibility rule under the CEAS.[64] The subsequent legal basis of the returns from Greece to Turkey has been the bilateral readmission Protocol between Greece and Turkey. At the heart of the EU–Turkey deal was a 'one for one' offer – for every Syrian being returned to Turkey from the Greek islands, another Syrian will be resettled from Turkey to the EU, taking into account the UN vulnerability criteria.[65]

As with Libya, although to a much lesser extent, the presumption of Turkey as safe for returns of asylum seekers has been strongly challenged by NGOs and scholars.[66] The reasons behind this are twofold. Firstly, Turkey has reserved to the Refugee Convention with a geographical limitation that grants refugee

60 See analysis in Cantor et al, 'Externalisation, Access to Territorial Asylum and International Law' (n 1) 136–138.

61 EU–Turkey Statement (18 March 2016) <https://www.consilium.europa.eu/en/press/press-releases/2016/03/18/eu-turkey-statement/> accessed 17 October 2024.

62 Michelle McEwen, 'Refugee Resettlement in Crisis: The Failure of the EU–Turkey Deal and the Case for Burden-Sharing' (Spring 2017) Issue 2 Swarthmore International Relations Journal 20.

63 Steven Peers, 'The Draft EU/Turkey Deal on Migration and Refugees: Is It Legal?' (16 March 2026) <http://eulawanalysis.blogspot.com/2016/03/the-draft-euturkey-deal-on-migration.html> accessed 17 October 2024.

64 Directive 2013/32/EU of 26 June 2013 on common procedures for granting and withdrawing international protection (recast).

65 EU–Turkey Statement.

66 Elizabeth Collet 'The Paradox of the EU–Turkey Refugee Deal' Migration Policy Institute (March 2016).

protection only to refugees coming from Europe.[67] Therefore, asylum seekers, subject to returns under the EU Turkey Statement, who in their majority are from Syria and other non-European nationalities, are granted under Turkish law some 'conditional refugee status' and are allowed to reside in Turkey only temporarily until they are resettled.[68] Secondly, the overall human rights situation in the country deteriorated following the attempted Turkish military coup in 2016. The coup triggered a state of emergency and derogation from the European Convention on Human Rights (ECHR).[69] The lack of international protection to non-EU nationals under Turkish law and the general human rights situation in the country suffice to challenge the characterisation of Turkey as a safe third country for all returnees without individual assessment.

While Turkey unilaterally suspended the Greece-Turkey Readmission Protocol in 2018 following tensions between the two states,[70] and while all transfers under the Statement were suspended in 2020 due to COVID-19, the knock-on effects of the Statement continue to impact the rights of asylum seekers in both Turkey and Greece. The EU–Turkey Statement is an illustrative example of how the EU asylum policy is premised on externalisation and responsibility shifting, either onto the frontline Member States at the external borders or to third countries in the region.[71]

The Statement turned Greece into a buffer zone for the EU's migration and refugee policy. Still today, as the President of the European Commission, Ursula von der Leyen, framed it, Greece is the EU's 'shield' in the management of external borders.[72] The EU–Turkey Statement was used by Greece over the years to pass a series of law reforms that have been negatively impacted on

67 Law No. 6458 of 2013 on Foreigners and International Protection, Article 61. Unofficial translation can be found at <https://www.refworld.org/cgibin/texis/vtx/rwmain?docid=5a1d828f4>.

68 Law No. 6458 of 2013 on Foreigners and International Protection, Article 62.

69 'Measures taken under the state of emergency in Turkey' Statement by Mr Nils Muižnieks, the Council of Europe's Commissioner for Human Rights (27 July 2016) <https://www.coe.int/en/web/portal/full-news/-/asset_publisher/y5xQt7QdunzT/content/measures-taken-under-the-state-of-emergency-in-turkey> accessed 17 October 2024.

70 Turkey suspends 'migrant readmission' deal with Greece (June 2018) <https://www.hurriyetdailynews.com/turkey-suspends-refugee-readmission-deal-with-greece-132955>.

71 https://www.asileproject.eu/why-the-eu-turkey-statement-should-never-serve-as-a-blueprint/ accessed 17 October 2024.

72 Alastair Jamieson, 'Greece is 'Europe's shield' in migrant crisis, says EU chief von der Leyen on visit to Turkey border' (Euronews March 4 2020) <https://www.euronews.com/2020/03/03/greece-migrant-crisis-is-an-attack-by-turkey-on-the-eu-austria> accessed 17 October 2024.

asylum seekers who are detained in camps on the islands and deprived of adequate living standards.[73] Greece has expanded the use of safe third countries in national asylum legislation by introducing a national list of safe third countries, which designates Turkey as safe for all applicants coming from Somalia, Pakistan and Bangladesh, whose asylum applications subsequently become inadmissible.[74] The legality however of this Act has been recently contested before the Greek Council of State since Turkey has not accepted transfers since 2019, leaving individuals from these three nationalities, whose applications are deemed inadmissible, in limbo.[75]

The EU–Turkey Statement showcases the fragility of STC and readmission arrangements and their impact on asylum seekers as well as on geopolitical relations in the region. The Statement was concluded in the wider framework of EU–Turkey relations and discussions on visa liberalisations and Turkey's accession to the EU. From an intra-EU solidarity and responsibility sharing perspective, the pressure upon Greece during 2015 and 2016 was not met with tangible responsibility sharing commitments by the EU Member States. It seems that the flexible solidarity measures established in the new Pact will not relieve frontline states' reception systems without a permanent large-scale relocation mechanism at the EU level. To conclude, the EU–Turkey Statement is another example of international cooperation on asylum at the regional level, designed to serve responsibility shifting objectives. What is

73 Angeliki Dimitriadi 'No Turning Back: Greece and the EU–Turkey Statement Seven Years On' Global Public Policy Institute (Policy Paper September 2023) 4–6 <https://gppi.net/media/ASILE_2023_Greece.pdf> accessed 17 October 2024.

74 The Joint Ministerial Decision 42799/2021 established a national list of safe third countries. Joint Ministerial Decision No. 42799/2021, (Government Gazette 2425 / B / 7-6-2021), Designation of third countries that are characterized as safe and compilation of a national list, according to the provisions of article 86 of Law 4636/2019 <https://www.e-nomothesia.gr/kat-allodapoi/prosphuges-politiko-asulo/koine-upourgike-apophase-42799-2021.html> accessed 17 October 2024.

75 The legality of the Greek Joint Ministerial Decision No. 42799/2021 has been contested before the Greek Council of State in its decision No. 177/2023, who favoured its annulment. The Greek Council of State further requested the CJEU for a preliminary ruling on the interpretation of EU Directive 2013/32 under the preliminary ruling procedure of Art 267 TFEU. The CJEU found that while Article 38 of Directive 2013/32/EU does not preclude legislation of a Member State designating a third country as generally safe, Member States may not, however, issue a decision rejecting an application for asylum as inadmissible, on the basis of the concept of 'safe third country' in case <https://rsaegean.org/en/cjeu-ruling-on-the-concept-of-safe-third-country/#:~:text=The%20Court%20accepted%2C%20however%2C%20that,those%20applicants%20to%20its%20territory> accessed 17 October 2024.

more, its implementation has also led to violations of fundamental rights at Europe's borders.[76]

3.2 *Australia's Offshore Processing Agreements with Nauru and Papua New Guinea*

If there is one country that has been pioneering the externalisation of international protection responsibilities to third countries, it is Australia. Australia has operated a systematic offshore processing regime for asylum claims, in partnerships with third countries in the Pacific region, such as Nauru and Papua New Guinea (PNG).[77] Nauru and PNG are not the only countries in the region with which Australia has built a sophisticated cooperation-based regime. For example, Indonesia cooperates with Australia in the form of stopping asylum seekers from leaving for Australia by boat. Cooperation, in this case, takes the form of funding, equipping and training, which comes at the expense of asylum seekers' ability to seek protection in the region.[78] Australia also cooperates with Sri Lanka, a refugee-producing country, and concluded a deal with Malaysia for the forcible transfers of intercepted asylum seekers, which the Australian High Court found to be illegal.[79] The discussion here focuses on Australia's offshore processing agreements with Nauru and PNG as two bilateral agreements that have been notoriously questionable with respect to their legality under international law and their responsibility shifting objectives.

Australia's offshore processing regime in cooperation with Nauru and PNG developed in the early 2000s and can be divided for purposes of the analysis into two periods: the 'Pacific Solution', operationalised between 2001 and 2007, and the 'Operation Sovereign Borders', the offshore processing resumed by Australia in 2013.[80] The policy in both instances is about the maritime

---

76 UN Human Rights Council (UNHRC), Report on Means to Address the Human Rights Impact of Pushbacks of Migrants on Land and at Sea: Report of the Special Rapporteur on the Human Rights of Migrants, UN doc A/ HRC/47/30 (12 May 2021).

77 Jane McAdam, 'Extraterritorial Processing in Europe Is 'regional protection' the answer, and if not, what is?' Policy Brief 1 (2015) Andrew & Renata Kaldor Centre for International Refugee Law 9.

78 On Australia – Indonesia cooperation See Antje Missbach 'Doors and fences: Controlling Indonesia's porous borders and policing asylum seekers' (2014) 35 The Singapore's Journal of Geography, 228–244; Nikolas Feith Tan 'The Status of Asylum Seekers in Indonesia' (2016) 28 International Journal of Refugee Law 365 https://doi.org/10.1093/ijrl/eew045.

79 Plaintiff M70/2011 and Plaintiff M106/2011 v Minister for Immigration and Citizenship [2011] HCA 32 (31 August 2011).

80 Australia government, Operation Sovereign Borders <https://osb.homeaffairs.gov.au> accessed 17 October 2024.

interception and forcible transfer of asylum seekers bound for Australia to Nauru and PNG for the purposes of asylum processing and protection.

Australia's bilateral arrangements have been framed by regional power asymmetries in the Asia-Pacific region. These power asymmetries are a useful lens that explains why PNG and a micro-state like Nauru accepted to become processing centres for Australia, despite the concomitant mass influx of aliens as well as the social and political cost of hosting asylum seekers. Power relations also illustrate the context in which externalisation and responsibility shifting take place. In this context, the two host states were countries dependent on Australia's aid, a fact that makes them willing to consent to deals that offer financial assistance, even if the arrangements are legally dubious and bound to raise serious legal concerns by the international community.

The selection of these two states was therefore strategic. Both Nauru, one of the world's smallest countries, and PNG, before gaining full independence, were trusteeships under the Administration of Australia.[81] This hierarchical power relationship allowed Australia to use its 'extremely poor, politically unstable and socially vulnerable neighbours' so as to transfer asylum seekers in exchange for money, preventing Nauru and PNG from bargaining on equal terms.[82] To offset the onus of essentially warehousing intercepted asylum seekers, Australia offered, in exchange, to both countries free medical care, educational opportunities and sports ovals.[83]

Australia's model of offshore processing kicked-off after the Tampa incident in 2001, involving a Norwegian freighter. The MV Tampa, having rescued 443 asylum seekers, was denied entry to and disembarkation at Australia's Christmas Island, the closest port of safety at the time. The passengers were transferred to a navy vessel and were forcibly removed to detention camps in Nauru. The incident marked the beginning of Australia's offshore processing policy development, championed as the 'Pacific Solution'.[84] In an amendment

81 For a discussion on Australia's historic ties to Papua New Guinea and Nauru, See Savitri Taylor 'The Pacific Solution or Pacific Nightmare; The Difference between Burden Shifting and Responsibility Sharing' (2005) 6 Asian Pacific Law and Policy Journal 1, 19–31.

82 Ibid., 32.

83 Tara Magner 'The less than Pacific Solution for Asylum Seekers in Australia' (2004) 16 International Journal of Refugee Law 53 https://doi.org/10.1093/ijrl/16.1.53.

84 Janet Philips, 'The 'Pacific Solution' revisited: a statistical guide to the asylum-seeker caseloads on Nauru and Manus Island' Background Note (September 2012) Australian Parliament <https://www.aph.gov.au/About_Parliament/Parliamentary_Departments/Parliamentary_Library/pubs/BN/2012-2013/PacificSolution#_Toc334509636> accessed 17 October 2024.

to the Migration Act of 2001, the Minister of Immigration unilaterally designated PNG and Nauru as incontestably safe for the processing of asylum claims, and that all asylum seekers bound for Australia would be, going forwards, transferred to these two countries.[85]

From 2001 to 2017, a series of Memoranda of Understanding were signed between Australia and the two countries.[86] These bilateral STC arrangements have been widely criticised and condemned for resulting in serious human rights violations against detainees in Nauru and Manus Island. The detainees were subject to unjust and prolonged detention and degrading treatment, in direct violation of international human rights law.[87] For those detained in the processing facilities, UNHCR reported serious levels of abuse, self-harm and neglect.[88] The transfer of the asylum seekers, offshore Australia, was even characterised as a 'discriminatory and arbitrary punishment for seeking asylum'.[89]

Australia denied any legal responsibility for the state of the asylum seekers in Nauru and on Manus Island. UNHCR, on the contrary, asserted that international law requires Australia to remain responsible for those who have sought its protection – *a fortiori* because it is Australia that 'designed, financed and managed the system in which these two developing and under-resourced

---

85 198 A of the Migration Act as inserted by the Migration Amendment (Excision from the Migration Zone) (Consequential Provisions) Act 2001.

86 2012 Memorandum of Understanding between the Republic of Nauru and the Commonwealth of Australia, relating to the transfer to and assessment of persons in Nauru, and related issues <https://dfat.gov.au/geo/nauru/pages/memorandum-of-understanding-between-the-republic-of-nauru-and-the-commonwealth-of-australia-relating-to-the-transfer-to-and.aspx> 2012 Memorandum of Understanding between the Government of the Independent State of Papua New Guinea and the Government of Australia, relating to the transfer to, and assessment and settlement in, Papua New Guinea of certain persons, and related issues <https://dfat.gov.au/geo/papua-new-guinea/Documents/joint-mou-20130806.pdf> accessed 17 October 2024.

87 Human Rights Council, Twenty-eighth Session 'Report of the Special Rapporteur on Torture and Other Cruel, Inhuman or Degrading Treatment or Punishment, Mr. Juan E. Méndez' A/HRC/28/68/Add.1 (6 March 2015), paras 16–31.

88 UNHCR Submission on the Inquiry into the Serious Allegations of Abuse, Self-harm and Neglect of Asylum-seekers in Relation to the Nauru Regional Processing Centre, and any like Allegations in Relation to the Manus Regional Processing Centre Referred to the Senate Legal and Constitutional Affairs Committee (12 November 2016) <https://www.refworld.org/legal/natlegcomments/unhcr/2016/en/116653> accessed 17 October 2024.

89 Jared L Lacertosa, 'Unfriendly Shores: An Examination of Australia's "Pacific Solution" under International Law' (2014) 40 Brooklyn Journal of International Law 321, 356.

countries participate'.[90] The legality of Australia's offshore processing regime, in light of the extended human rights violations, has been scrupulously assessed against international human rights law standards.[91] Literature has also explored Australia's responsibility in international law under the rules of the law of state responsibility.[92]

In April 2016, PNG's Supreme Court ruled that the detention of asylum seekers under the bilateral agreement breached the right to liberty under PNG's constitutional order.[93] The Court found that the persons on Manus Island Regional Processing Centre were forcefully brought into PNG, held against their will and that the administrative arrangements between the two sovereign countries were in breach of PNG's constitutional guarantee of liberty of all persons.[94] Following this ruling, the processing centre on Manus Island formally closed in October 2017. This was indeed a landmark decision coming from the Highest Court of the partnering state.

In 2018, the Migration Act was amended and a legislation on the urgent medical evacuation and transfer of refugees and asylum seekers in mainland Australia was passed in 2019, known as the Medevac Bill.[95] As positive as this move is, in response to the new law, Australian Prime Minister Scott Morrison announced the reopening of Christmas Island's detention centre, declaring that refugees and asylum seekers needing medical transfer will not be sent

90 UNHCR Urges Australia to evacuate offshore facilities as health situation deteriorates (12 October 2018) <https://www.unhcr.org/uk/news/briefing-notes/unhcr-urges-australia-evacuate-shore-facilities-health-situation-deteriorates> accessed 17 October 2024.

91 See indicatively, Amy Nethery, Rosa Holman, 'Secrecy and Human Rights Abuse in Australia's Offshore Immigration Detention Centres' (2016) 20 The International Journal of Human Rights 177; Sergio Carrera, Elspeth Guild, 'Offshore Processing of Asylum Applications Out of sight, Out of Mind?' CEPS Commentary (Brussels: CEPS, 27 January 2017).

92 See Indicatively, Hathaway, Gameltoft-Hansen 'Non Refoulement in A World of Cooperative Deterrence' (n 5); Savitri Taylor, 'Australian Funded Care and Maintain ace of Asylum-Seekers in Indonesia and Papua New Guinea, All care but no Responsibility?' 337; Nikolas Feith-Tan, 'State Responsibility and Migration Control: Australia's international deterrence model' in *Human Rights and the Dark Side of Globalisation* (n 18) 225; Azadeh Dastyari, Asher Hirsch, 'The ring of steel: extraterritorial migration controls in Indonesia and Libya and the complicity of Australia and Italy' (2019) 19 Human Rights Law Review 435 https://doi.org/10.1093/hrlr/ngz024.

93 Supreme Court of Papua New Guinea, *Namah v Pato* (Minister for Foreign Affairs and Immigrations) para 74.

94 Ibid.

95 Migration Amendment (Urgent Medical Treatment) Bill 2018.

to mainland Australia, but will first be sent to Christmas Island, where they will be further assessed.[96]

The Pacific Solution and the Operation Sovereign Borders were Australia's response to large-scale arrivals of asylum seekers in the region. The arrangements were purported to have been concluded in the name of cooperation and responsibility sharing.[97] The overtly stated purpose of the Operation Sovereign Borders was, as its name suggested, border control of illegal migration as a sovereign act. The cooperation of Nauru and PNG was easily bought at a price, given the countries' existing power asymmetries and financial dependence on Australia. Australia's bilateral offshore processing arrangements were therefore an example of the language of responsibility sharing being used as 'a deceptive rhetorical veil,' whilst, in reality, they had been tantamount to responsibility shifting.[98] Despite their human rights implications and the high costs of maintaining the offshore processing regime, Australia's asylum policies have had knock on effects outside the region, with countries around the world considering similar arrangements.[99]

3.3 *The US–Canada Safe Third Country Agreement*

In 2004, Canada entered into a bilateral Safe Third Country Agreement (STCA) with the US.[100] For a long period of time, Canada had been hailed as a leader in refugee protection standards worldwide.[101] It had traditionally been seen as a destination country – and a particularly welcoming one[102] – with high rates of approval of asylum applications.[103] In contrast, the US, also a traditional

---

96 'Tropical location' used to lure doctors to Christmas Island for refugee medical transfers https://reliefweb.int/report/christmas-island-australia/tropical-location-used-lure-doctors-christmas-island-refugee, accessed 17 October 2024.

97 Taylor 'The Pacific Solution or Pacific Nightmare; The Difference between Burden Shifting and Responsibility Sharing' (n 81) 31.

98 Ibid., 36.

99 The UK-Rwanda deal sought to imitate the Australian model. Italy has recently signed a deal with Albania on maritime interception and offshore processing.

100 Agreement Between the Government of the United States of America and the Government of Canada for Cooperation in the Examination of Refugee Status Claims from Nationals of Third Countries (December 5, 2002) (US-Canada STC Agreement).

101 Efrat Arbel, Alletta Brenner, 'Bordering on Failure Canada-US Border Policy and the Politics of Refugee Exclusion' Harvard Immigration and Law Clinic, Harvard Law School (November 2014), 104.

102 The Peoples of Canada won in 1986 the Nansen Medal Award for their work on the causes of refugees. <https://www.latimes.com/archives/la-xpm-1986-10-07-mn-5066-story.html>, accessed 17 October 2024.

103 Andrew F Moore, 'Unsafe in America: A Review of the US Safe Third Country Agreement' (2007) 47 Santa Clara Law Review 201, 208.

destination and resettlement country, has always had more restrictive asylum policies in place, in particular for refugees coming from Central America.[104] Following the landmark case of Singh[105] before the Supreme Court, Canada revitalised its national asylum system and established a tribunal process that gave every asylum seeker the opportunity to have their claim assessed on its merits.[106] Since the conclusion of the STCA with the US, there has been a shift towards increasingly restrictive and exclusionary policies on asylum in Canada.[107]

The STCA is a bilateral agreement that constitutes an arrangement for sharing and determining responsibility for asylum applications between the two neighbouring countries and which, for the purposes of the agreement, have designated each other as safe. It can be seen, therefore, as a bilateral framework on responsibility sharing for asylum between two countries of the Global North and relatively equal partners.

Under the Agreement, '[t]he Party of the country of last presence shall examine, in accordance with its refugee status determination system, the refugee status claim of any person who arrives at a land border, port of entry […] and makes a refugee status claim'.[108] Until recently, the STAC applied only at official entry points and land borders. This loophole has been used by asylum seekers over the years to resort to irregular crossings into Canada from unofficial points so that they can lodge a claim.

Over the years, the STCA has been challenged on the ground that it acts as a deterrent that has resulted in the irregular crossing of borders and, more specifically, on the ground that the US cannot be considered a safe country, at least for a certain category of refugees.[109] In 2007, the Canadian Council for Refugees, Amnesty International and the Canadian Council for Churches, challenged the designation of the US as a safe country.[110] The Federal Court,

---

104 Arbel and Brenner, 'Bordering on Failure Canada-US Border Policy and the Politics of Refugee Exclusion' (n 101) 105.

105 *Singh v Canada* (Minister of Employment and Immigration), [1985] 1 S.C.R. 177.

106 Arbel and Brenner, 'Bordering on Failure Canada-US Border Policy and the Politics of Refugee Exclusion' (n 101) 104.

107 Ibid., 105.

108 US-Canada STC Agreement, Article 4 (1).

109 Ben Proctor, 'Fleeing to Canada on Foot: Reviewing the Canada-U.S. Safe Third Country Agreement' Wilson Centre, Canada Institute (4 April 2017) 8. <https://www.wilsoncenter.org/sites/default/files/media/documents/article/fleeing_to_canada_on_foot_stca_final_04-04-2017.pdf ?> accessed 17 October 2024.

110 Canadian Council for Refugees, Canadian Council of Churches, Amnesty International, and John Doe (Applicants) v. Her Majesty the Queen (Respondent) *Canadian Council for Refugees v. Canada*, [2007] F.C.J. No. 1583, 2007 FC 1262.

having granted the coalition of organisations legal standing in the proceedings, found that the US does not comply with its *non-refoulement* obligations under the Refugee Convention and the Convention against Torture,[111] and that the application of the safe third country rule, in the context of this bilateral STCA, violates refugees rights under the Canadian Charter and international law.[112] Although the decision was later overturned by Canada's Federal Court of Appeal on technical grounds, what is important is that, in the first instance, the Court did challenge the legality of the agreement determining that the US is not a safe country for all refugees.[113]

Under the Trump Administration, the 2017 Executive Order on Immigration under the Zero Tolerance Policy included a travel ban for several Muslim-majority countries, under which refugees are punished for illegal entry, in contravention of Article 31 of the Refugee Convention,[114] with either expedited removal or detention in substandard conditions and with no access to counsel.[115] Because of the operation of the STCA, these refugees had no prospect of applying for asylum in Canada, unless they attempted an illegal crossing. These changes in the US asylum policy have rendered the US no longer safe within the meaning of the bilateral STCA.[116]

A second challenge of the STCA was lodged by the Canadian Council for Refugees, Amnesty International and other applicants before the Federal Court of Canada in 2017, seeking to have the Agreement declared unconstitutional under Canadian law.[117] The case was about refugee claimants who

---

111 Convention Against Torture and Other Cruel, Inhuman and Degrading Treatment or Punishment (1984) UNTS Vol 1465, 85 (CAT); Article 3 (1).

112 *Canadian Council for Refugees v. Canada*, para 239–240.

113 Ibid. 338. For an in-depth scholarly analysis on the legality of the US-Canada STC Agreement under international law See Moore, 'Unsafe in America: A Review of the US Safe Third Country Agreement' (n 103).

114 Attorney General Announces Zero-Tolerance Policy for Criminal Illegal Entry <https://www.justice.gov/opa/pr/attorney-general-announces-zero-tolerance-policy-criminal-illegal-entry> accessed 17 October 2024.

115 Attorney General Announces Zero-Tolerance Policy for Criminal Illegal Entry <https://www.justice.gov/opa/pr/attorney-general-announces-zero-tolerance-policy-criminal-illegal-entry> accessed 17 October 2024.

116 Contesting the Designation of the US as a Safe Third Country (19 May 2017) Amnesty International Canada and Canadian Council for Refugees <https://ccrweb.ca/sites/ccrweb.ca/files/stca-submission-2017.pdf> accessed 17 October 2024

117 *The Canadian Council for Refugees Amnesty International, the Canadian Council of Churches v. The Minister of Immigration, Refugees and Citizenship and the Minister of Public Safety and Emergency Preparedness*, and *Nedira Jemal Mustefa v. The Minister of Immigration, Refugees and Citizenship and the Minister of Public Safety and Emergency Preparedness* and *Mohammad Majd Maher, Homsi Hala Maher Homsi Karam Maher*

reached Canada from US entry points and filed claims for asylum on gender-based persecution and sexual violence, but were returned to the US on the basis of the STCA. Upon return, they were detained by US Immigration officials. The applicants asked the Court, *inter alia*, to declare that Canada needs to consider rescinding the STCA with the US and, as an interim measure, to immediately suspend the agreement.

The Federal Court of Appeal gave its decision in July 2020 and found that 'ineligible STCA claimants are returned to the US by Canadian officials, where they are immediately imprisoned by US authorities.[118] The Court also held that the '"sharing of responsibility" objective of the STCA should entail some guarantee of access to a fair refugee process' and that, in this case, it had not, as applicants were removed to the US without any assessment of their risks or the substance of their refugee claims.[119] Finally, the Court held that 'Canada cannot turn a blind eye to the consequences that befell' applicants who are removed to the US because of the operation of the STCA,[120] and given that the provisions enacting the agreement infringed upon constitutional guarantees, particularly Section 7 of the Canadian Charter of Rights and Freedoms concerning the life, liberty and security of the person, the Court invalidated the STCA.[121]

The Canadian Government appealed the decision before the Supreme Court, which, in June 2023, delivered its decision and found partly in favour of the government. The Court found that the STCA as a legislative scheme does not breach Section 7 of the Charter because of the legal safeguards, namely the safety valves that may be used on a case-by-case basis.[122] However, the Supreme Court returned the appellants' claims on Section 15 of the Charter regarding equality before the law, to the Federal Court, for determination, due to the lack of factual findings on which the Supreme Court could rely, the complexity of the record and conflicting evidence, and the profound seriousness of the matter.[123]

Homsi Reda Yassin Al Nahass v The Minister of Immigration, Refugees and Citizenship and the Minister of Public Safety and Emergency Preparedness. Federal Court of Canada 2020 FC 770 22 July 2020.

118 Ibid., para 103.

119 Ibid., para 128.

120 Ibid.

121 Ibid, Conclusion.

122 *Canadian Council for Refugees v. Canada (Citizenship and Immigration)*, 2023 SCC 17 (June 16, 2024) para 163.

123 Ibid., para 178.

While the legal challenge to the STCA was ongoing, in March 2023, the US and Canada expanded through an additional Protocol, the application of the STCA to all crossings across the entire land border, including internal waterways, so that all applicants who have crossed irregularly from the US to Canada will be returned to the US unless they met one of the exceptions specified under the Agreement.[124] This amendment removed the procedural loophole on which asylum seekers had relied upon to lodge claims in Canada.

The US-Canada STCA is a unique example of a North-North responsibility sharing arrangement, where the two countries are both parties to the Refugee Convention, have similar, but not identical, international protection standards on paper at least and are equal partners in international relations. From a responsibility sharing perspective, the STCA decreased the number of asylum applications in Canada.[125] A report claimed that the effects of the STCA have been felt unevenly, as the implementation of the agreement has resulted in large numbers of asylum seekers being kept in the US and out of Canada.[126] The same report sheds light into the different motivations behind the conclusion of the Agreement between the two countries:

> While the Agreement was designed as a "burden sharing mechanism" (...) the United States (...) entered the agreement primarily to fortify the border, whilst Canada entered into the Agreement to deter asylum seekers from making refugee claims in Canada.[127]

Canada has thus insulated itself from excessive asylum responsibilities that it would otherwise have towards refugees arriving irregularly from the US. Considering the recent amendment of the STCA and the Supreme Court's ruling on its constitutionality insofar as Section 4 of the Charter is concerned, the possibility of reaching Canada and applying for asylum is now impossible for the majority of asylum seekers, who found themselves subject to US' restrictive asylum policies.

---

124 *Additional Protocol to the Agreement between The Government of Canada and the Government of the United States of America For cooperation in the examination of refugee status claims from nationals of third countries* (signed on 29 March 2022, as modified 24 March 2024).

125 Moore, 'Unsafe in America: A Review of the US Safe Third Country Agreement', 210.

126 Arbel, Brenner, 'Bordering on Failure Canada-US Border Policy and the Politics of Refugee Exclusion' (n 101) 66.

127 Ibid.

4 Conclusions

The increasing focus of the Global North on the externalisation of asylum and migration control has had a negative impact on the provision of refugee protection, by defining approaches to asylum.[128] The conclusion of safe third-country agreements, like the ones discussed in this chapter, has been facilitated by existing power asymmetries between states, where the consent of partner states has been secured through financial or other incentives that use asylum and migration control as bargaining chips.

While states are free to cooperate against *quid pro quo* arrangements in pursuit of their legitimate interests, including border control, international law places certain limits to international cooperation. The foregoing discussion of the five safe third-country agreements has shown that these practices fall short of international law standards on international cooperation in refugee matters. Firstly, these arrangements have resulted in numerous violations of refugee rights at states' land and sea borders, going against the letter and spirit of the Refugee Convention. Secondly, they constitute a bad faith implementation of the duty to cooperate towards fair responsibility sharing under international refugee law. While some of these agreements employ the language of responsibility sharing and international protection standards on paper, in practice, their true and primary objective is refugee containment and responsibility shifting.

What is more, such agreements negatively impact on interstate relations in the long term, as they exacerbate current inequities in the allocation of protection responsibilities, undermining the fairness of the international refugee law regime. As illustrated in the context of the EU, frontline Member States that were disproportionately affected by Dublin's operation and large-scale arrivals were left without meaningful assistance and support from their fellow central and northern Member States. In the absence of such assistance, countries such as Italy and Greece have adopted even more restrictive asylum policies. For all these reasons, cooperative arrangements that shift responsibilities onto other states, restrict access to asylum and result in refugee rights violations constitute prohibitive forms of international cooperation under the Refugee Convention.

128 Crisp, 'A New Asylum Paradigm? Globalization, Migration and the Uncertain Future of the International Refugee Regime' UNHCR New Issues on Refugee Research, Working Paper No. 100. (December 2003).

CHAPTER 4

Comprehensive Approaches to International Cooperation and Responsibility Sharing

In the life of the international refugee law regime, there have been instances of international cooperation that have made a positive contribution to refugee protection and have sought to redistribute responsibilities between states in cases of mass influx. This chapter discusses the Comprehensive Plan of Action for Indochinese Refugees (CPA) and the International Conference on Central American Refugees (CIREFCA). While these arrangements have been rather context specific, *ad hoc* and emergency-driven, they are widely seen as overall successful instances of responsibility sharing in the practice of states. The purpose of the discussion is to identify the common factors that contributed to the relative success of these arrangements, outside of the unique political junctures and regional specificities, so as to draw somewhat 'universal' lessons and elements of best practice.

The chapter also discusses the UN Convention Plus Initiative, a 2009 UNHCR-led process that sought to fill the responsibility sharing gap of the Refugee Convention through a normative framework at the UN level. While unsuccessful, its treatment in this chapter showcases what went wrong in the process of negotiating a framework on responsibility sharing and whether the lessons learned were incorporated into the negotiation and conclusion of the Global Compact on Refugees. The chapter concludes with a discussion of the responsibility sharing modalities of the Refugee Compact, identifying shortcomings as well as elements of best practice.

1 The Comprehensive Plan of Action for the Indochinese Refugees (CPA)

A 'textbook' example of meaningful international cooperation and responsibility sharing took place between 1979 and 1993 during the Indochinese exodus. This process involved the cooperation among countries of origin, coun-

 | DOI:10.1163/9789004547711_005

tries in the region – assuming a first-asylum role – and countries outside the region, assuming a resettlement role.[1]

From the very beginning, the Indochinese refugee crisis became the business and foreign policy consideration of all anti-communist states in the West, particularly the US, which responded to the plight of the labelled 'boat people' with liberal admission policies.[2] The Indochinese refugees were individuals who fled Vietnam, Cambodia and Laos. A conference in Geneva was convened in 1979 to come up with what has been characterised as a model of 'universal' responsibility sharing.[3] Under this model, states assumed different protection roles; states in the region assumed first-asylum responsibilities and states further afar in the Global North undertook explicit commitments to resettle, with an exception of Japan, which responded to responsibility sharing demands only through increased financial contributions.[4]

Asylum in the region however quickly became somewhat contingent upon resettlement elsewhere. While as a matter of international law, the provision of international protection is not legally contingent on responsibility sharing, in the context of the Vietnamese exodus, the neighbouring countries, namely Malaysia, Thailand and Indonesia, only offered temporary protection due to the explicit resettlement commitments on the part of Western states.[5] Western countries, such as the US, Australia, Canada and France, contributed to the responsibility sharing effort with resettlement quotas that were the result of a market-based model consisting of both immigration and humanitarian criteria.[6]

As new flows of Indochinese refugees continued to emerge in the region, Western states became sceptical about the genuine refugee status of the Indo-

---

1 Alexander Betts, 'Comprehensive Plans of Action: Insights from CIREFCA and the Indochinese CPA' New Issues in Refugee Research, Working Paper 102 (UNHCR 2006), 27.

2 Astri Surhke, 'Burden Sharing during Refugee Emergencies: The Logic of Collective versus National Action' (1998) 11 Journal of Refugee Studies 396 405 https://doi.org/10.1093/jrs/11.4.396.

3 UN General Assembly Meeting on Refugees and Displaced Persons in South-East Asia, convened by the Secretary-General of the United Nations at Geneva, on 20 and 21 July 1979, and subsequent developments: Report of the Secretary-General, 7 November 1979, A/34/627 (34th session, agenda item 83) <https://www.refworld.org/docid/3ae68f420.html> accessed 17 October 2024; Asha Hans, Astri Surhke, 'Responsibility Sharing' in James Hathaway (ed) *Reconceiving International Refugee Law* (Martinus Nijhoff Publishers 1997) 87, 100.

4 Surhke, 'Burden Sharing during Refugee Emergencies: The Logic of Collective versus National Action' (n 2) 405.

5 Ibid.

6 Hans, Surhrke 'Responsibility Sharing' (n 3), 100.

chinese people, as well as the openness of their resettlement policies. All the while, neighbouring countries in the region responded with excessive use of deterrence measures and *refoulement*.[7]

A second Geneva Conference was called in 1989 by the UN Secretary General at the time, to respond to the new waves of Indochinese refugees.[8] The Comprehensive Plan of Action (CPA) agreed upon during the Conference was premised upon individual refugee status determination, whereby the Vietnamese had to prove their refugee status after an agreed cut-off date.[9] The cut-off date varied across the neighbouring countries.[10] This meant that from the date of the cut-off, the Vietnamese were not considered *de facto* refugees. A negative outcome of this change was that those who fell short of refugee status were voluntarily repatriated to Vietnam with the help and monitoring of UNHCR,[11] under what has been described as a controversial process from a human rights perspective.[12] The failure of the human rights mandate of the CPA was strongly observed in the phase of the individual determination process, which did not offer the individual asylum-seeker the benefit of doubt.[13] UNHCR essentially became a 'broker' between the countries of first-asylum and the countries of origin and resettlement in an effort to afford durable solutions.[14]

The Steering Committee of the International Conference on Indochinese Refugees,[15] chaired by UNHCR and comprising of government representatives,

---

7 Volker Türk, Madeline Garlick, 'From Burdens and Responsibilities to Opportunities: The Comprehensive Refugee Response Framework and a Global Compact on Refugees' (2016) 28 International Journal of Refugee Law 656, 667 https://doi.org/10.1093/ijrl/eew043.

8 Declaration and Comprehensive Plan of Action of the International Conference on Indochinese Refugees, Report of the Secretary General UNGA A/44/523 (1989) (44th session, item 111 c).

9 Hans, Surhrke 'Responsibility Sharing' (n 3) 101.

10 Betts, 'Comprehensive Plans of Action: Insights from CIREFCA and the Indochinese CPA' (n 1) 34.

11 Türk, Garlick, 'From Burdens and Responsibilities to Opportunities; The Comprehensive Refugee Response Framework and a Global Compact on Refugees' (n 7) 668.

12 W Courtland Robinson, 'The Comprehensive Plan of Action for Indochinese Refugees 1989–1997 Sharing the Burden and Passing the Buck' (2004) 17 Journal of Refugee Studies 319 https://doi.org/10.1093/jrs/17.3.319.

13 Arthur C Helton, 'Refugee Determination under the Comprehensive Plan of Action: Overview and Assessment' (1993) 5 International Journal of Refugee Law 544, 557 https://doi.org/10.1093/ijrl/5.4.544.

14 Ibid.

15 International Conference on Indo-Chinese Refugees: resolution/adopted by the General Assembly A/RES/44/138, para 6.

worked towards identifying resettlement quotas. Countries outside the region pledged their commitments under a three-year target timeline.[16] UNHCR provided statistics on past contributions, helping states to identify their targets and a fair share. For the purposes of implementing the CPA, UNHCR circulated a responsibility sharing distribution formula, identifying the proportion of resettlement quotas for each resettlement state. Betts has commented on UNHCR's attempt to stress how effective protection of the Indochinese was factually dependent on responsibility sharing.

> [i]s illustrative of the way in which UNHCR managed to credibly convey to states that without each contributing their 'fair share', the whole process would fail. In other words, free riding was not an option if states hoped to meet their individual or collective interests.[17]

Certain criteria informed the resettlement process beyond the pledged quotas. The caseload of refugees with social ties to third countries would be resettled there and the caseload of refugees lacking such ties would be equitably shared among the rest of the states.[18] The US's significant leadership role in this large-scale resettlement and the sense of responsibility they felt towards its erstwhile allies were other important geopolitical factors.[19]

To be sure, the CPA was far from a flawless scheme of international cooperation in refugee protection. Arthur Helton, a significant player in the CPA's implementation, concluded in his own overview and assessment that, in the end, humanitarian considerations were overridden by migration control objectives.[20] Further, the CPA was very much a product of a certain political juncture.[21] When considering however what universal lessons or elements of best practice can be drawn for the purposes of responsibility sharing, the CPA

16 Betts, 'Comprehensive Plans of Action: Insights from CIREFCA and the Indochinese CPA' (n 1) 40.

17 Ibid.

18 Ibid.

19 James C Hathaway and Alexander Neve, 'Making International Refugee Law Relevant Again', 1997) 10 Harvard Human Rights Journal 115, 193.

20 Helton 'Refugee Determination under the Comprehensive Plan of Action: Overview and Assessment' (n 13) 558; Hathaway has also criticized the human rights situation under the CPA as falling short of complying with international human rights standards. James C Hathaway 'Labelling the "Boat People": The Failure of the Human Rights Mandate of the Comprehensive Plan of Action for Indochinese Refugees' (1993) 15 Human Rights Quarterly 686.

21 Suhrke, 'Burden Sharing during Refugee Emergencies: The Logic of Collective versus National Action' (n 2) 408.

process combined two important characteristics that are not context or region specific.

Firstly, the CPA sought to link asylum and refugee protection to a durable solution. The essence of international protection is realised in securing the full gamut of Convention rights as well as a permanent solution to refugeehood. Under the CPA, responsibility sharing on the part of the international community went beyond mere financial assistance to asylum states in the region during the emergency and the initial stage of protection from *non-refoulement.* It extended to physical responsibility sharing, with states in the Global North admitting a fair share of the refugees through resettlement. Crucially, among the determinative criteria for refugee resettlement, existing social ties of refugees to third states were considered in the allocation of resettlement quotas, making it an example of relatively successful preference matching.

Secondly, the CPA framed the plight of the Indochinese refugees as a common but differentiated responsibility by providing for different protection roles for different states, laying down interlocking, interdependent and *differentiated* commitments, voluntarily pledged by states. In the context of the CPA, the international community came to recognise for all sorts of reasons, including geopolitical ones, that effective protection of the Indochinese refugees required countries in the region and outside the region to undertake a fair share. To this end, the effective use of linkages in other issue areas, including peace and security in the region, eliminated the risk of free riding.

Despite its emergency-driven and *ad hoc* nature, the CPA was an overall positive instance of international cooperation towards responsibility sharing. It implemented a loose framework of common but differentiated responsibilities, which meant different protection roles for states at different times, linking refugee protection to durable solutions. States of the Global North meaningfully contribute their fair share, not only by financing international protection costs at the emergency phase, but also by providing large-scale resettlement, in line with their capacities.

2 The International Conference on Central American Refugees (CIREFCA)

In the Central American context, CIREFCA was a process that arose out of the Esquipulas Peace Agreement of 1987. The Agreement marked the end of long-standing conflicts in Costa Rica, El Salvador, Honduras, Guatemala and Nicaragua.[22] The Conference on Central American Refugees,[23] like the CPA, focused on providing solutions, but unlike the CPA, the solutions were provided at the regional level. CIREFCA can be understood better as seen as part of a *process*.[24] Unlike the CPA, which was framed around the migration-asylum nexus, CIREFCA aimed at bridging the gap between humanitarian relief and development.[25] The Central American Peace and Development Process was about long-term assistance to the displaced and post-conflict development in the region. The protection of refugees was positively linked to issues of peace and development, making the case for an integrated developmental approach to forced displacement.[26]

The Conference, under the auspices of UNHCR and the United Nations Development Programme (UNDP) took place in Guatemala City in 1989 and resulted in a Declaration and a Concerted Plan of Action, explicitly conceived as a follow-up process to the 1984 Cartagena Declaration.[27] The Plan focused on voluntary repatriation, local integration of refugees and their contribution to economic development.[28] The integrated developmental approach, dynamically adapted from country to country, depending on whether the state was a source of refugees or a country of asylum, offered self-reliance to the refugees, development opportunities to the host communities and secured stability in the region. Further, CIREFCA, as a process, played an important normative role in the region by contributing to the development and dissemination of international protection norms, strengthening regional solidarity between states and offering joint responsibilities for refugees.[29]

Innovative responsibility sharing approaches in the region did not end with CIREFCA. The Brazil and Mexico Declarations and Plans of Action discussed earlier framed responsibility sharing against 'an ostensibly south-south prin-

---

22 UNGA Annex, Procedure for the Establishment of a Firm and Lasting Peace in Central America (Esquipulas II) A/RES/42/521 (31 August 1987) (CIREFCA).

23 International Conference on Central American Refugees: resolution / adopted by the General Assembly UNGA A/RES/47/103 (6 December 1992).

24 Türk, Garlick, 'From Burdens and Responsibilities to The Comprehensive Refugee Response Framework and a Global Compact on Refugees' (n 7) 668. Emphasis added.

25 Betts, 'Comprehensive Plans of Action: Insights from CIREFCA and the Indochinese CPA' (n 1) 50.

26 Ibid.

27 Declaration and Concerted Plan of Action in Favour of Central American Refugees, Returnees and Displaced Persons, (CIREFCA) 30 May 1989, A 89/13/Rev.1.

28 CIREFCA, para 19.

29 Alexander Betts, Paul Collier, *Refuge Transforming a Broken Refugee System* (Allen Lane Penguin 2017) 150.

ciple of "common but differentiated responsibility".[30] States of origin, transit and destination within this region have assumed distinct protection roles to refugee situations. In light of this, responsibility sharing in Latin America links refugee protection to comprehensive solutions and humanitarianism with development by expanding labour mobility programmes where refugees can freely move to third countries and have access to gainful employment, promoting economic self-sufficiency.[31] This is the well-known 'Cartagena Spirit' of regional solidarity between states that is built on context-specific regional shared values but also on an understanding of refugee protection in the region as a common responsibility.[32]

3 Pulling the Threads Together: Identifying Elements of Best Practice

The CPA and the CIREFCA processes were products of a strongly influenced Cold War-sentiment in the history of refugee protection that saw the UN and states assume priority for refugees for various interests, including both humanitarian and geopolitical. In this sense, they were unique products of a certain historical juncture. Having said this, there are some elements of best practice in both the CPA and CIREFCA that can have universal application.

Both processes were *cooperative* because they involved the cooperation between a wide range of countries, including countries of origin, asylum, resettlement and/or donor countries. They were *comprehensive*, for they simultaneously adopted a range of protection roles and durable solutions, and they were *collaborative* in terms of working across UN agencies, including development actors and civil society organisations.[33] This element of intra-agency collaboration is evidenced today in UNHCR's 'multi-stakeholder' or 'whole of society' approach to refugee situations.[34] Finally, and importantly, both processes operationalised responsibility sharing against a framework of common but differentiated responsibilities. States of origin, asylum and destination

30 David Cantor, 'Responsibility-sharing in the refugee field: lessons from Latin America' (2018) Policy Brief: Pisa Observatory on European Migration Law 5. See Discussion in Chapter 3.

31 See 2014 Brazil Plan of Action.

32 Stefania E Barichello, 'Responsibility Sharing in Latin America', in Satvinder Juss (ed) *Research Handbook of International Refugee Law* (Edward Elgar 2019) 111.

33 Betts, 'Comprehensive Plans of Action: Insights from CIREFCA and the Indochinese CPA' (n 1) 5.

34 Volker Türk, 'The Promise and Potential of the Global Compact on Refugees' (2019) 30 International Journal of Refugee Law 575 https://doi.org/10.1093/ijrl/eey068.

came together from the initial emergency phase to the provision of durable solutions, with each state contributing to either physical and/or financial responsibility sharing.

4 UNHCR Convention Plus Initiative

The Convention Plus Initiative (2002–2005) was a three-year, UNHCR-led project, which brought states together to negotiate a normative framework on international responsibility sharing for refugees.[35] It can be seen as the precursor to the Global Compact on Refugees, in the sense that it was a UNHCR-led effort at filling the gap of responsibility sharing with a framework. The "Plus", intended to be a number of generic and special soft law agreements, was based on three identified priority strands: the strategic use of resettlement; more effective targeted development assistance to support durable solutions for refugees; and clarification of the responsibilities of states in the event of irregular secondary movements.[36] These generic agreements would then be applied to context-specific protracted refugee situations.

Although the Convention Plus failed to meet its objective, it nonetheless enriched UNHCR's and states' experience by offering valuable lessons.[37] Two distinct tools were used by UNHCR to bring states together to agree on what would have been differentiated commitments to refugee protection; firstly, a 'common but differentiated' approach to refugee protection, where different states assume different roles in and the use of issue linkages; and secondly, a bargaining technique that links asylum and refugee protection to other state interests such as migration control and development.[38]

From the outset, responsibility sharing under the Convention Plus Initiative was framed as a Global North-Global South dialogue. There was however a rather strict division of labour between donor states in the Global North that

35 UNHCR *Convention Plus at a Glance* <https://www.unhcr.org/sites/default/files/legacy-pdf/403b30684.pdf> accessed 17 October 2024.

36 Ibid.

37 The only tangible output of Convention Plus was the Multilateral Framework of Understandings on Resettlement. UNHCR Multilateral Framework of Understandings on Resettlement (Forum/2004/6) (16 September 2004) <https://www.refworld.org/policy/strategy/unhcr/2004/en/19171> accessed 17 October 2024.

38 Alexander Betts, Jean Francois Durieux 'Convention Plus Initiative as a Norm Setting Exercise' (2007) 20 Journal of Refugee Studies 509, 522 https://doi.org/10.1093/jrs/fem010.

finance refugee protection and Southern states that host the refugees. The issue of linkages in the Convention Plus was played as follows: UNHCR appealed to Northern states to commit to responsibility sharing on the basis of their strong interests in halting irregular secondary movements using the asylum – migration nexus, and to the Southern states by persuading them that development assistance from the North would only come to benefit their local populations if they make local integration and self-sufficiency for refugees a viable option.[39]

The shortcomings of the Convention Plus have been highlighted in literature.[40] Three of them, however, are important to this study as they illustrate the challenge of responsibility sharing: the lack of transparency during the negotiations, the conditionality of the targeted development assistance to refugee host countries and the failure to make the necessary structural adjustment that would infuse an idea of fairness in the global refugee regime.

Firstly, the negotiations on development assistance by donor countries were conducted behind closed doors, going against elemental considerations of procedural fairness and equal participation. The refugee host states and would-be recipients of development assistance were excluded from the negotiations, which were, in turn, led by donor states pursuing a refugee-containment agenda.[41]

Secondly, refugee host states requested that any targeted assistance for refugee protection be *additional* to that of poverty eradication and other developmental needs, so that the aid does not become conditioned on readmission agreements.[42] The request was not met by donor states, which made clear that no additional funding for refugee self-reliance would be allocated, and any targeted development assistance would come from already allocated and earmarked budgets.[43] Elemental considerations of fairness would warrant that refugee-targeted assistance to developing countries should not be linked to streamlined development aid since refugee host states are undertaking the lion's share of the common responsibility to protect refugees. Conditioning development aid on readmission agreements further polarised states across

39 Alexander Betts, Protection By Persuasion, *International Cooperation in the Refugee Regime* (Cornell University Press 2009).

40 For a comprehensive critique of the Convention Plus, See Marjoleine, Zeick, 'Doomed to Fail from the Outset? UNHCR's Convention Plus Initiative Revisited' (2009) 21 International Journal of Refugee Law 387 https://doi.org/10.1093/ijrl/eep011.

41 Ibid., 411.

42 Betts, *Protection by Persuasion* (n 39) 170.

43 Ibid., 171.

the North-South divide, ultimately hindering the conclusion of a normative framework.[44]

Finally, the Convention Plus Initiative did not deliver on what its name suggested and perhaps what the expectation might have been at the time; to come up with a normative framework that would correct the resulting inequities in the allocation of responsibilities, and optimise fair sharing by making the structural adjustment to the Refugee Convention with 'a universal instrument that would build upon and supplement the 1951 Convention'.[45]

5 The Global Compact on Refugees: A Framework towards a More Equitable and Fair Responsibility Sharing?

The Global Compact on Refugees resulted from two years of intense negotiations led by UNHCR that sought to replace the *ad hoc* approaches that have traditionally characterised refugee responsibility sharing at the UN level with a comprehensive framework. Unlike the Convention Plus Initiative, the expectations from the beginning were more modest, and the outcome in the form of a 'Compact' was pre-agreed in the New York Declaration for Refugees and Migrants.[46] Having said that, in the negotiations leading up to the UN Summit, the then High Commissioner for Refugees Antonio Guterres had remarked on the missing protocol on 'international solidarity and burden sharing' that would supplement the Refugee Convention.[47] Despite the momentum, political appetite was not conducive to a binding instrument. In the end, the originally intended 'Global Compact on Responsibility Sharing' was reduced to the 'Global Compact on Refugees'.[48]

The Compact builds on the operational practice of UNHCR developed over the years. In contrast to the Convention Plus initiative, the negotiations

44 Zeick, 'Doomed to Fail from the Outset? UNHCR's Convention Plus Initiative Revisited' (n 40) 404.

45 Ibid., 415.

46 New York Declaration for Refugees and Migrants UN Doc A/RES/71/1 (3 October 2016).

47 Antonio Guterres, 'Closing Remarks at the Session of the 66th Executive Committee of the High Commissioner's Programme' speech delivered on the 9th October 2015 <https://www.unhcr.org/en-au/excom/speeches/562f4a5415/closing%20remarks-%2066thsession-executive-committee-high-commissioners-programme.html> accessed 17 October 2024.

48 See Zero Draft of the Global Compact on Responsibility Sharing for Refugees, 30 June 2016 <http://www.unhcr.org/events/conferences/578369114/zero-draft-global-compact-responsibility-sharing-refugees.html> accessed 17 October 2024.

of the Global Compact on Refugees were inclusive and participatory by taking a whole of society approach to the refugee problem. Unlike the Convention Plus, the Global Compact on Refugees does not reduce responsibility sharing to a problem of assistance between donor and refugee hosts states. It recognises the various roles states can play in refugee protection and solutions.

The Compact made some important pronouncements and introduced positive elements to the responsibility sharing at the UN level. Firstly, it framed the contemporary refugee challenge as the 'common concern of humankind', reaffirming the community interest nature of refugee protection, underscoring the institutional responsibility of the international community. Even if merely declaratory, this is nonetheless an important reframing. The Compact emphasises what is already widely accepted by states, especially by refugee host states, namely that responsibility sharing is in practice the *sine qua non* for a fair and effective international protection regime.[49]

For the first time, the idea of refugee protection as a 'common but differentiated responsibility' that has been somehow part and parcel of past responsibility sharing arrangements, like the ones discussed here, guides the responsibility sharing arrangement at the UN level. Importantly, the Compact has borrowed from the language and processes of contemporary instruments of climate change law and policy.[50] The use of the CBDRRC language as well the Compact's implementation mechanisms, like the Follow up and Review and the global stocktaking, mirror certain processes of the UNFCCC and the Paris Agreement on Climate Change.[51]

On the downside, responsibility sharing in the Global Compact era remains however a voluntary undertaking. The whole edifice of the Compact as well as its implementation rests in the good will of states that choose to participate in the Global Refugee Forums and UNHCR's leadership in monitoring the implementation of the pledges. The Compact, by ascribing to a rather broad conception of responsibility sharing, further obfuscated a common conceptual understanding of the term by opening up contributions against an extensive list of 'Areas of Support' that go beyond the provision of international protection and solutions and include contributions to root causes and early prevention.[52]

---

49 Geoff Gilbert, 'Not Bound but Committed Operationalizing the Global Compact on Refugees' (2019) 59 International Migration IOM 28 https://doi.org/10.1111/imig.12632.

50 See Chapter 6.

51 Global Compact para 101–105. See discussion in Chapter 6, pp. 117–123.

52 Global Compact paras 7–8 and 49–100.

With respect to solutions, commentators have challenged the focus on voluntary repatriation as the preferred solution. Zeick, in a critique of the Convention Plus Initiative, stressed that 'voluntary repatriation has little or nothing to do with burden sharing', as voluntary return, if and when it happens, does not actually correct the uneven distributions of refugee-related responsibilities resulting from the responsibility sharing gap.[53] Further, insistence on voluntary repatriation can be particularly harmful to refugees if circumstances in the countries of origin are not conducive to such return.[54]

The Compact's implementation in the past six years has been rather slow, and global responsibility sharing for refugees today remains highly inequitable if measured against states' relative capacities.[55] There has been little redistribution of asylum-related responsibilities that would reflect a fair share, as the developing countries continue to disproportionately host more refugees vis-à-vis their capacities. From the pledges made during the Global Refugee Forum in 2019, only one-third was fulfilled while the majority of the pledges made were towards policy harmonisation.[56] In terms of financial sharing, USD 26.4 billion was the targeted refugee development assistance to middle- and low-income countries in 2020–2021 but this has been unevenly distributed across refugee situations.[57] Global resettlement needs are reported not to have been met while only a small number of refugees have accessed third-country solutions.[58]

To conclude, the Compact, neither by design nor implementation, can fill the responsibility sharing gap of the Refugee Convention. The Compact did not make the necessary structural adjustment to the international refugee law regime so that responsibility sharing comes under a legally binding framework. This does not mean that the Compact is to be discarded. On the contrary, the Global Compact on Refugees and the responsibility sharing processes it has set in motion can serve as the blueprint upon which a protocol on responsibility sharing can be advanced. Importantly, the Compact brought a version of the principle of CBDRRC from international environmental law while also drawing from multilateral processes in the field of environmental protection that merit further study and attention.

---

53 Zeick, 'Doomed to Fail from the Outset? UNHCR's Convention Plus Initiative Revisited' (n 40) 41.

54 Ibid, 415.

55 2023 Global Compact on Refugees, Indicator Report, 14 <https://www.unhcr.org/media/2023-global-compact-refugees-indicator-report> accessed 17 October 2024.

56 Ibid,14, Figure 34.

57 Ibid.,11.

58 Ibid.,14.

PART 2

A Proposal

CHAPTER 5

Fairness and the Practice of Differential Treatment in International Law

The second part of the study turns into international environmental law where the principle of CBDRRC has been the guiding principle framing responsibility sharing in multilateral environmental agreements (MEAs). While the CBDRRC principle was explicitly formulated in international environmental law, the wider practice of differential treatment has long been a key feature of multilateral law-making. This chapter traces the practice of differential treatment as an application of fairness in international law. It argues that elements of differentiation, either at the level of treaty obligations or treaty implementation, permeate international legal regimes and that differential treatment has served as a legal device for forging international cooperation and responsibility sharing in the protection of community interests. This is illustrated by the discussion of international trade law, international law of the sea, international human rights law and international environmental law, where the principle of CBDRRC was explicitly articulated.

1 Differential Treatment in International Law

The principle of 'common but differentiated responsibilities', as it was first articulated in the 1992 Rio Declaration on Environment and Development, captures the essence of differential treatment in international law.[1] While explicitly articulated in international environmental law, some commentators situate the origins of a broader practice of differential and non-uniform treatment in law to the Treaty of Versailles.[2]

---

1 1992 Rio Declaration on Environment and Development as Principle 7; Philippe Cullet, 'Differential Treatment in International Law: Towards a New Paradigm of Inter-State Relations', (1999) 10 European Journal of International Law 549, 577.

2 Cristopher D Stone, 'Common But Differentiated Responsibilities in International Law' (2004) 98 American Journal of International Law 276, 278. Stone refers to the 1919 Constitution of the International Labour Organisation.

 | DOI:10.1163/9789004547711_006

The doctrine of differential treatment emerged in international law as a legal construct for remedying the inherent inequalities and competing interests among states that international law had been previously blind to.[3] On a theoretical level, differentiation in law stems from an idea of substantive equality or distributive justice among states.[4] This is in contrast to the legal equality of sovereign states that requires their strict and uniform legal treatment.[5] On a practical level, differentiation has also been a tool for ensuring broader participation in multilateral treaty regimes where international cooperation and responsibility sharing are essential to achieve common goals.[6] The role of differential treatment is hence generally understood as twofold; a distributive one, insofar as states are not substantively equals, and a facilitating one, insofar as it strengthens international cooperation and responsibility sharing towards common goals.[7]

2 Differential Treatment in International Development and Trade Law

When the international community acquired a more heterogeneous composition, following decolonisation in the 1960s, it became clear that formal legal equality, as a legal corollary of sovereign equality, could not and should not always be upheld.[8] Developing states had different social and economic priorities and therefore the central challenge was to accommodate such diverse priorities and realities within context-specific legal regimes on international cooperation and responsibility sharing in the various community interest areas of the UN.

The developing countries started to voice their concerns about control over the economic resources of their territories, arguing that political independence had not brought economic independence with it. The states of Asia, Africa and Latin America had, as their central preoccupation and primary

3 Antonio Cassese, *International Law in a Divided World* (Oxford Clarendon Press 1986) 351.
4 Cullet, 'Differential Treatment in International Law: Towards a New Paradigm of Inter-State Relations' (n 1) 553.
5 Dinah Shelton, 'Equity', in Daniel Bodansky, Jutta Brunnée, Ellen Hey (eds) *The Oxford Handbook of International Environmental Law* (Oxford University Press 2007) 646.
6 Cullet, 'Differential Treatment in International Law: Towards a New Paradigm of Inter-State Relations' (n 1) 550.
7 Ibid., 558.
8 Ibid., 564.

mission, their economic development.[9] In 1964, a negotiating block of developing countries, the G-77/China, under the auspices of United Nations Conference on Trade and Development (UNCTAD), started putting before international fora the demand to remedy economic stagnation during the colonial rule and to assist the less economically advanced states to become economically independent.

At the same time, alternative normative prescriptions for a new international legal system that would respect and promote the interests of Global South states appeared in academic discourse. The birth of the law of development signified a nascent approach to international law, with developing countries calling for a regime of positive discrimination, unilateral and non-reciprocal preferences, and for a new set of principles and rules on the international order.[10] Around the same time, the emergence of Third World Approaches to International Law (TWAIL), an academic and intellectual movement, began to confront colonialism and question international law as a system that legitimises, produces and sustains the subordination of the Third World by the West.[11]

It was the 1970s, when demands for a new set of international principles and rules culminated in the establishment of the New International Economic Order (NIEO).[12] The three fundamentals of the NIEO were the protection of the economies of developing countries, positive discrimination and non-reciprocity in law by means of application of the principle of preferential treatment.[13] Despite the short life of the NIEO movement, the dialogue between the North and the South was shaped by the NIEO rhetoric.[14] The year of 1974 was dedicated at the UN to the establishment of a NIEO. The adoption

9 Lavanya Rajamani *Differential Treatment in International Environmental Law* (Oxford University Press 2006) 4.

10 Maurice Flory, 'Adapting International Law to the Development of the Third World' (1982) 26 Journal of African Law 12, 15; Ahmed Mahiou, 'Development, International Law' Max Plank Encyclopaedia of Public International Law (2013).

11 See Makau Mutua, 'What is TWAIL' (2000) 94 Proceedings of America Society of International Law, 31–38

12 Daniel Barstow Magraw, 'Existing Legal Treatment of the Developing Countries: Differential, Contextual and Absolute Norms' (1990) 1 Colorado Journal International Environmental Law and Policy 69, 74.

13 Wil D Verwey, 'The Principles of a New International Economic Order and the Law on General Agreement on Trade and Tariffs' (1990) 3 Leiden Journal of International Law 117, 123 https://doi.org/10.1017/S0922156500001436.

14 Cullet, 'Differential Treatment in International Law: Towards a New Paradigm of Inter-State Relations' (n 1) 566. Rajamani, *Differential Treatment in International Environmental Law* (n 9) 19.

of the UN General Assembly Declaration on the Establishment of a New International Economic Order,[15] the Programme of Action on the NIEO,[16] and the adoption of the Charter of Economic Rights and Duties of States[17] were the three instruments and outcomes of the NIEO movement. The UNGA Declaration on the Establishment of a New International Economic Order was founded in respect for the principles of, *inter alia*, 'the broadest co-operation of all the States members of the international community based on equity' and 'preferential and non-reciprocal treatment for developing countries, wherever feasible, in all fields of international economic co-operation, whenever possible'.[18]

All three NIEO resolutions repeatedly affirmed the role of international law in ensuring fairness and equity, with the latter dictating that individual characteristics of developing countries must be taken into account.[19] References to equity throughout texts of the NIEO instruments, such as 'equitable sharing, equitable prices and equitable terms of trade', reflected a concerted effort 'to apply the principle of distributive justice to construct new legal and political arrangements to allow developing countries to overcome the inheritance of their colonial past'.[20] The quest for differential treatment in international law thus emanated from a conception of distributive justice that militates that the pervasive inequalities in 'economic capacity or lack of development to tackle a given problem'[21] among the subjects of law, warrants special attention or special treatment in international law.[22]

Within international trade law, the claim for distributive justice was pursued by developing countries through a request for preferential treatment. Preferential treatment in trade agreements, namely granting special rights and privileges to the developing countries, was only one of the earliest instances of differential treatment within international law in favour of developing

15 Declaration on the Establishment of New International Economic Order UNGA A/Res/s-63201 (S-VI) (1974) Sixth Special Session.

16 Ibid.

17 Charter of Economic Rights and Duties of States', UNGA Resolution 'A/Res/29/3281 December 1974.

18 Declaration on the Establishment of New International Economic Order, paragraph 4 (b), (n). 1974 Charter of Economic Rights and Duties of States, Article 25.

19 Magraw, 'Legal Treatment of the Developing Countries, Differential, Contextual and Absolute Norms' (n 12) 78.

20 Shelton, 'Equity' (n 5) 650.

21 Ibid., 647.

22 Tuula Honkonen, *The Common But Differentiated Responsibility Principle in Multilateral Environmental Agreements* (2009 Kluwer Law International) 40–41.

countries.[23] During the life of the NIEO movement, the General Agreement on Tariffs and Trade (GATT) tried to accommodate some of the demands of developing countries for non-reciprocity and preferential treatment. In 1964, the GATT was revised to include special provisions for developing countries.[24] In 1979, the GATT established a permanent legal basis for preferential treatment of developing countries, commonly known as the 'Enabling Clause'. This provided for derogation from 'the most favoured nation clause', namely GATT's Article 1 non-discrimination provision.[25] The contracting states adopted the 'Decision on Differential and More Favourable Treatment, Reciprocity and Fuller Participation of Developing Countries', which granted preferential tariffs to developing countries.[26]

Notwithstanding the changes to GATT, the economic and social discrepancies between developed and developing countries were not reduced and the profits of the vast majority of developing countries were very limited.[27] Even if the NIEO rhetoric managed to influence, in principle, the regulatory framework on international trade, in practice, trade concessions by means of preferential treatment of the developing countries were merely discretionary, 'an entitlement whose implementability is not guaranteed by a corresponding obligation to the extent necessary to make it a substantive right'.[28]

The developing countries' claim for preferential treatment did not flourish because developed states were not prepared to commit to legally binding, non–reciprocal preferential standards nor to any form of wealth redistribution. The NIEO rhetoric did not make it beyond the early 1980s when a *laissez faire* approach to the global regulatory market was introduced and where development became synonymous with structural adjustment policies.[29] The early 1990s witnessed the demise of preferential treatment of developing countries in the global trade arena, especially since the establishment of the

---

23 Verwey 'The Principles of a New International Economic Order and The Law on General Agreement on Tariffs and Trade (GATT)' (n 13) 123.

24 1948 General Agreement on Tariffs and Trade (GATT) Part IV Goods, Article XXXVI (8) which recognized for the first time the principle of non-reciprocity in tariff negotiations or renegotiations.

25 GATT Decision of 28 November 1979 (L/4903).

26 Differential and More Favourable Treatment, Reciprocity and Fuller Participation of Developing Countries' 28 November 1979, GATT BISD 1980, 203–205.

27 Verwey 'The Principles of a New International Economic Order and The Law on General Agreement on Tariffs and Trade (GATT)' (n 13)140.

28 Ibid., 141.

29 Cullet, 'Differential Treatment in International Law: Towards a New Paradigm of Inter-State Relations' (n 1) 568.

World Trade Organisation (WTO).[30] In light of emerging global environmental challenges on the side and the quest to develop on the part of the developing states, differential treatment took the form of 'mutually accepted non-reciprocity'.[31]

3 Differential Treatment in the International Law of the Sea

The negotiations on the United Nations Convention on the Law of the Sea (UNCLOS) were influenced by the NIEO rhetoric and relevant debates before the UN General Assembly.[32] This is evident in the UNCLOS Preamble, which reflects the quest for a 'just and equitable international economic order' that takes into account the special interests of developing states.[33] UNCLOS recognises, in various provisions, the different needs and capacities of various states, including developing, landlocked or geographically disadvantaged.[34] Differential treatment at the level of legal obligations and at the level of implementation of common standards appear in the subsequent regimes of the deep seabed and marine pollution.[35]

In the context of the deep seabed, differentiated commitments ensure broad participation and an equitable benefit-sharing among states. UNCLOS establishes that the mineral resources of the deep seabed, termed as 'the

30 GATT Multilateral Trade Negotiations (the Uruguay Round): Marrakesh Agreement Establishing the Multilateral Trade Organization (World Trade Organization), 15 December 1993.

31 Cullet, 'Differential Treatment in International Law: Towards a New Paradigm of Inter-State Relations' (n1) 556.

32 United Nations Convention on the Law of the Sea (adopted Montego Bay, 10 December 198 and entered into force 16 November 1994) 1833 UNTS 397 (UNCLOS); Honkonen, *The Common But Differentiated Responsibility Principle in Multilateral Environmental Agreements* (n 22) 48.

33 UNCLOS, Preamble.

34 UNCLOS, Article 202, 203 266, 267 268; See also Section 5 and 7 of the Annex to the 1994 Agreement provide for transfer of technology and economic assistance. Agreement Relating to the Implementation of Part XI of the United Nations Convention on the Law of the Sea of 10 December 1982, July 1994.

35 For a detailed analysis on CBDRRC in the Law of the Sea, See Richard Barnes 'Global Solidarity, Differentiated Responsibilities and the Law of the Sea' and Tara Davenport 'Differentiated Rights and Responsibilities in Activities in the Area – From Wealth Redistribution to Marne Environmental Protection' in Maarten den Heijer, Harmen van der Wilt (eds) *Global Solidarity and Common But Differentiated* Responsibilities (2020) Netherlands Yearbook of International Law, 107–142 and 147–183 respectively.

Area', are the 'common heritage of mankind'[36] and, as such, all activities in the Area shall be carried out for the benefit of mankind as a whole, irrespective of the geographical location of states, whether coastal or land-locked, and taking particular consideration of the interests and needs of developing states.[37]

The principle of the 'common heritage of mankind' is a well-known doctrinal expression of community interests in international law with regard to the use of natural resources beyond national jurisdiction.[38] The institutionalisation of the common heritage of mankind principle in UNCLOS and its application to the legal regime on the deep seabed aims, at least in principle, to correct the distribution of resources as the consequence of geography and advances an equitable sharing of financial and other economic benefits derived from activities in the Area.[39] As a consequence, there is a community obligation on the part of individual states to cooperate with each other and with the International Seabed Authority (ISA), which acts as a trustee on behalf of mankind as a whole.[40] The legal regime on the deep seabed thus fosters community interests and 'instantiates its vision of 'common but differentiated responsibilities'[41] by acknowledging the disadvantaged geographic location of some of the developing landlocked states[42] and by ensuring broad participation and a fair distribution of financial benefits. Commentators have, however, stressed that there are still several matters regarding the deep seabed that require further implementation, without which equitable benefit sharing from activities in the Area will remain aspirational.[43]

An idea of differential treatment permeates the legal regime on prevention, reduction and control of marine pollution under UNCLOS. Prevention and control of marine pollution is dependent on cooperative arrangements to

36 UNCLOS, Article 136.

37 UNCLOS, Article 140.

38 Simma, 'From Bilateralism to Community Interest in International Law' in *Collected Courses of the Hague Academy of International Law* (Hague Academy of International Law 1994) 234, 240.

39 UNCLOS, Article 140, (2).

40 UNCLOS, Article 153; Rüdiger Wolfrum, 'Identifying Community Interests in International Law: Common Spaces and Beyond' in Eyal Benvenisti, Georg Nolte (eds), *Community Interests Across International Law* (Oxford University Press 2018) 26.

41 Volker Roeben, 'Responsibility in International Law' (2012) 16 Max Planck Yearbook of United Nations Law 99.

42 UNCLOS, Article 148.

43 Davenport 'Differentiated Rights and Responsibilities in Activities in the Area – From Wealth Redistribution to Marne Environmental Protection' (n 35) 181.

achieve common standards.[44] In pursuit of this objective, the capabilities of developing countries should be taken into consideration in the adoption of applicable legal standards.[45] To that end, UNCLOS lays down contextual obligations adjusting the various marine pollution measures, to be taken against an idea of differentiated responsibility based on capabilities. In addition, an explicit call for preferential treatment of developing countries is found in the provisions of technical and financial assistance. Developing states shall be granted preference by international organisations in the allocation of funds and technical assistance to enable them to meet their environmental protection requirements.[46]

To conclude, differential treatment in UNCLOS takes the form of contextual norms at the level of implementation of treaty obligations. A right for preferential treatment can be made by developing countries insofar as financial and technical assistance is concerned in the field of marine pollution. There is therefore, at least in principle, an attempt by UNCLOS to address fairness considerations in resource and burden sharing, and differential treatment is one such legal device.

4 Differential Treatment in International Human Rights Law

While areas beyond national jurisdiction make stronger cases for the existence of community interests and hence, common responsibilities and community interests, as already argued, are not reserved solely for such areas. They can also be found in predominantly territorial legal regimes such as the protection of human rights. In fact, the legal protection of human rights is the primary evidence of a community interest-oriented international legal order.[47]

It should not therefore be surprising that an element of differentiation structurally permeates international human rights instruments. This is done through the use of contextual norms within the structure of legal obligations.[48] A contextual norm provides, on the face of it, identical treatment to

44 Barnes 'Global Solidarity, Differentiated Responsibilities and the Law of the Sea' (n 35) 126.

45 UNCLOS, Article 194 (1).

46 UNCLOS, Articles 202–203.

47 Simma, 'From Bilateralism to Community Interest in international law' (n 38) 234.

48 See the distinction of norms into 'differential, contextual and absolute' in Magraw, 'Legal Treatment of the Developing Countries, Differential, Contextual and Absolute Norms' (n 12) 74.

all states-parties, but its implementation requires or allows for the consideration of characteristics that may vary from state to state.[49] On its face, the idea of differentiation in human rights obligations might seem problematic, given that human rights treaties are not about reciprocal and bilateral obligations between states, but codify a universal set of minimum standards of rights and freedoms for all individuals.[50] The 1966 International Covenant on Economic, Social and Cultural Rights (ICESCR) is an illustrative example of a human rights instrument that allows for differentiation at the level of implementation of treaty obligations.[51] Article 2 (1) of the ICESCR recognizes the particular socio-economic level of each state and requires states to take steps:

> [I]ndividually and through international cooperation, especially economic and technical, to the maximum of its available resources with a view to achieving progressively the full realization of the rights recognized in the present Covenant by all appropriate means, including particularly the adoption of legislative measures.[52]

The recognition of the fact that full enjoyment of socioeconomic rights in a contracting state depends on its resources and capacities does not mean that the rights protected thereunder are not universal or that they can be subject to unfettered restrictions and abuse.[53] It does not mean either that states that cannot ensure the full gamut of socioeconomic rights are relieved from their legal obligations. It simply stresses the fact that developing countries, in particular, may need more time as well as international assistance to ensure the full realisation of Covenant rights to their people. That is why the implementation of the ICESCR requires international cooperation and the provision of assistance to developing countries. To be sure, the absence of international assistance does not relieve developing state-parties from the Covenant's obligations. As the Committee on Economic, Social and Cultural Rights explains in its General Comment on the nature of the obligation of Article 2:

---

49 Ibid.

50 Human Rights Committee, General Comment 24 'Issues Relating to Reservations Made Upon Ratification or Accession to the Covenant or the Optional Protocols Thereto, or in Relation to Declarations under Article 41 of the Covenant' Fifty-second Session (4 November 1994) CCPR/C/21/Rev.1/Add.6 at 17.

51 Rajamani, *Differential Treatment in International Environmental Law* (n 9) 23.

52 International Covenant on Economic, Social and Cultural Rights (adopted 16 December 1966, entered into force 3 January 1976) 993 UNTS 3 (ICESCR) Article 2 (1).

53 Rajamani, *Differential Treatment in International Environmental Law* (n 9) 22.

> the concept of progressive realization constitutes a recognition of the fact that full realization of all economic, social and cultural rights will generally not be able to be achieved in a short period of time. In this sense, the obligations on socio-economic rights differ significantly from the obligation contained in Article 2 of the International Covenant on Civil and Political Rights, which 'embodies an immediate obligation to respect and ensure all of the relevant rights.[54]

The progressive realisation principle infuses thus the necessary flexibility and represents a contextual form of differentiation between subjects of law, responding to factual inequalities, by giving states-parties a margin of appreciation at the level of implementation.[55] At the same time, this margin of appreciation is not unfettered but there are legal safeguards. As the ESCR Committee has stressed, there is a 'minimum core' of obligations' for each Covenant right that must be, at minimum, fulfilled.[56] By strictly limiting differentiation at the level of implementation, the Covenant takes heed of the sociopolitical context while ensuring broad participation to the treaty.

5 Differential Treatment in International Environmental Law: Common but Differentiated Responsibilities and Respective Capabilities

The principle of common but differentiated responsibilities was explicitly articulated as such in international environmental law. It is most correctly captured in its full extension as the principle of 'common but differentiated responsibilities and respective capabilities' (CBDRRC).

The need to differentiate between states of the Global North and the Global South emerged over a 'dialogue of dissonance' as to whose responsibility should be the protection of the environment and how to regulate environmental protection while considering the pressing developmental needs of developing countries.[57] Shedding light to this dissonance clarifies the

54 CESCR General Comment No. 3: The Nature of States Parties' Obligations (Art. 2, Para. 1, of the Covenant) UN doc E/1991/23 (14 December 1990).
55 Magraw, Legal Treatment of the Developing Countries, Differential, Contextual and Absolute Norms' (n 12) 81.
56 CESCR General Comment No. 3: The Nature of States Parties' Obligations (Art. 2, Para. 1, of the Covenant) UN doc E/1991/23 (14 December 1990), para 10.
57 Rajamani, *Differential Treatment in International Environmental* Law (n 9) 54.

principle's origins, normative foundations and contours. This dissonance was present during the second United Nations Conference on Environment and Development (UNCED) that took place in Rio in 1992.[58] Developing countries sought access to the global market, trade, technology and development assistance, whilst the developed countries sought progress on climate change, biodiversity, fisheries issues and forest loss.[59] The delicate balance of regulating such competing interests was ultimately achieved through the 'inchoate', at the time, concept of 'sustainable development', first articulated in the 1987 Brundtland Report.[60] The Rio Declaration incorporated international environmental law's key guiding principles: the polluter pays principle,[61] the precautionary principle[62] and, for the first time, the principle of 'common but differentiated responsibilities'. Principle 7 of the Rio Declaration reads:

> [I]n view of the different contributions to global environmental degradation, States have common but differentiated responsibilities. The developed countries acknowledge the responsibility that they bear in the international pursuit of sustainable development in view of the pressures their societies place on the global environment and of the technologies and financial resources they command.[63]

Effectively, CBDRRC became the guiding principle for responsibility sharing on issues related to sustainable development and the environment.[64] The principle's rationale is that all states have a common responsibility to protect the environment, but the subsequent individual responsibilities understood as commitments to take action are further differentiated on the basis of different contributions to environmental degradation. In addition, fairness considerations warrant that in order for developing countries to take action for the

58 United Nations Conference on Environment and Development (UNCED), Earth Summit Rio de Janeiro, Brazil 3–14 June 1992.

59 Lavanya Rajamani, 'The Changing Fortunes of Differential Treatment in the Evolution of International Environmental law' (2012) 88 International Affairs 605, 609 https://doi.org/10.1111/j.1468-2346.2012.01091.x.

60 UN Report on the World Commission on Environment and Development Our Common Future (1987) United Nations.

61 Rio Declaration, Principle 16.

62 Rio Declaration, Principle 15.

63 Rio Declaration, Principle 7.

64 Philippe Sands, *Principles of International Environmental Law* (Cambridge University Press 2nd edition 2003) 231.

environment, there needs to be provision for the transfer of substantial quantities of financial and technological assistance.[65]

Some of the key multilateral environmental agreements (MEAS) that protect community interests are framed on the principle of CBDRRC. The first multilateral environmental agreement that provided for differential treatment of the developing countries was the international legal regime on the protection of the ozone layer. The depletion of the ozone layer was initially a problem predominantly impacting the Northern hemisphere.[66] Uncoordinated, unilateral action from specific countries resulted in a 'free rider' effect that urgently needed the conclusion of a cooperative framework that would address it.[67] The Vienna Convention on the Protection of the Ozone Layer did not contain any substantive obligations for the states parties.[68] Rather concluded as a framework convention, it sketched the general framework on responsibility sharing.[69] In accordance with the provisions of the Convention, and given the gradual global consensus on the gravity of the problem, developed and developing countries concluded a second legal instrument, the 1987 Montreal Protocol on Substances that Deplete the Ozone Layer.[70] The Montreal Protocol is considered to be a success story in terms of a fair responsibility sharing framework within a treaty regime.[71]

The Protocol introduced specific targets for the reduction of ozone-depleting substances, while differentiated between developed and developing state parties. Developing countries were granted longer implementation periods such as delayed compliance schedules and permission to adopt different base years.[72] Under the Protocol, financial and technological assistance is a condition for developing countries' compliance with the Proto-

65 Ibid., Principle 9.

66 Louis P Oliva, 'The International Struggle to Save the Ozone Layer' (1989) 7 Pace Environmental Law Review 213, 219.

67 Thomas Franck, *Fairness in International Law and Institutions* (Oxford University Press 1998) 382.

68 Vienna Convention on the Protection of the Ozone Layer (adopted 22 March 1985, entered into force 22 September 1988) 1513 UNTS 293.

69 Catherine Redgwell 'International Environmental Law' in M Evans (ed) *International Law* (Oxford University Press 2018) 694.

70 Montreal Protocol on Substances that Deplete the Ozone Layer (adopted 16 September 1987, entered into force 1 January 1989) 1522 UNTS 3. (Montreal Protocol)

71 Rajamani, 'The Changing Fortunes of Differential Treatment in the Evolution of International Environmental law' (n 59) 608

72 Montreal Protocol, Preamble, Article 5 (3) (a).

col.[73] Within such a flexible responsibility sharing structure, states accommodated the special claims of least developing countries for economic development through the controlled use of chlorofluorocarbons (CFCs), enabled resource transfer from the North to the South in the form of financial and technological assistance and crafted a legal regime on costs and benefits allocation against fairness and efficiency. The developed countries secured the much-needed cooperation of the least developing countries in the regime because the fairness discourse 'played an openly acknowledged part' in the negotiations.[74]

Another environmental matter that qualified in the 1990s as an area of common concern was the continuing loss of biodiversity and the urgent need for its conservation. The 1992 Convention on Biological Diversity establishes differentiated responsibilities between developed and developing states.[75] Developing countries are tasked with the protection of their biodiversity while their social and economic priorities are taken into consideration.[76] Effective protection of the biodiversity in the Global South depends on finance and bio-technology transfer from the developed countries.[77] While developing countries' legal obligations to the Biodiversity Convention stand, irrespective of whether resources from developed countries are actually transferred, the Convention acknowledges that implementation of the treaty by developing countries becomes factually dependent on the commitment of the developed country to redistribute resources.[78] Although the Biodiversity Convention is not explicitly grounded in the CBDRRC principle, its underlying *fairness problematique* is reflected in the provisions that differentiate between developed and developing countries at the level of treaty obligations and in the provisions on resource redistribution.

Another instance where the limited capabilities and resources of the developing countries are acknowledged and catered for within the legal framework is the 1989 Basel Convention on Hazardous Waste.[79] The legal regime of the

---

73 Montreal Protocol, Articles 5 (5), Article 6, Article 10 A; Rajamani, 'The Changing Fortunes of Differential Treatment in the Evolution of International Environmental law' (n 59) 608.

74 Franck, *Fairness in International Law and Institutions* (n 67) 386.

75 The Convention on Biological Diversity (5 June 1992) 1760 UNTS 69; Hereinafter, Biodiversity Convention. Preamble, recital 2.

76 Biodiversity Convention, Article 20 (4).

77 Ibid., Article 16 (2), Article 20 (1).

78 Ibid., Article 20 (4).

79 The Basel Convention on the Control of Transboundary Movements of Hazardous Wastes and their Disposal, (adopted in 1989 and it came into force in 1992), 1673 UNTS

Basel Convention is, however, different to that of the Ozone Layer and Biodiversity Conventions. It differs because it is not a legal regime that establishes a general framework for the protection of a community interest. The Basel Convention seeks to control the outsourcing of hazardous waste to developing countries that are financially, as well as technologically, ill-equipped to manage the waste in an environmentally sound way.[80] The Basel Convention therefore provides for different rights and obligations between states of import (developing) and states of export (developed). As one commentator notes, the Basel Convention, in Article 6, 'codifies procedural justice' by providing developing countries with an absolute right to refuse any import of hazardous waste, unless they expressly consent to it.[81] In this way, the Basel Convention alleviates the pressure developing countries are often faced with and reduce the environmental burdens borne by these financially and technologically ill-equipped countries to manage them.[82]

To conclude, differential treatment and its doctrinal expression, the principle of CBDRRC, structures responsibility sharing arrangements in multilateral environmental agreements. CBDRRC can be seen as an application of fairness to the extent that the inherit inequalities of states determine the extent and breadth of the legal obligations under the relevant treaty.

6 Conclusions: Differential Treatment as an Application of Fairness in International Law

The discussion of the practice of differential treatment in international trade law, international law of the sea, international environmental law and international human rights law illustrates the important role which fairness considerations have played in the conclusion and implementation of the respective legal regimes. The practice of differential treatment is thus an application of fairness in international law that warrants that, in certain cases, the mate-

126. (Basel Convention). Jutta Brunnée, 'Common Areas, Common Heritage, and Common Concern' in Bodansky, Brunnée, Hey (eds) *The Oxford Handbook of International Environmental Law* (n 5) 565.

80 The Convention provides that transboundary movements can only take place if certain conditions are met and if they are in accordance with certain procedures. Basel Convention, Preamble, & Article 14 (2).

81 Basel Convention, Article 6; Lisa Widawsky, 'In my Backyard: How Enabling Hazardous Waste Trade to Developing Nations Can Improve the Basel Convention's Ability to Achieve Environmental Justice' (2008) 38 Environmental Law 577, 595.

82 Ibid.

rial inequalities of states ought to be taken into account within the law's distributive aspects.[83] Commentators argue that the doctrinal expression of differential treatment, namely the principle of CBDRRC, as developed in international environmental law, reflects Rawlsian conceptions of justice as fairness in international relations.

> Reciprocity under cooperation, governed by the principles of justice, can be seen as a corresponding idea to common responsibility, and the 'everyone doing his/her fair share' as referring both to the requirement to participate in common action and to differentiated obligations when justice would require that.[84]

As this chapter has demonstrated, international law today serves procedural and distributive fairness. Multilateral environmental treaties affording longer implementation periods to developing countries or equal participation to the deep seabed regime serve notions of procedural fairness. Legal regimes that provide for equitable and sustainable distribution of resources like the deep seabed regime or promote resource redistribution from the Global North to the Global South in the form of trade preferences and concessionary lending, serve procedural as well as distributive fairness, even if not explicitly articulated as such.[85] The language of international law is rife with references to equity and equitable outcomes that incorporate conceptions of fairness and justice.[86] In the words of one commentator:

> The language of sharing responsibilities for collective problems, of taking account of the relative position and capacities of developed and developing countries in the establishment and implementation of international regimes is the idiom of fairness in relations between states.[87]

---

83 Thomas Pogge, *Realizing Rawls* (Cornell University Press, Ithaca 1998 NY).

84 Honkonen, *The Common But Differentiated Responsibility Principle in Multilateral Environmental Agreements* (n 22) 85.

85 Franck, Fair*ness in International Law and Institutions* (n 67) 436.

86 Henry Shue writes that what diplomats and lawyers call equity incorporates important aspects of what ordinary people everywhere call fairness. Henry Shue, 'Global Environment and International Inequality' (1999) 75 International Affairs 531; Christine Batruch, 'Hot Air as Precedent for Developing Countries? Equity Considerations' (1999) 17 UCLA Journal of Environmental Law Policy 45, 48.

87 Fridrich Soltau, *Fairness in International Climate Change Law and Policy* (Cambridge University Press 2009) 189.

To conclude, the perception by states of a legal regime as distributively and/or procedurally fair determines the breadth of participation and impacts on compliance. The unfairness of the international refugee law regime impacts on interstate relations as well as on the availability and quality of refugee protection, as Chapter 1 illustrated.[88] A protocol on responsibility sharing should therefore strive to correct the unequal distribution of protection responsibilities, as a consequence of geography, and enhance the international refuge law regime's distributive and procedural fairness. The study of the international legal regime on climate change offers useful lessons and inspiration into how considerations of fairness were structurally integrated in one of the most progressive responsibility sharing arrangements through the principle of CBDRRC.

88 Matthew J Gibney, 'Refugees and Justice between States' (2015) 14 European Journal of Political Theory 448, 449 https://doi.org/10.1177/1474885115585325.

CHAPTER 6

Responsibility Sharing in the Legal Regime on Climate Change

1 Common but Differentiated Responsibilities and Respective Capabilities (CBDRRC) in the United Nations Framework Convention for Climate Change (UNFCCC)

Climate change, also known as global warming, refers to the phenomenon of the extraordinary warming of the earth's atmosphere by increased concentrations of trapped Greenhouse Gas (GHG) emissions. It is predominantly a human-induced environmental phenomenon that requires collective action. During the negotiations of the United Nations Framework Convention for Climate Change (UNFCCC), the incorporation of the principle of CBDRRC within the multilateral treaty and the ensuing legal obligations became a contested matter amongst developed and developing countries.[1]

Under the UNFCCC, international cooperation to combat climate change extends across four pillars, namely: (1) mitigation – actions to limit or prevent the rising of the earth's temperature rising through the reduction of GHG emissions, (2) adaptation – actions to limit the harmful effects of climate change by adjusting ecological, social, or economic systems in response to actual or expected climatic stimuli, (3) financial support and technology transfer to developing countries for both mitigation and adaptation actions and (4) international oversight.[2]

Principle 7 of the Rio Declaration formulated the principle of CBDRRC as the guiding principle for international cooperation and responsibility sharing in the area of environmental protection. The principle was further positivised when it was included within the UNFCCC.[3]

The Preamble to the UNFCCC framed the problem of climate change as a common concern by acknowledging its global nature and 'calls for the wider possible cooperation by all countries (…) in accordance with their common

1 United Nations Framework Convention on Climate Change (adopted May 1992, entered into force March 1994) 1771 UNTS 107 (UNFCCC).

2 Daniel Bodansky, Jutta Brunnée, Lavanya Rajamani, *International Climate Change Law* (Oxford University Press 2018) 12–16.

3 UNFCCC, Preamble, Article 3.

 | DOI:10.1163/9789004547711_007

but differentiated responsibilities *and 'respective capabilities'*.[4] Article 3 of the UNFCCC titled 'Principles' also includes other environmental law principles, namely the precautionary principle, the principle of sustainable development and the principle of equity. It is widely acknowledged by environmental law commentators that their function *qua* principles in the operative part of the treaty is to guide the parties in their actions to achieve the Convention's objective and implement its provisions.[5]

Comparing Rio Principle 7 to UNFCCC Article 3, one notes that the principle's formulation is extended to include states' capabilities to respond to climate change, placing additional responsibilities on developed countries. Article 3 of the UNFCCC reads:

> The Parties should protect the climate system for the benefit of present and future generations of humankind, on the basis of equity and in accordance with their common but differentiated responsibilities and respective capabilities. Accordingly, the developed country Parties should take the lead in combating climate change and the adverse effects thereof.[6]

This addition was made following developed countries' insistence on the projected and expected rapid economic development of some of the developing countries, warranting a more dynamic differentiation in relation to mitigation commitments.[7] The allocation of responsibility on the basis of historic contributions to the climate's degradation remained in the UNFCCC, but existing resources and capacities became qualifying factors that determine the extent and breadth of the commitments.[8]

The UNFCCC divided the state parties rigidly as Annex I and non-Annex I countries.[9] Annex I countries, namely the developed countries, have a legal obligation under the treaty to adopt national mitigation policies and measures

4 UNFCCC, Preamble recital 6. Emphasis added.

5 Bodansky, Brunnée, Rajamani, *International Climate Change Law* (n 2) 127.

6 UNFCCC, Article 6.

7 Ibid., 128.

8 Michael Weisslitz, 'Rethinking the Equitable Principle of Common but Differentiated Responsibility: Differential Versus Absolute Norms of Compliance and Contribution in the Global Climate Change Context' (2002) 13 *Colorado Journal of International Environmental Law and Policy* 473, 476.

9 There were however provisions on review of the Annexes that could lead in amendments by a three-quarter majority. See UNFCCC, Articles 15, 16, 17.

to limit their GHG emissions as well as to report on their progress.[10] The treaty did not however concretise this obligation further by setting emission reduction targets. This is due to the treaty model. The UNFCCC was concluded as a Framework Convention which forms part of international environmental law's toolkit in ensuring broad participation to treaty regimes. The treaty therefore only established the general principles and overarching legal framework that would guide responsibility sharing and left the formulation of more specific obligations, such as mitigation targets, to be determined at a later stage by the parties in subsequent instruments.

2 Operationalising CBDRRC under the UNFCCC

2.1 *Responsibility Sharing in the Kyoto Protocol: A Rigid Differentiation in Mitigation Commitments between the Parties*

The Kyoto Protocol was concluded in 1997 by the parties to the UNFCCC as a supplementary instrument to the Convention focusing almost entirely on strengthening mitigation commitments of developed countries (Annex I).[11] To this end, it established internationally negotiated, legally binding quantitative emission reduction targets and timetables for developed countries whilst excluding developing countries from any legally binding commitments on mitigation.[12]

During the course of the Kyoto negotiations, a suggestion was made by some developed countries, in particular the US, that the major economies among developing countries should also, at least voluntarily if not as a matter of legal obligation, assume country-specific emission reduction commitments. To put pressure, the US refused to reach its Kyoto targets and ratify the Protocol, unless major developing country emitters, such as China, India and Mexico, also undertook mitigation actions on a voluntary basis.[13] The G7 strongly opposed such a scenario as going squarely against the principle of CBDRRC.[14] As a result, the US openly rejected the Kyoto Protocol in 2001.

10 UNFCCC, Article 4 (2) (b).

11 Kyoto Protocol to the United Nations Framework Convention on Climate Change 2303 UNTS 162.

12 Ibid., Article 3, 10.

13 This was based on a Resolution that passed in the US Senate that forbid the US from signing any subsequent legal agreement additional to the UNFCCC. See discussion in Paul G Harris, 'Common but Differentiated Responsibility: The Kyoto Protocol and United States Policy' (1999) 7 N.Y.U. Environmental Law Journal 27, 42.

14 Ibid., 35.

Article 3 of the Kyoto Protocol established a legal obligation of result for each developed country party to achieve its emission targets.[15] The Kyoto targets were incorporated in Annex B of the Protocol and were not uniform for developed states but reflected historic contributions as well as capacities.[16] Although the targets were negotiated top-down during the Kyoto international conference, they were largely predetermined at the national level.[17] Commentators noted that the Kyoto targets were as much a result of politics as well as a lack of agreement on the objective criteria and indicators for sharing the responsibilities.[18] Some of the proposed criteria for sharing the responsibilities for climate change included CO_2 emissions per capita, GDP per capita or CO_2 emissions per unit of GDP.[19] The absence of agreement on indicators, in turn, led to a pledged-based process that reflected each state's national interests.[20] If it were to draw an analogy here, a similar Kyoto-style approach to refugee responsibility sharing would be pre-determined refugee quotas against objective indicators.[21]

Deeply controversial in many ways and overtly ambitious, the Kyoto Protocol has been hailed as one of the most ambitious environmental treaties ever negotiated.[22] The Protocol introduced, inter alia, the legalisation of the carbon market[23] and the establishment of the Clean Development Mechanism, shaping the future direction of the international legal regime on climate. Most crucially, the Protocol somewhat accidentally defined the trajectory of the CBDRRC principle.

The sharp classification of countries into developed and developing was not going to be sustainable in the long term as it did not reflect existing realities, with certain developing countries becoming major emitters without legal obligations to undertake mitigation actions. As a result of these changing circumstances, the bifurcated rigid approach to differentiation in Kyoto was re-

15 Some initial targets did change during the diplomatic negotiations to reflect greater commitments on the part of certain states. Bodansky, Brunnée, Rajamani, *International Climate Change Law* (n 2) 172.

16 Kyoto Protocol, Annex B.

17 Bodansky, Brunnée, Rajamani, *International Climate Change Law* (n 2) 172.

18 Lasse Ringius, Asbjorn Torvanger and Bjart Holtsmark 'Can multi-criteria rules fairly distribute climate burdens OECD results from three burden sharing rules' (1998) 26 Energy Policy 777.

19 Ibid.

20 Tuula Honkonen, *The Common But Differentiated Responsibility Principle in Multilateral Environmental Agreements* (2009 Kluwer Law International) 130.

21 See discussion of scholarly proposals of Grahl Madsen, Chimni and Schuck in Chapter 7.

22 Bodansky, Brunnée, Rajamani, *International Climate Change Law* (n 2) 161.

23 The Protocol also included provisions on emissions trading. Kyoto Protocol, Article 17.

placed with a more flexible and dynamic differentiation and a reinterpretation of the CBDRRC principle.

2.2 *Responsibility Sharing Post-Kyoto: CBDRRC Revisited*

In the years that followed the conclusion and the entry into force of the Kyoto Protocol, the Parties to the UNFCCC reviewed the future of the climate change regime. This was due to the unwillingness of many developed states to undertake new targets unless major developing country emitters also accepted their share of responsibility. In response to this, the Bali Road Map was adopted by the 13th Conference of the Parties (COP) in December 2007.[24] The Bali Action Plan launched a *process*, a dialogue that would enable 'the full, effective and sustained implementation of the Convention through long-term cooperative action' up to and beyond 2012, 'in order to reach an agreed outcome and adopt a decision'.[25]

The Bali Action Plan opted for an outcome rather than a legally binding instrument.[26] For the first time, it required developing countries to undertake 'nationally appropriate mitigation actions in the context of sustainable development supported and enabled by technology, financing and capacity-building, in a measurable, reportable and verifiable manner'.[27] Under this re-interpretation of the CBDRRC principle, the developing countries were now to contribute to the global mitigation effort in a manner equivalent to their capabilities.

In 2009, the COP took 'note' of a political accord that was reached in Copenhagen.[28] The Copenhagen Accord was a soft law instrument which nonetheless normatively influenced the future of responsibility sharing for climate change. The Copenhagen Accord introduced a re-interpretation of the CBDRRC principle with regard to mitigation commitments which signalled a

24 Decision 1/CP.13, Bali Action Plan, in Report of the Conference of the Parties on its thirteenth session, held in Bali from 3 to 15 December 2007. Addendum. Part Two: Action taken by the Conference of the Parties at its thirteenth session, FCCC/CP/2007/6/Add.1 (14 March 2008) <https://unfccc.int/resource/docs/2007/cop13/eng/06a01.pdf> accessed 17 October 2024 (Bali Action Plan)

25 Ibid., 3.

26 It could have been a legally binding instrument, a soft law instrument or a decision of the Conference of the Parties. Lavanya Rajamani, 'From Berlin to Bali, Killing Protocol Softly?' (2008) International and Comparatively Law Quarterly 918.

27 Bali Action Plan, para 1 (b) ii.

28 The COP took note of the Copenhagen Accord rather than endorsed in as a COP decision. Report of the Conference of the Parties on its 15th Session held in Copenhagen from 7 to 19 December 2009, Addendum. UN Doc FCCC/CP/2009/11, 4. (Copenhagen Accord) <https://unfccc.int/resource/docs/2009/cop15/eng/11a01.pdf> accessed 17 October 2024.

departure from the one-sided, rigid operationalisation of CBDRRC à la Kyoto-style, towards a bottom-up process of pledge and review.[29] Under the Accord, *all* states parties to the UNFCCC, irrespective of their development levels, committed to undertake mitigation commitments that would subsequently be part of some international scrutiny towards the ambitious objective of limiting the global average temperature to 2 degrees Celsius.[30] With regard to the principle of CBDRRC, the Accord emphasised the *common* responsibility to protect the climate, requiring mitigation action by all parties to the regime rather than solely focusing on differentiation between historical emitters and developing countries.[31]

Developed countries pledged to undertake economy-wide emissions reduction targets subject to international monitoring, review and verification, while developing countries committed to undertake national mitigation actions.[32] The ideological dissonance between developed and developing countries re-emerged over the financial responsibilities of the developed country parties vis-à-vis developing ones. Developed states saw the provision of assistance as 'an implicit quid pro quo' for developing states' mitigation commitments whilst the latter saw it as a form of compensation for historical carbon emissions.[33]

The changing character of the principle of CBDRRC was reiterated and endorsed in the subsequent COP Decisions arising out of the Ad Hoc Working Groups on long term cooperative action.[34] In 2014, the CBDRRC principle acquired an additional qualifier. The Lima Call for Climate Action Decision expressed the urgent need to conclude 'an ambitious agreement in 2015 that reflects the principle of common but differentiated responsibilities and respective capabilities, *in light of different national circumstances*'.[35] It further

29 Copenhagen Accord, para 4.

30 Ibid., para 1.

31 Daniel Bodansky, 'The Copenhagen Climate Change Conference: A Postmortem' (2010) 104 The American Journal of International Law 230, 240.

32 Copenhagen Accord, para 4 and para 6 respectively.

33 Bodansky, 'The Copenhagen Climate Change Conference: A Postmortem' (n 30) 237.

34 Report of the Conference of the Parties on its sixteenth session, held in Cancun from 29 November to 10 December 2010, Addendum, Part Two: Action taken by the Conference of the Parties at its sixteenth session Outcome of the work of the Ad Hoc Working Group on Long Term Cooperative Action under the Convention of 2010 Decision 1/CP.16/ UNFCCC/CP/2010/7 <https://unfccc.int/documents/6525> accessed 17 October 2024 (The Cancun Agreements).

35 UNFCCC, 'Decision 1/CP.20 Lima Call for Climate Action' (2 February 2015) FCCC/CP/ 2014/10/Add.1 para 3 <https://unfccc.int/resource/docs/2014/cop20/eng/10a03.pdf> accessed 17 October 2024 (Lima Call for Climate Action).

urged developed countries to provide and mobilise enhanced financial support to developing countries especially those that are vulnerable to the adverse effects of climate change and which require complementary support.[36]

Against the above, the principle's interpretation changed through time. It started in Rio as encapsulating an idea of corrective fairness which then required historical emitters to take responsibility and mitigate the harm done while developing states achieve their economic development. Gradually, the rationale for differentiating responsibility sharing commitments on the basis of contributions to harm evolved to a more dynamic, less rigid approach focusing on capabilities and capacities. This change meant that developing countries, especially major emitters, were to take mitigation commitments equivalent to their contributions as well as capacities. The next section discusses whether this dynamic evolution of the CBDRRC principle was the litmus test for its continued relevance.

2.3 *Responsibility Sharing in the Paris Agreement: CBDRRC* Sur Mesure

The principle's dynamics were put to test during the negotiations of a post 2020 climate change law regime in Paris in 2015. The Paris Agreement reintroduced CBDRRC in the context of a multilateral treaty and reaffirmed the principle within a legal regime of universal obligations defined by prevalent asymmetries, vulnerabilities and different levels of socio-economic realities.[37]

The Paris Agreement has the very ambitious objective to hold the increase in global temperature to well-below 2 degrees Celsius above pre-industrial levels, and to pursue efforts to limit the temperature increase towards 1.5 degrees Celsius.[38] The Agreement contains a distinct version of CBDRRC. The basis for differentiation in states' legal obligations under the treaty and their subsequent mitigation targets is no longer focused on the contribution to harm but the respective capabilities and national circumstances of each state party.[39]

36 Ibid., para 4.

37 UNFCCC, Decision 1/CP/.21 'Adoption of the Paris Agreement' (entered into force 29 January 2016) FCCC/CP/2015/10/Add.1, Annex. (Paris Agreement); Mariama Williams, Manuel F Montes, 'Common But Differentiated Responsibilities: Which way Forwards?' (2016) 59 Dialogue, 114.

38 Paris Agreement, Art 2 (1).

39 Ibid., Article 2 (2); Lavanya Rajamani, 'Ambition and Differentiation in the 2015 Paris Agreement: Interpretative Possibilities and Underlying Politics' (2016) 45 International and Comparative Law Quarterly 493, 511 https://doi.org/10.1017/S0020589316000130.

The responsibility sharing arrangement in the Paris Agreement is still normatively premised on a conception of fairness expressed by the CBDRRC principle and operationalised via a bottom-up self-differentiation tailored to each state's national circumstances and capabilities. With respect to mitigation commitments, each state party can self-differentiate and determine its commitments when pledging its Nationally Determined Circumstances (NDCs).[40] Furthermore, whilst developed countries are still normatively expected to continue to take the lead in climate action because of their greater capacities and resources,[41] the text of the agreement 'leaves little room for tailoring commitments to differentiated responsibilities for environmental harm'.[42] Crucially, the Paris Agreement opened up differentiation beyond mitigation across all pillars of climate action, namely adaptation, finance, technology transfer and capacity building.[43]

On a parallel reading of the Paris Agreement and the Global Compact on Refugees, responsibility sharing in the Compact is premised on a version of the CBDRRC principle that mirrors the language of the Paris Agreement.[44] As already argued, the Compact's implementation mechanisms and the processes it has set in motion mirror some of the modalities of the Paris Agreement. A closer look at the Agreement's legal design and operationalisation of the CBDRRC principle is therefore imperative to understand the principle's potential in guiding the global refugee responsibility sharing effort.

The Paris version of CBDRRC serves an idea of fairness as proportionality since mitigation commitments ought to somehow reflect the state's capabilities and national circumstances. The fairness of each contribution is not assessed against an internationally agreed list of objective indicators but is 'self-assessed' by the submitting party. For example, when states submitted their first rounds of NDCs in 2015 and 2016, they included in their submissions a narrative on how their NDCs were reflective of their CBDRRC.[45] The

40 Paris Agreement, Article 4 (2).

41 Ibid., Article 4 (4).

42 Rajamani, 'Ambition and Differentiation in the 2015 Paris Agreement: Interpretative Possibilities and Underlying Politics' (n 39) 511.

43 Daniel Bodansky, 'The Paris Climate Change Agreement: A New Hope?' (2016) 110 American Journal of International Law 288, 300 https://doi.org/10.5305/amerjintelaw.110.2.0288.

44 Global Compact on Refugees para 1 and 4.

45 Nicholas Chan, 'Contributions and the Paris Agreement: Fairness and Equity in a Bottom-Up Architecture' (2016) 39 Ethics and International Affairs 291, 301 https://doi.org/10.1017/S0892679416000228.

lack of agreement over objective indicators that has characterised the climate change regime persisted in Paris. It is notable that a Synthesis Report on the Aggregate Effect of the Intended Nationally Determined Contributions (INDCs) of the Parties prepared by the UNFCCC Secretariat in 2016 claimed that: '[s]ome Parties noted that no single indicator can reflect fairness or a globally equitable distribution of efforts'.[46] Some parties justified their NDCs in light of their particular, 'social, economic and geographical factors', while others relied on more specific criteria, such as 'responsibility, capability and historical responsibility, based on climate justice, share of emissions, development and/or technological capacity, mitigation potential, cost of mitigation actions, etc.'.[47] This is useful to bear in mind when discussing fairness indicators to measure capacities for refugee protection. Even in the context of climate change, where objective indicators could seemingly be agreed upon given that GHG emissions can be quantifiable, international agreement has proved elusive.

In the first instance, such conception of fairness is endowed with a great degree of subjectivity that is ultimately determined by national self-interests. This was however intentional in order to enable broad participation to the treaty while reflecting 'practical international politics' in the legal design of a responsibility sharing arrangement.[48] Having said that, the Paris Agreement codifies a procedural obligation of each party to submit its NDCs in a public record which further acts as a mechanism for transparency and review of the global responsibility sharing effort.[49] This bottom-up self-differentiation was an innovative way of overcoming competing conceptions of fairness if mitigation commitments were to be determined top down against predetermined quotas. While the NDCs are not legally binding in the sense that failure to achieve them will not incur violation of the treaty provisions, procedural fairness is ensured since participation to responsibility sharing is a legal obligation.

46 Conference of the Parties Twenty-second session Marrakech, 7–18 November 2016 Aggregate effect of the intended nationally determined contributions: an update Synthesis report by the secretariat FCCC/CP/2016/2 (2 May 2016) para 25 <https://unfccc.int/resource/docs/2016/cop22/eng/02.pdf> accessed 17 October 2024.

47 Ibid.

48 Rajamani, 'Ambition and Differentiation in the 2015 Paris Agreement: Interpretative Possibilities and Underlying Politics' (n 39) 514.

49 The NDCs communicated by Parties shall be recorded in a public registry maintained by the secretariat. Paris Agreement, Article 4 (12). See discussion below Section 4.2.

3 CBDRRC and Financial Assistance to the Developing Countries

Financial assistance to developing countries has been an important feature and often a condition for the conclusion and implementation of most multilateral environmental agreements as discussed in the previous chapter. This section focuses on the responsibilities of developed states with regard to financial responsibility sharing under the Paris Agreement.

Developing countries have always sought to secure the necessary financial, technology and capacity building resources in order to undertake and meet mitigation commitments under the climate change regime. Indeed, financial commitments on the part of developed states have been the *quid pro quo* for developing countries' cooperation and participation to the responsibility sharing effort in the first place.[50] All climate change law instruments, including the Paris Agreement, provide for some commitments on financial assistance on the part of developed countries.[51] Under the UNFCCC, developed countries are to provide 'new and additional financial resources to meet the full costs incurred by developing countries in meeting their commitments'.[52] To this end, a financial mechanism is established that would mobilise finance on a grant or at least concessional basis.[53] The treaty recognises the conditionality of such funding for the compliance with the obligations:

> The extent to which developing country Parties will effectively implement their commitments under the Convention will depend on the effective implementation by developed country Parties of their commitments under the Convention related to financial resources and transfer of technology.[54]

Likewise, Article 9 (1) of the Paris Agreement stipulates that developed countries *shall* provide financial resources to assist developing country parties with respect to both mitigation and adaptation, in continuation of their existing obligations under the UNFCCC. This provision establishes what has been de-

50 Bodansky, Brunnée, Rajamani, *International Climate Change Law* (n 2) 138.

51 UNFCCC, Article 4 (3), 4 (4), 11. Kyoto Protocol, Article 11. Paris Agreement, Articles 9, 10, 11.

52 UNFCCC, Article 4 (3).

53 Ibid., Article 11.

54 Ibid., Article 4 (7).

scribed as *a collective* legal obligation on the part of developed parties to provide financial assistance to developing countries.[55] Some commentators have noted that the provision's formulation in passive terms further blurs what is expected of each individual developed state.[56] Notably, regarding the financing of adaptation needs of the least developed countries, small island states that are most vulnerable to the adverse effects of climate change effects and the ones with the most limited capacities, the Paris Agreement encourages developed states to commit to grant-based resources.[57]

Whether financial assistance from developed states, including capacity building and relevant technology transfer, is conditional to developing countries' compliance with the Paris Agreement is a contested matter. The majority of commentators acknowledge that there is a factual necessity between financial responsibility sharing from developed countries and developing states' mitigation and adaptation action, the absence of which does not affect the legal obligations of developing countries under the treaty.[58] In other words, compliance with the treaty is not legally contingent upon receipt of support, and the provision of Article 9 just offers context for effective implementation.[59] In practice, however, many of the developing countries' pledged NDCs have been made partly or wholly conditional upon international assistance. Dominica's NDCs read:

> This contribution is conditional upon receiving timely access to international climate change financing, technology development and transfer, and capacity building support for priority adaptation and mitigation measures. Dominica's INDC will remain provisional pending confirmation of timely access to international climate change financing, technology development and transfer, and capacity building support for priority adaptation and mitigation measures detailed in this

55 Lavanya Rajamani, 'The 2015 Paris Agreement: Interplay Between Hard, Soft and Non-Obligations' (2016) 28 Journal of Environmental Law 337, 353; https://doi.org/10.1093/jel/eqw015; Daniel Bodansky, 'The Legal Character of the Paris Agreement' (2016) 25 Review of European Comparative and International Environmental Law 142, 145–146 https://doi.org/10.1111/reel.12154.

56 Rajamani, 'The 2015 Paris Agreement: Interplay Between Hard, Soft and Non Obligations' (n 55) 353.

57 Paris Agreement, Article 9 (4).

58 Bodansky, Brunnée, Rajamani, *International Climate Change Law* (n 2) 131.

59 Ibid.

> INDC. Dependent upon COP21 outcomes, Dominica reserves the right to revise the INDC.[60]

Zambia's NDC states:

> This emission reduction is conditional and subject to the availability of international support in form of finance, technology and capacity building. The total budget for implementing both components is estimated at US$ 50 billion by the year 2030, out of this USD 35 billion is expected to come from external sources while $15 billion will be mobilized from domestic sources.[61]

Therefore, despite the lack of legal conditionality within the treaty, developing countries have explicitly based their mitigation and adaptation commitments on their receipt of support from the international community. Some commentators have highlighted the risk that the conditionality of the NDC s – though justified by fairness considerations, factual circumstances and resources – could eventually become the Paris Agreement's Achilles' heel.[62]

What is important to note regarding the obligations on financial assistance in the Paris Agreement is that the treaty acknowledges the functional, if not legal, conditionality between such assistance to developing countries and effective implementation of the Agreement. The limited capacities of the least developing countries and their special adaptation needs are especially catered for in the legal agreement. This is done through a collective obligation on the part of developed states as a whole to mobilise climate change finance. Drawing a parallel to the international refugee law regime, similar issues are present regarding financial responsibility sharing and low-income refugee host states. While compliance with the Refugee Convention is not and should not be conditioned upon the receipt of financial assistance from Western states, a responsibility sharing framework that serves elemental considerations of fair-

60 Dominica's 2020 INDC <https://www4.unfccc.int/sites/submissions/INDC/Published%20Documents/Dominica/1/Commonwealth%20of%20Dominica-%20Intended%20Nationally%20Determined%20Contributions%20(INDC).pdf> accessed 17 October 2024.

61 Zambia's 2020 NDCs <https://www4.unfccc.int/sites/submissions/INDC/Published%20Documents/Zambia/1/FINAL+ZAMBIA'S+INDC_1.pdf> accessed 17 October 2024.

62 Pieter Pauw, Paula Castro, Jonathan Pickering, Shikha Bhasin 'Conditional nationally determined contributions in the Paris Agreement: foothold for equity or Achilles heel? (2020) 20 Climate Policy 468, 481 <https://www.tandfonline.com/doi/full/10.1080/14693062.2019.1635874> accessed 17 October 2024.

ness should provide for some financial commitments on the part of the international community vis-à-vis refugee host states.

4 The Legal Architecture of the Paris Agreement

Much of the Paris Agreement's provisions would not have been agreed upon without the innovative legal design and creative lawyering that took place. This section studies in more depth the legal architecture of the Paris Agreement as a model example of a multilateral instrument on responsibility sharing, the 'art and craft'[63] of which helped overcome political unwillingness, ideological conundrums and collective action problems.[64]

The Paris Agreement is built upon a hybrid legal architecture of bottom-up and top-down treaty obligations. During the negotiations, the issue of the legal form of the instrument *per se*, the differentiation in states' mitigation, adaption and finance commitments, as well as the binding nature of each of its provisions, were central and highly vexed maters.[65] The treaty includes a wide range of provisions that span across a spectrum of legal obligations which commentators have described as 'hard law, soft law, and non-law'.[66]

The Durban platform for Enhanced Action that launched the mandate on the negotiations for what came to be the Paris Agreement provided for the conclusion of either a 'protocol, another legal instrument or an agreed outcome with legal force under the Convention'.[67] The fact that the Paris Agreement was not concluded as a 'protocol' was in deference to the American

63 The term 'art and craft' is used in the title of a book written by the prominent American environmental lawyer Daniel Bodansky who has participated in all multilateral negotiations on climate change for the past ten years. Daniel Bodanksy, *The Art and Craft of International Environmental Law* (Harvard University Press 2011).

64 Ibid., 271.

65 Lavanya Rajamani, Jacob Werksman, 'The Legal Character and Operational Relevance of the Paris Agreement's Temperature Goal' (2018) 376 Philosophical Transactions of The Royal Society 1, 13 https://doi.org/10.1098/rsta.2016.0458.

66 'Non-law' provisions have been termed those that set mere aspirations and provide context. Rajamani, 'The 2015 Paris Agreement: Interplay Between Hard, Soft and Non-Obligations' (n 55) 356; Bodansky, 'The Legal Character of the Paris Agreement' (n 54) 147.

67 Report of the Conference of the Parties on its seventeenth session, held in Durban from 28 November to 11 December 2011 Addendum Part Two: Action taken by the Conference of the Parties at its seventeenth session Decision 1/CP.17 Establishing of an Ad Hoc Working Group on a Durban Platform for Enhanced Action, 2. (Durban Platform for Action).

political sensitivities withstanding from the Kyoto Protocol nomenclature.[68] The Paris Agreement is a multilateral treaty under the definition of Article 2 (1) (a) of the VCLT.[69] As the VCLT specifies, the particular designation of an instrument does not affect its legal status.[70] The delicate balance of bottom-up and top-down obligations is examined next.

4.1 *Responsibility Sharing Bottom-Up*

The NDCs, namely the responsibility sharing commitments, are fundamental building blocks of the Paris Agreement. The provision of Article 4 subjects each party to a legal obligation to 'prepare, communicate and maintain successive nationally determined contributions that it intends to achieve' in line with their CBDRRC.[71] Crafted as a procedural obligation of conduct,[72] it does not obligate the parties to achieve their NDCs, intentionally falling short of creating an obligation of result.[73] Article 4 nonetheless imposes a good faith expectation on the parties that they will take the necessary measures to implement their submitted NDCs.[74]

The way NDCs are constructed in Paris offers each party with the flexibility and latitude to choose the content of their mitigation commitments. The lessons learned from Kyoto was that states would never again accept to be bound by pre-determined emission targets and hence only a more flexible, bottom-up approach to differentiation would be able to secure widespread agreement. The Paris Agreement yet differentiates between the parties by setting different normative expectations between developed and developing countries, as well as amongst developing countries. For example, Article 4 (4) reinstates the practice that developed counties are encouraged *but not obligated* to continue taking the lead by undertaking economy-wide absolute emission reduction targets and developing countries are encouraged to do

---

68 Lavanya Rajamani, 'The Devilish Details: Key Legal Issues in the 2015 Climate Negotiations' (2015) 78 Modern Law Review 826.

69 VCLT, Article 2 (1) (a).

70 Ibid.

71 Paris Agreement, Article 4.

72 Rajamani, Werksman, 'The Legal Character and Operational Relevance of the Paris Agreement's Temperature Goal' (n 64) 6.

73 During the negotiations, the US, China and India opposed any legally binding obligation of result that would require the Parties to achieve their NDCs. Rajamani, 'The 2015 Paris Agreement: Interplay Between Hard, Soft and Non-Obligations' (n 54) 353.

74 Rajamani, Werksman, 'The Legal Character and Operational Relevance of the Paris Agreement's Temperature Goal' (n 64) 6.

the same over time, 'in light of different national circumstances'.[75] Commentators have highlighted that this was because the provision of Article 4 does not create new obligations for developed countries other than the ones they have already assumed voluntarily.[76]

Article 4 (3) sets a normative expectation for each party to progress its NDCs to reflect the highest possible ambition, in accordance with its CBDRRC.[77] Developed countries are therefore normatively expected by the treaty to be more ambitious with their emission reduction targets due to their resources and capabilities.[78] The level of ambition in the submitted NDCs will ultimately vary as well among the developing countries as they too differ in national circumstances.[79] Finally, and as discussed earlier, Article 9 (1) of the Paris Agreement codifies a collective obligation of financial responsibility sharing on the part of developed states as a whole, in continuation of their existing obligations under the UNFCCC.

At first, the latitude which the parties are offered in relation to mitigation commitments might seem counterintuitive to fairness considerations. After all, the NDCs are not legally binding and the parties are merely expected to achieve them. In assessing whether a legal obligation to undertake mitigation commitments, coupled with a good faith expectation to implement the pledges, is sufficient to achieve the ambitious objective of the Paris Agreement, one needs to look at the treaty as a whole. While the nature of the legal obligations are admittedly 'softened', with the core of obligations to be procedural in character, the Paris Agreement provides for a unique oversight system in the areas of transparency, review and implementation that tames the parties' increased flexibility by placing a strong emphasis on procedure and public reporting, both serving an important function in the protection of community interest.[80]

4.2 *Obligations on Transparency and Reporting*

To ensure effective implementation, the Paris Agreement sketches a rigorous oversight system that complements and completes its legal architecture. The

75 Paris Agreement, Article 4 (4).

76 Rajamani, 'The 2015 Paris Agreement: Interplay Between Hard, Soft and Non-Obligations' (n 55) 355.

77 Paris Agreement, Article 4 (3).

78 This can be inferred from a combined reading of Articles 4 (3), (4) and (5).

79 Ibid., Article 4 (4).

80 Jutta Brunnée, 'International Environmental Law and Community Interests Procedural Aspects', in Eyal Benvenisti, Georg Nolte (eds) *Community Interests Across International Environmental Law* (Oxford University Press) 155.

way the oversight system is structured stems from the rationale that 'peer and public pressure can be as effective as legal obligation in influencing behaviour'.[81] The legal obligations on mitigation and financial support are further bolstered by respective legal obligations on transparency and reporting.[82]

The purpose of the transparency framework is the tracking of individual and collective progress towards the Agreement's objective. To this end, the treaty codifies an individual obligation of information sharing. In relation to mitigation action in particular, each party *shall* provide a national inventory report of anthropogenic emissions by sources and removals by sinks, as well as report on its progress towards achieving its NDCs.[83] In contrast to reporting on adaptation measures, which allows for a certain discretion, there is no such margin regarding reporting in relation to mitigation actions.[84]

In addition, each party is required to report on why it considers its NDCs to be fair and ambitious, how they reflect their CBDRRC and how they contribute to the objective of the Agreement as set out in Article 2.[85] Additionally, developed countries are also required to report on financial, technology transfer and capacity building support provided to developing countries.[86] This requirement bolsters the collective obligation to provide financial resources to assist developing country parties with mitigation and adaptation under Article 9, adding an extra layer of transparency and monitoring in climate finance.

Beyond the transparency function of information sharing, reporting obligations constitute a self-examination on the part of each state party that contributes to the overall assessment and tracking of collective progress towards the treaty's objectives.[87] What is more, and in the absence of internationally agreed indicators for assessing the fairness of each party's contributions to the global mitigation effort, the NDCs become 'public claims of fairness' further

81 Bodansky, Brunnée, Rajamani, *International Climate Change Law* (n 2) 242.

82 Rajamani, 'The 2015 Paris Agreement: Interplay Between Hard, Soft and Non-Obligations' (n 55) 353.

83 Paris Agreement, Article 13 (7) (a) (b).

84 Ibid., Article 13 (8).

85 Information to facilitate clarity, transparency and understanding of nationally determined contributions is referred to in the Conference of the Parties Twenty-fourth session in Katowice, (14 December 2018) Preparations for the implementation of the Paris Agreement and the first session of the Conference of the Parties serving as the meeting of the Parties to the Paris Agreement, Decision 1/CP.21, FCCC/CP/2018/L.22. Annex I. para 6 and para 7. <https://unfccc.int/sites/default/files/resource/l22_0.pdf> accessed 17 October 2017.

86 Articles 13 (9), (10) and (11).

87 Bodansky, *The Art and Craft of International Environmental Law* (n 63) 239.

subjected to international scrutiny so as 'to become socially accepted as being genuinely fair and ambitious'.[88]

The reporting and transparency framework is complemented with a global stocktake that takes place every five years.[89] The stocktake encourages the parties to adopt more ambitious NDCs while taking stock of the collective progress made.[90] A downside of this review mechanism is that implementation is only limited to the assessment of collective progress, insulating the parties from an assessment of their individual mitigation efforts. The first global stock change confirmed that the international community is far from achieving the Paris Agreement's objectives. The submitted NDCs are insufficient against the magnitude of the climate challenge.[91] Despite the innovative legal design, the challenge of responsibility sharing for climate change 'will likely persist given the disparities among countries in wealth, historical and per capita emissions and circumstances'.[92]

4.3 *Implementation and Compliance*

Completing the oversight system, the Paris Agreement provides for a mechanism on implementation and compliance.[93] Article 15 establishes a standing Committee of Experts that operates in a non-adversarial and non-punitive way. Briefly, the Committee of Experts can initiate proceedings regarding non-compliance, with several binding procedural obligations that would otherwise escape review.[94]

More importantly, the Committee may not address the 'content of the contributions, communications, information and reports' of the Parties.[95] The

88 Emphasis in the original. Chan 'Climate Contributions and the Paris Agreement: Fairness and Equity in a Bottom-Up Architecture' (n 44) 298.

89 Paris Agreement, Article 14.

90 Ibid. Article 14 combined with Article 4 (3).

91 Report of the Conference of the Parties serving as the meeting of the Parties to the Paris Agreement on its fifth session, held in the United Arab Emirates from 30 November to 13 December 2023 (15 March 2024) UN FCCC/PA/CMA/2023/16/Add.1 Decision 1/CMA.5 I, 3 <https://unfccc.int/documents/637073> assessed 17 October 2024.

92 Bodansky, Brunnée, Rajamani, *International Climate Change Law* (n 2) 361.

93 Paris Agreement, Article 15 (2).

94 Rajamani, Bodansky, 'The Paris Rulebook: Balancing International Prescriptiveness with National Discretion', (2019) 68 International and Comparative Law Quarterly 1023, 1039 https://doi.org/10.1017/S0020589319000320.

95 Report of the Conference of the Parties serving as the meeting of the Parties to the Paris Agreement on the third part of its first session, held in Katowice from 2 to 15 December 2018 Addendum Part two: Action taken by the Conference of the Parties serving as the meeting of the Parties to the Paris Agreement Decision 20/CMA.1 Modalities and

compliance procedure may only consider the breach of the procedural obligation, namely the omission to submit an NDC or a national inventory report.[96] The compliance measures the Committee can take are 'soft' in nature and they include, *inter alia*, opening a dialogue with the Party concerned, in order to make recommendations for the development of an action plan, assist the concerned party, if necessary, or issue findings in relation to matters of implementation and compliance.[97] The oversight system is facilitative in character and preserves considerable autonomy, flexibility and discretion for states.

4.4 *The Paris Agreement: A Model Treaty for Responsibility Sharing*

The Paris Agreement represents a model treaty with a distinct hybrid legal design that takes a pragmatic yet principled approach to responsibility sharing for climate change. It codifies a light package of obligations that serve predominantly a conception of procedural fairness while the rest of the treaty provisions set normative expectations against a very ambitious, if not aspirational, goal. Its hybrid legal architecture offered a solution to vexed matters of 'bindingness, prescriptiveness, and differentiation' common in the area of responsibility sharing.[98] The bottom-up approach to global mitigation efforts was instrumental in reducing the perceived costs of sovereignty that would arise from the conclusion of a binding legal instrument.[99] The treaty has a unique oversight system of transparency and reporting which is key in building trust between the parties. For these reasons, the Paris Agreement can be seen as a model legal framework for responsibility sharing that can be replicated in other fields of international law protecting community interest and facing similar challenges.

5 Conclusions: Lessons from International Climate Change Law

The detailed study of the legal regime on climate change has unfolded true potential for the *de lege ferenda* development of international refugee law.

---

procedures for the effective operation of the committee to facilitate implementation and promote compliance referred to in Article 15, paragraph 2, of the Paris Agreement FCCC/PA/CMA/2018/3/Add.2, para 23 <https://unfccc.int/sites/default/files/resource/cma2018_3_add2_new_advance.pdf> accessed 17 October 2024.

96 Ibid.

97 Ibid., paras 28–31.

98 Daniel Bodansky, Lavanya Rajamani 'The Issues that Never Die' (2018) 12 Carbon and Climate Law Review 184, 190.

99 Bodansky, Brunnée, Rajamani, *International Climate Change Law* (n 1) 212.

International climate change law has been shaped by competing interests between developed and developing countries over economic development on the one hand and environmental protection on the other. From this perspective, it has faced similar challenges to any other field of international law where collective action problems hinder the protection of community interests.

The principle of CBDRRC has had its own unique trajectory in the context of climate change where it dynamically evolved over the years, adapting to social and economic realities. At times, it was the subject of intense controversy between states. In some ways, it continues to be so today. Yet, it remains the normative bedrock for global responsibility under the UNFCCC.[100] CBDRRC reflects claims of interstate as well as intergenerational fairness and serves both procedural and substantive fairness, as it seeks to fairly distribute the burden of addressing climate change while securing the climate for future generations.[101] Two of the most widely accepted principles of fairness are obliquely embedded within the doctrine; the *contribution to the problem* principle and *the capacity or capability to respond and take measures*.[102] What is more, distributive fairness under the CBDRRC principle warrants that developed countries', because of the financial resources as well as historic contribution to the problem, assume additional responsibilities of financial assistance in helping developing states meeting their commitments.

In light of the above, there is value in taking the principle of CBDRRC as the guiding principle of a protocol on responsibility sharing for refugees. Its value lies in the principle's normative foundations to fairness and its adaptation would require first an appraisement of the fairness *problematique* in the international refugee law regime. This is *a fortiori* imperative as the Global Compact on Refugees promotes a CBDRRC approach to refugee responsibility sharing, evidently borrowing from principles and processes of international climate change law. The art of the possible is illustrated by the study of the Paris Agreement's legal architecture and the way it addressed vexed matters of fairness, differentiation and prescriptiveness in matters of responsibility sharing by adopting a pragmatic yet principled approach.

---

100 Brunnée, 'International Environmental Law and Community Interests Procedural Aspects', (n 80) 166.

101 Cinammon P Carlane, JD Colavecchio, 'Balancing Equity and Effectiveness: The Paris Agreement & the Future of International Climate Change Law' (2019) 27 N.Y.U. Environmental Law Journal 108, 117.

102 Friedrich Soltau, *Fairness in International Climate Change Law and Policy* (Cambridge University Press 2019) 133.

CHAPTER 7

A Proposal for a Protocol on Responsibility Sharing: Common but Differentiated Responsibilities in International Refugee Law

This chapter is the culmination of what this book has argued thus far, namely that the responsibility sharing gap of the Refugee Convention cannot be comprehensively filled without further legal development. For as long as there is a disjuncture between the institutional obligation of the international community to protect the refugees and the individual obligations of states the gap will remain. The only way to sync the two is by making the necessary 'structural adjustment' to the international refugee law regime with a legally binding framework on responsibility sharing.[1] Using the prescriptive lens of enlightened positivism, this chapter puts forward a proposal for a second Protocol to the Refugee Convention on Responsibility Sharing premised on common but differentiated legal obligations.

1 The Proposal

To be sure, the originality of this proposal does not lie in its law reform nature. Proposals on a binding framework on responsibility sharing or on some sort of binding contributions to refugee protection have been made by scholars and policy makers throughout the life of the international refugee law regime. From Hathaway and Neve's reformulation project in the 1990s to Wall's recent proposal on a Framework Convention, scholarship has problematised on how to best fill in the responsibility sharing gap and maximise fair sharing.[2] Hath-

1 Marjoleine, Zeick, 'Doomed to Fail from the Outset? UNHCR's Convention Plus Initiative Revisited' (2009) 21 International Journal of Refugee Law 387, 403 https://doi.org/10.1093/ijrl/eep011.

2 See indicatively James C Hathaway and Alexander Neve, 'Making International Refugee Law Relevant Again', 1997) 10 Harvard Human Rights Journal 115, 204; James Hathaway, 'The Global Co-Op Out on Refugees' (2018) 30 International Journal of Refugee Law 591 https://doi.org/10.1093/ijrl/eey062; A Grahl-Madsen, 'Further Development of International Refugee Law', (1965) 35 Nordic Journal of International Law 159; Matthew J Gibney, 'Refugees and Justice Between States' (2015) 14 European Journal of Political Theory 448, 452 https://doi.org/10.1177/1474885115585325; Peter Schuck, 'Refugee Burden Sharing: A Modest Proposal'

 | DOI:10.1163/9789004547711_008

away and Neve submitted a detailed proposal for a UN administered, binding allocational mechanism premised on a logic of 'common but differentiated responsibility' whereby states in the refugee region would provide asylum for the duration of risk, and extra regional states would be legally bound to support the system through funding as well as resettlement.[3] While questions of legal design were left out of the original study, Hathaway, in a reformulation of the original proposal, added that an optional protocol on responsibility sharing would be the best means to vest such a framework.[4] Schuck also proposed a binding allocation mechanism in which an international agency would allocate binding refugee quotas against states' capacities that could be further traded among states.[5] Schuck did not elaborate on the legal architecture that could vest such mechanism and his study attracted most criticism for its refugee commodification risk and its market-based approach to refugee protection.[6]

More recently, Harley has proposed moving towards legal commitments with regard to both resettlement and refugee financing in different ways.[7] Regarding financial sharing, Harley has recommended that one option is to amend UNHCR's funding model from voluntary to binding contributions through payments via the UN General Assembly, and another option would be the creation of a global refugee fund where states would contribute in accordance with their capacity to pay.[8] Regarding resettlement, Harley has suggested that an additional protocol on resettlement that would allocate quotas to states based on agreed fairness indicators would be the ideal way forward.[9]

Wall has proposed the conclusion of a 'Framework Convention on Refugee Responsibility Sharing' inspired by the international legal regime on climate change. Wall's proposal focuses on the framework convention as a model treaty for incremental regime building rather than the codification of specific

---

(1997) 22 Yale Journal of International Law 243; Patrick Wall, 'A New Link in the Chain: Could a Framework Convention for Refugee Responsibility Sharing Fulfill the Promise of the 1967 Protocol?' (2017) 29 International Journal of Refugee Law 201 https://doi.org/10.1093/ijrl/eex025; Tristan Harley, 'Innovations in Responsibility Sharing for Refugees' World Refugee Council Research Paper No. 14 (May 2019).

3 Hathaway, Neve, 'Making International Refugee Law Relevant Again' (n 2) 145.

4 Hathaway 'The Global Co-Op Out on Refugees' (n 2) 599.

5 Schuck, 'Refugee Burden Sharing: A Modest Proposal' (n 2) 277–288.

6 Debora Anker, Joan Fitzpatrick, Andrew Shacknove 'Crisis and Cure: A Reply to Hathaway/Neve and Schuck' (1998) 11 Harvard Human Rights Journal 295–310.

7 Harley, 'Innovation in Responsibility Sharing for Refugees', (n 2) 1.

8 Ibid., 12.

9 Ibid., 13.

obligations of responsibility sharing. While a version of the CBDRRC principle would frame the responsibility sharing effort under the Convention, contributions to responsibility sharing would retain their voluntary nature.[10] Borrowing from climate change policy, Wall's proposed convention mirrors the architecture of the UNFCCC and constitutes an elaborate proposal on a formal yet 'lean' institutional structure for a responsibility sharing framework that would be implemented bottom-up.[11]

What is missing however from *de lege ferenda* proposals like the ones discussed above is an explicit engagement with a notion of fairness and its role in the international refugee law regime. This is *a fortiori* the case with scholarly proposals that advocate for a CBDRRC approach to refugee responsibility sharing without engaging with the principle's contours and fairness *problematique* that require unpacking in the context of refugee protection. Considerations of fairness are not only integral to the debate on how to share refugee protection responsibilities more equitably between states but permeate the global refugee law regime which cannot insulate itself from broader questions of global justice.

This proposal sketches out the key building blocks for a Protocol on Responsibility Sharing that would complement the Refugee Convention and the 1976 Protocol and fill in the responsibility sharing gap. I believe the contribution of this proposal is twofold. Firstly, it problematises with what role for fairness and what conception of fairness could normatively vest a binding responsibility sharing arrangement in international law. The quest for fairness however is modest and stays within the confines of legal positivism, even if enlightened, reflecting the practical realities of international law making rather than ideal conceptions of justice. In the proposed Protocol on Responsibility Sharing, the principle of CBDRRC is adapted to international refugee law and becomes the legal device and framework against which a minimal package of responsibility sharing obligations are codified.

Secondly, the proposal focuses on questions of legal design which are central to the art and craft of a Protocol that caters for both principle and pragmatism since responsibility sharing has traditionally been seen by states as an area within their *domaine réservé*. I have sought to demonstrate how vexed

10 Wall, 'A New Link in the Chain: Could a Framework Convention for Refugee Responsibility Sharing Fulfil the Promise of the 1967 Protocol?' (n 2) 227.

11 Ibid. Wall proposes the establishment of the following bodies under the treaty: a conference of the parties with two subsequent bodies one advisory and the other for monitoring implementation.

matters of fairness, differentiation in resources and capacities and prescriptiveness of the obligations can be accommodated within one single legal instrument. Finally, it is argued that a Protocol on Responsibility Sharing is not that long a stretch as the processes and implementation mechanisms proposed here are already part and parcel of the Global Compact on Refugees machinery.

2 Anticipating the Feasibility Objection

It is anticipated that a proposal on a protocol on responsibility sharing would be *prima facie* challenged, if not plainly rejected, on feasibility grounds. In the current climate of externalisation and responsibility shifting practices that this study has discussed in detail, a proposal for further multilateral law making might come across as wishful legal thinking or even naïve.

It has been supported by scholars that 'new binding obligations on international cooperation are not politically palatable in the refugee context at present' and that 'states are generally unwilling to relinquish discretion in determining the extent to which they wish to support refugees' outside of their territories.[12] Having said this, commentators do agree on the need for some sort of binding obligations of responsibility sharing if it were to fill in the responsibility sharing gap. Policy makers and UNHCR have also acknowledged that ultimately a second protocol to the Refugee Convention would be required if it were to correct the resulting inequitable sharing of responsibilities. In a 2004 study on enhancing cooperation for mass influx situations, UNHCR suggested:

> [I]t may be worth considering an instrument on this issue, for instance, in the form of a Second Protocol to the 1951 Convention. As with the 1967 Protocol, such a Protocol could be open to accession by non-Convention States, a number of which already host large numbers of refugees and would arguably stand to benefit from better governance of mass influxes across the globe. The focus of a new instrument would be

12 Rebecca Dowd, Jane McAdam 'International Cooperation and Responsibility Sharing to Combat Climate Change: Lessons for International Refugee Law' (2017) 18 Melbourne Journal of International Law 180, 216; Harley, 'Innovations in Responsibility Sharing for Refugees' (n 2) 14; Meltem Ineli-Giger, 'The Global Compact on Refugees and Burden Sharing: Will the Compact Address the Normative Gap Concerning Burden Sharing?' (2019) 38 Refugee Survey Quarterly 115, 129 https://doi.org/10.1093/rsq/hdz003.

on putting in place practical guidelines for better management of asylum demands and problems in mass influx situations within a burden-sharing framework.[13]

Among the guiding parameters of such protocol would be the 'specific recognition of the differing capacities of States to contribute to assistance and solutions, and the need for an equitable distribution of burdens and responsibilities'.[14] The former High Commissioner for Refugees, Antonio Guterres, famously said in one of his speeches, 'if there is one Protocol that is yet to be drafted to complement the 1951 Convention, it is one on international solidarity and burden sharing'.[15] Volker Türk, former Assistant High Commissioner at UNHCR who led the negotiations of the Global Compact, noted in an academic publication that an additional protocol to the Refugee Convention would be the ideal means to fill the gap, and that the Global Compact was and should be seen as the feasible intermediary step.[16]

It is also true that the current climate is not conducive to proposals for multilateral law-making, especially today when multilateralism seems to be losing ground and appeal due to an ever growing nationalism.[17] Even if multilateralism's appeal might be in decline as some scholars caution, international lawyers' response should be a defence of multilateral law making which is in fact required for the protection of community interests.[18] As Hathaway aptly puts it, the best defence of multilateralism would be 'a good offence', which in the case of the responsibility sharing gap entails a defence for a binding instrument that accommodates states' legitimate interests and refugee and host communities' humanitarian and developmental needs.[19] Ultimately, the feasi-

13 Ensuring International Protection and Enhancing International Cooperation in Mass Influx Situations: Advance Summary Findings of the Study Commissioned by UNHCR (2004) (2004) EC/54/SC/CRP. (11 June 2004), para 12.

14 Ibid.

15 Opening Remarks at the 66th Session of the Executive Committee of the High Commissioner's Programme. António Guterres, United Nations High Commissioner for Refugees (Geneva, 5 October 2015).

16 Volker Türk, Madeline Garlick, 'From Burdens and Responsibilities to Opportunities: The Comprehensive Refugee Response Framework and a Global Compact on Refugees' (2016) 28 International Journal of Refugee Law 656, 678 https://doi.org/10.1093/ijrl/eew043.

17 Harlan G Cohen, 'Multilateralism's Life-Cycle' (2018) 112 American Journal of International Law 47, 48 https://doi.org/10.1017/ajil.2018.11.

18 Ibid.

19 Hathaway, 'The Global Co-Op Out on Refugees' (n 2) 596.

bility of any proposal for a treaty lies with the costs of entering into such an agreement. As already discussed, academic proposals on responsibility sharing have been either vague and inattentive to legal design or overtly prescriptive, going too far as to suggest binding pre-determined quotas. With an exception to Wall, most of the scholarly proposals on a binding instrument have left questions of legal design unaddressed.

A protocol on responsibility sharing does not need to establish a central allocation mechanism of pre-determined quotas. Binding quotas are not politically feasible, do not guarantee compliance nor address fairness considerations. The intra EU relocation experience under the CEAS illustrated this point.[20] Crucially, an important distinction often neglected in law reform proposals is the one between the binding nature of the instrument and the legal character of its constituent provisions. The Paris Agreement is a model treaty where this distinction between the legal form of the instrument and the prescriptiveness of the treaty obligations is illustrated.

Arguments against a legal instrument on responsibility sharing have also been made from the perspective of effectiveness. Betts, Costello and Zaun argue that effective responsibility sharing is unlikely to be achieved through a single legal mechanism or centralised allocation system.[21] They add that there must be 'complementary – political, analytical, and operational – mechanisms' in place that will also provide for situation specific responses.[22] It goes without saying that no legal instrument on its own, however it is crafted, can achieve fairness in refugee responsibility sharing and respond to global challenges such as the management of forced displacement. That would be too much to expect from international law in any given scenario. The necessity and complementarity of situation specific operational responses in the short term is uncontested. So too is the need to fill in the responsibility sharing gap left by the Refugee Convention with a principled yet pragmatic framework that sets in motion a process towards a more equitable sharing of the common responsibility to protect refugees.

---

20 See Discussion in Chapter 3 pp. 47–48.

21 Alexander Betts, Cathryn Costello and Natascha Zaun, 'A Fair Share Refugees and Responsibility-Sharing' Report 2017:10, 6 <https://www.rsc.ox.ac.uk/publications/a-fair-share-refugees-and-responsibility-sharing> accessed 17 October 2024.

22 Ibid.

3 Fairness and the International Refugee Law Regime

3.1 *Fairness between States*

Fairness considerations on how to share refugees more equitably among states conceptually underpin the debate on refugee responsibility sharing. The effective operation of the international refugee law regime is also dependent on the regime's procedural and distributive fairness. It has been the 'urgent need' for fairness, or the lack thereof, that brought states to the negotiating table to discuss ways for redistributing the collective responsibility to protect refugees more equitably and more predictably.[23] Fairness considerations were prominent to the refugee responsibility sharing debate during the UNHCR Convention Plus Initiative that framed responsibility sharing as a matter of North-South cooperation.[24] More recently, 'the fundamental unfairness and inequity of the international refugee regime for hosts states and their communities' was one of the reasons that led to the adoption of the New York Declaration on Refugees and Migrants, and the subsequent conclusion of the Global Compact on Refugee.[25]

Fair and equitable have become synonymous terms in the context of international cooperation and responsibility sharing for refugees.[26] It is precisely this synonymous relationship that manifests itself in the interchangeable use of both terms in international refugee law and policy. One might argue that the use of such words by states in particular are mere perfunctory statements, corresponding at best to a factual acknowledgement that some states host a disproportionate number of refugees compared to others. That is not the case, however, for large refugee host states that undertake the lion's share of the common institutional responsibility to protect refugees.[27]

A conception of fairness therefore acquires normative salience in the context of international cooperation and responsibility sharing. As two commentators write:

---

23 Global Compact on Refugees, para 1.

24 See Chapter 4, Section 4

25 Harley, 'Innovations in Responsibility Sharing for Refugees' (n 2) 1.

26 Pieter Pauw, Steffen Bauer, Carmen Richerzhagen, Clara Brandi, Hanna Schmole 'Different Perspectives on Differentiated Responsibilities; A State-of-the-Art Review of the Notion of Common but Differentiated Responsibilities in International Negotiations' (German Development Institute Discussion Paper 6/2014), 6.

27 See Statements by countries hosting large numbers of Syrian refugees in 2013, UNHCR Executive Committee, 64th session, Summary Record of the 666th Meeting, UN Doc A/AC.96/SR.666 (14 October 2013) paras 15–35.

> justice would argue for no one state to be disproportionately affected by refugee flows because it is likely that the burdened state was not the cause of the flow and it is burdened simply because of propinquity.[28]

Unpacking the fairness *problematique* in the international refugee law regime is not without challenge. Fairness can be said to be an inherently 'contested concept' as multiple and often competing conceptions of fairness can derive from the broader concept.[29] This is *a fortiori* the case in international law where the international community consists of sovereign states, each state with its own plausible conception of fairness informed and shaped by its economic and social circumstances.[30] Thomas Franck, in *Fairness in International Law*, adverted to the subjective nature of fairness which, in his view, can only be fulfilled in the reality of international law in a process of public discourse, reasoning and negotiation. He writes:

> fairness is relative and subjective (...) a human, subjective contingent quality which merely captures in one word a process of discourse, reasoning and negotiation leading, if successful to an agreed formula located at a conceptual intersection between various plausible formulas for allocation.[31]

Political theorists have grappled with various conceptions of fairness and have developed subsequent distributive principles that seek to resolve issues of resource or burden allocation in the protection of community interests.[32] Amongst the most popular are the egalitarian principle of per capita distribution, the needs-based principle – reflecting the conception that the distribu-

28 Alexander Aleinikoff and Steven Poellot, 'The Responsibility to Solve: The International Community and Protracted Refugee Situations', (2014) 54 Virginia Journal of International Law 196, 213.

29 Gallie introduced the term 'essentially contested concepts' as conceptual tool to explore the multiple understandings and interpretations certain abstract evaluative notions can take. WB Gallie, 'Essentially Contested Concepts' (1955–1956) 56 Proceedings of the Aristotelian Society 167. Since Gallie, the concept/conception distinction has been used in Political Sciences and International Relations. Rawls for example in his Theory of Justice employs this distinction when advancing his own conception of justice as fairness. John Rawls, A *Theory of Justice* (Harvard University Press 1971) 5.

30 Friedrich Soltau, *Fairness in International Climate Change Law and Policy* (Cambridge University Press 2019) 144.

31 Thomas Franck, *Fairness in International Law and Institutions* (Oxford University Press 1998) 14.

32 Ibid.

tion of benefits should accord priority to the poorest or most at risk -, the contribution to the harm/problem principle – evident in 'the polluter pays' doctrine of international environmental law – and finally, the capabilities-based principle – prescribing that the greater the ability to take action, the greater the share of responsibility.[33] As the previous chapter discussed, the principle of CBDRRC is an application of fairness in international law and encapsulates two of the aforementioned principles, the contribution to harm and the capacity to take action.

Another crucial distinction that adds conceptual clarity to the quest for fair responsibility sharing of refugee protection responsibilities is that between *fairness principles* and *burden sharing formulae.* Fairness principles are the ones mentioned above which embody different normative conceptions of fairness. *Burden sharing formulae*, on the other hand, are methodologies or indicators that measure fairness against so-called objective metrics such as GDP, landmass and population size.[34] If we were to draw this schematically, on top of the pyramid would sit the abstract and contested concept of fairness, under it would be the principles reflecting the various conceptions and at the bottom would sit the specific burden sharing formulae or indicators that measure or assess a fair share.

Scholars have proposed various indicators that could measure a fair share of refugee protection responsibilities while also acknowledging that there exists considerable disagreement. Miller notes that states 'can reasonably disagree' on what indicators shall be used to determine a fair share of refugee protection.[35] Likewise, Owen finds that the lack of uniform agreement among states on what should be the criteria for a fair distribution is yet another challenge to face.[36] Gibney, on the other hand, contends that this disagreement is overrated and that three indicators used in UNHCR reports, namely GDP, population size and the total numbers of refugees are widely accepted economic metrics.[37] Similarly, Grahl-Madsen proposed to allocate refugee quotas in the

33 These principles are summarised in Soltau *Fairness in International Climate Change Law and Policy* (n 30) 153. See also Lasse Ringius, Asbjorn Torvanger and Bjart Holtsmark 'Can Multi-Criteria Rules Fairly Distribute climate Burdens: OECD Results From Three Burden Sharing Rules' (1998) 26 Energy Policy 77, 781.

34 Soltau, *Fairness in International Climate Change Law and Policy* (n 30) 163.

35 David Miller, 'David Owen on Global Justice, National Responsibility and Transnational Power: A Reply' (2011) 37 Review of International Studies 2029, 2033.

36 David Owen 'Refugees, Fairness and Taking Up the Slack: On Justice and the International Refugee Regime' (2016) 3 Moral Philosophy and Politics, 141.

37 Gibney 'Refugee and Justice Between States' (n 2) 457.

EU on the basis of the absorptive capacities of Member states.[38] Harley has questioned the accuracy of certain objective metrics as their methodologies often discount the contributions that states make to refugees in their territory.[39] Some economists have even questioned the presumed objective nature of economic metrics as they are constructed out of certain sets of assumptions and prejudices.[40]

Sarnata Reynolds and Juan Pablo Vacatello developed a global model that measures the capacity of the 193 governments who voted in favour of the Global Compact on Refugees to physically protect and financially support refugees and host communities.[41] The model was developed with an aim to provide the Global Compact with a concrete model for equitable and predictable responsibility sharing based on each nation's capacity to receive and/or care for refugees.[42] Their methodology starts with data collected from GDP and population density, which offer a preliminary baseline number of fair share to each state. This is subsequently adjusted twice, once to reflect rankings on the Human Development Index and the second time to reflect data from the Fragile States Index.[43] Under their model, some states are removed altogether from receiving any share due to their fragility levels. In the end, these percentages are converted to refugee quotas against the number of refugees in need of international protection provided in UNHCR statistics.[44] Such model can be a useful tool when measuring states' contributions to refugee protection against relative capacities.

Hathaway, in his original proposal distinguished between states' role and criteria for physical and financial responsibility sharing. Physical security, functional compatibility, cultural harmony and geographical proximity are the suggested indicators for sharing refugees more equitably within the region of origin.[45] With regard to the roles of states outside the region, their primary responsibility would be sharing the costs of protection and contribute to re-

38 Grahl-Madsen, 'Further Development of International Refugee Law', (1965) 35 Nordic Journal of International Law (n 2) 165.

39 Harley, 'Innovations to Responsibility Sharing' (n 2) 8.

40 Rutger Bregman, *Utopia for Realists* (Bloomsbury 2017) 123.

41 Sarnata Reynolds, Juan Pablo Vacatello, 'Building a Lifeline: A Proposed Global Platform and Responsibility Sharing Model for the Global Compact on Refugees' (2019) 21. The Scholar St. Mary's Law Review on Race and Social Justice 325.

42 Ibid., 374.

43 Ibid., 342.

44 Ibid., 344.

45 Ibid.

settlement. Financial shares and resettlement quotas would be determined against an agreed formula based on economic metrics.[46]

Such proposals reflect a conception of fairness as proportionality since the various indicators and metrics measure the relatively objective capacity of each country to either host refugees or finance the costs of refugee protection in other states. Proposals that advocate for refugee quotas also serve a conception of corrective fairness as they seek to adjust the resulting imbalance by some form of refugee redistribution between states. While there seems to be a consensus between scholars and policy makers that each state's share of refugee protection responsibilities should reflect its capacities and resources, there is a lack of agreement on whether fair responsibility sharing should entail an element of redistribution of refugees as well or should be limited to a redistribution of the financial costs only. In the absence of a common understanding of responsibility sharing and given the risk of relinquishing authority over refugee admission policies, states have been reluctant to commit to refugee redistribution and pre-determined quotas.

The Global Compact on Refugees endorses this idea of proportional responsibility sharing reflected in the language of CBDRRC. States are encouraged to contribute to refugee protection and solutions in light of their capacities as well as national realities and priorities.[47] The pledges made under the Global Compact on Refugees have been measured by UNHCR against economic metrics within a broader indicator framework that corresponds to the Compact's four objectives.[48] The 2023 Global Indicator Report highlights that the current contributions to responsibility sharing do not actually reflect the relative capacities of states as no substantive redistribution of the responsibility to protect and provide solutions for refugees has been achieved, with the majority of refugees still being hosted in low-income countries with limited access to solutions.[49]

---

46 On financial sharing, the authors suggest the use of the UN funding model. Hathaway, Neve, 'Making International Refugee Law Relevant Again' (n 2) 207–209; Hathaway, 'The Global Co-Op Out on Refugees' (n 2) 597.

47 Global Compact on Refugees, paragraph 4.

48 The metrics are based on the Gini co-efficient that includes each country's population size, per capita wealth of the resident population as measured by the Gross National Income (GNI) per capita as adjusted to Purchasing Power Parity (PPP) and Human Development Index (HDI); Global Compact on Refugees Indicator Report (UNHCR 2023), p 62 <https://www.unhcr.org/media/2023-global-compact-refugees-indicator-report> accessed 17 October 2024.

49 Ibid.

3.2 *Fairness to Refugees: Some Ethical Considerations*

Within the fairness *problematique* comes also questions of fairness of the international refugee law regime vis-à-vis the refugees and how these can be accommodated within a responsibility sharing framework that caters primarily for states. Considerations of interstate fairness are given primacy in the debate on responsibility sharing and proposals on refugee redistribution have been criticised for showing a degree of indifference to refugee agency and for even promoting the commodification of refugees. Ethical considerations relating to refugee agency and refugee preferences have not received a great deal of attention from refugee law scholars.[50]

Noll argues that it is axiomatic that an equitable distribution of costs and responsibilities will ultimately deliver fairness vis-à-vis the refugees too as it 'will generate a maximum of openness towards protection seekers'.[51] Gibney's account of justice and refugee responsibility sharing defends that the preferences of refugees with respect to the country of asylum can be ignored in favour of the overriding goal of distributive justice between states which in his view is a normative goal of the Refugee Convention.[52] He is however cautious to qualify this by adding that states have a moral duty to send refugees to places where they are likely to flourish.[53] Ferracioli, in a similar spirit, defends that is 'morally permissible to deny refugees the right to choose the country of final destination given the importance of creating a regime that fares better in terms of distributive and procedural fairness'.[54]

Kuosmanen, writing on the ethics of trading refugee quotas, contends that if a refugee's preference for a particular country is not based on fundamental desires, such as a family reunification claim, then it is reasonable to override such a choice.[55] Conversely, Owen submits that any sharing of people between states should accommodate the legitimate preferences of refugees in order to be morally defensible.[56] A whole different discussion is

50 Tally Kritzman-Amir, 'Not in My Backyard, On the Morality of Responsibility Sharing in Refugee Law' (2009) 34 Brooklyn Journal of International Law 355, 363–772.

51 Gregor Noll, 'Risky games? A Theoretical Approach to Burden Sharing in the Asylum Field' (2003) 16 Journal of Refugee Studies 236, 249.

52 Gibney, 'Refugees and Justice Between States' (n 2) 457.

53 Ibid., 459–460.

54 Laura Ferracioli 'The Appeal and Danger of a New Refugee Convention' (2014) 40 Social Theory and Practice 123.

55 Jacob Kuosmanen, 'What (If Anything) is Wrong with Trading Refugee Quotas?' (2013) 19 Res Publica 103, 109.

56 David Owen 'Refugees and Responsibilities of Justice' (2018) 11 Global Justice: Theory and Practice Rhetoric 23, 37.

on what preferences can be said to be legitimate which Owen attempts to sketch in great detail.[57] Hathaway, whose proposal has been criticised for its commodification element, acknowledges the ethical concern of transferring refugees between states but invokes in his defence a utilitarian argument.[58]

> massive resources are now expended on the 15 per cent of refugees able to reach the developed world – disproportionately young, male, and mobile – while comparatively derisory resources are made available to the 85 per cent of refugees who remain closer to home.[59]

As a matter of international law, the Refugee Convention is silent as to whether the refugee has any choice with respect to the country of asylum. States and scholars have interpreted this silence in various ways. Goodwin-Gill and McAdam argue that international law appears to recognise a right to at least some choice about where asylum is sought, in particular when family members reside in another state.[60] Regional legal frameworks such as the CEAS have codified a right to family reunification.[61] Arguments in favour of a right to choose find support in UNHCR Executive Committee Conclusion No. 15, which states that 'the intentions of the asylum-seeker as regards the country in which he wishes to request asylum should as far as possible be taken into account'.[62] In the context of effective protection in secondary movements, UNHCR concluded that refugees do not have an unfettered right

57 Ibid.

58 For a critique of Hathaway's proposal See Satvinder Juss, 'Towards a Morally Legitimate Reform of Refugee Law: The Uses of Cultural Jurisprudence' (1998) 11 Harvard Human Rights Journal 311. BS Chimni, 'The Geopolitics of Refugee Studies: A View from the South' (1998) 11 Journal of Refugee Studies 350, 362–363 https://doi.org/10.1093/jrs/11.4.350-a; Anker, Fitzpatrick, Schacknove, 'Crisis and Cure: A Reply to Hathaway, Neve and Schuck' (n 6) 300.

59 Hathaway, 'The Global Co-Op Out on Refugees' (n 2) 603. A similar answer to the commodification objection has been given by Schuck in Shuck 'Refugee Burden Sharing: A Modest Proposal' (n 2) 276.

60 Guy Goodwin-Gill, Jane McAdam, Emma Dunlop, *The Refugee in International Law* (Oxford university Press 2021) 392.

61 Regulation (EU) 2024/1351 of the European Parliament and of the Council of 14 May 2024 on Asylum and Migration management.

62 UNHCR ExCom Conclusion No. 15 (1979) 'Refugees Without an Asylum Country', para iii.

to choose the country that will determine their asylum claim but their intentions ought to be taken into account.[63]

Arguments against a right to choose the country of asylum are based on the Refugee Convention's interpretation. Hathaway is of the view that until a refugee is actually admitted to a country's refugee status determination procedure 'at which point he or she becomes, in the language of the treaty, lawfully present, governments may lawfully assign their protection responsibilities to another country, even without the refugee's consent'.[64] He nonetheless recognises that there might be a moral obligation to design a responsibility sharing regime that maximises refugee agency.[65]

While international law does not codify an individual right for the refugee to choose the country of asylum, refugee and human rights instruments prescribe certain standards of treatment that refugee relocation, for the purposes of responsibility sharing, especially when not voluntary, should comply with.[66] From a moral standpoint, considering refugee preferences in relocation or resettlement processes would be the defensible stance.[67] There have been studies on integrating refugee preferences using sophisticated algorithms for preferences matching and on refugee participation and inclusion in decision making that maximises refugee agency while accommodating states' interests.[68]

63 UNHCR 'Summary Conclusions on the Concept of "Effective Protection" in the Context of Secondary Movements of Refugees and Asylum-Seekers' (Lisbon Expert Roundtable, 9–10 December 2002), para 11.

64 Provided that it is a rights-regarding allocation of responsibility. James Hathaway 'Why Refugee Law Matters' (2007) 8 Melnourne Journal of International Law 89, 101; Jens Vedsted-Hansen 'Non-Admission Policies and the Right to Protection: Refugees' Choice versus States' Exclusion?' in Frances Nicholson, Patrick Twomey, (eds) Refugee Rights and Realities: Evolving International Concepts and Regimes (Cambridge University Press 1999) 287.

65 Hathaway 'The Global Co Op Out on Refugees' (n 2) 603.

66 David Cantor, Nikolas-Feith Tan, Mariana Gkliati, Elizabeth Mavropoulou, Katherine Allinson, Sreetapa Chakrabarty, Maja Grundler, Lynn Hillary, Emilie McDonnell, Riona Moodley, Stephen Phillips, Annick Pijnenburg, Adel Reyhani,, Sophia Soares, Natasha Yacoub, 'Externalisation, Access to Territorial Asylum, and International Law' (2022) 34 International Journal of Refugee Law 120 https://doi.org/10.1093/ijrl/eeac023.

67 Gibney 'Refugees and Justice between States' (n 2) 461.

68 Tristan Harley, Harry Hobbs, 'The Meaningful Participation of Refugees in Decision-Making Processes: Questions of Law and Policy' (2020) 32 International Journal of Refugee Law 200; Kirk Bansak, Jeremy Ferwenda, Andrea Dillon, Dominik Hangartner, Duncan Lawrence, Jeremy Weinstein 'Improving Refugee Integration through Data Driven Algorithmic Assignment' (2018) 359 Science 325.

The challenge of synching fairness between states and fairness to refugees is a difficult one and this section has only scratched the surface so as to illustrate the tension between the two.[69] The proposed Protocol would only provide the overarching legal framework and the fact that its legal design is geared towards fairness between states is a limitation. Having said this, if a redistribution of the costs and benefits of hosting refugees is achieved and barriers to access to international protection that currently exist are dismantled by having more states contributing to refugee protection and solutions, then the international legal regime would fare better in terms of fairness towards refugees. Ultimately, as with any treaty, the extent to which responsibility sharing under the proposed Protocol would be implemented in a rights-regarding manner cannot be pre-determined at the level of legal design.

4 A Protocol on Refugee Responsibility Sharing

4.1 *Common but Differentiated Responsibilities and Respective Capabilities in International Refugee Law*

The responsibility sharing obligations of the proposed Protocol would be normatively guided by a version of the CBDRRC principle adapted to the international refugee law regime. As it stands in international environmental law, the principle differentiates states' legal obligations under the treaty against their contributions to environmental harm as well as their capabilities to act in mitigating the problem. Even in its latest reformulation of the principle in the Paris Agreement, responsibility on the basis of harm remains and thus major emitters are legally bound to undertake greater mitigation targets.

Bringing the principle of CBDRRC to international refugee law raises certain normative questions. Firstly, should wealthier states assume greater responsibilities in refugee protection and solutions because of their greater capacities and resources? As already discussed, there seems to be a consensus that contributions to responsibility sharing should in principle reflect proportionality and the relative capacities of states. Secondly, should countries of origin as well as countries that have indirectly contributed to refugee flows, for example through foreign policies, contribute more to responsibility sharing given their contribution to forced displacement? Finally, since the majority of refu-

---

69 On the ethics and the international refugee law regime, See Matthew J Gibney, 'Political Theory, Ethics and Forced Migration' in Elena Fiddian – Qasmiyeh and others (eds) *The Oxford Handbook of Refugee and Forced Migration Studies* (Oxford University Press 2014) 54; David Owen, 'Refugees and Responsibilities of Justice' (n 56) 23.

gees is hosted by countries, loosely termed as developing or least developed, would an application of the principle of CBDRRC warrant that they are somehow compensated for protecting the community interest and should the Protocol promote at minimum some sort of redistribution of resources towards this objective? These questions are addressed next.

4.2 *Responsibility Based on Contribution to Refugee Flows*

Arguments on the direct and indirect causal responsibility of states to refugee flows have always been present in the discourse of refugee protection and are worth rehearsing here. Zolberg et al. have argued that the Global North has a moral obligation to share asylum responsibilities because of its 'enormous resource capabilities relative to those of the South', as well as its 'co-responsibility' for upheavals and social conflicts in the Global South.[70] Schacknove and Byrne share this view and support that the Global North has, in its colonial past, historically contributed to refugee flows and continues to do so indirectly through its foreign policy.[71]

Regarding refugee producing countries, Owen claims that they have a general *moral* responsibility to contribute to the responsibility sharing efforts as well as a special one to compensate other states for their unjust conduct or omission.[72] He further explains:

> States that engage in unjust conduct to another state – conduct that foreseeably generates refugees – should be held responsible for the protection of these refugees, and discharging this responsibility should not be seen as a contribution to their share of general responsibility.[73]

Similarly, but from an international law point of view, Goodwin-Gill and Sazak have suggested that refugee-creating states have a legal responsibility to compensate asylum countries that face sometimes devastating financial demands.[74] They suggest that this could be done by UNHCR, which in turn could make effective use of the UN sanctions regime and the freezing of as-

---

70 Aristide R Zolberg, Astri Surkhe, Sergio Aguayo, *Escape from Violence, Conflict and The Refugee Crisis in the Developing World* (Oxford University Press 1993) 279.

71 Rosemary Byrne, Andrew Schacknove, 'The Safe Country Notion in European Asylum Law' (1996) Harvard Human Rights Journal 185, 212.

72 David Owen, *What do we Owe to Refugees?* (Polity 2020) 86. Emphasis added.

73 Ibid., 92.

74 Guy S Goodwin-Gill, Selim Can Sazak, 'Footing the Bill Refugee-Creating States' Responsibility to Pay' Foreign Affairs (29 July 2015) <https://www.foreignaffairs.com/articles/africa/2015-07-29/footing-bill> assessed 17 October 2024.

sets.[75] Such measure would ultimately generate some funds, even if nominal, that could be channelled to refugee assistance programmes.[76]

Legal arguments have been drawn from the law of state responsibility too as codified in the International Law Commissions' Draft Articles on Responsibility of States for Internationally Wrongful Acts (ARSIWA).[77] Such arguments seek to establish that responsibility for large scale refugee flows into other countries, in certain situations, may violate international law obligations and therefore amount to internationally wrongful acts for which the state responsible may be liable for compensating the 'injured' refugee host countries.[78]

Doctrinal explorations of the law of state responsibility, while useful for strengthening and closing accountability gaps for direct or indirect contribution to mass refugee flows, fall outside the scope of responsibility sharing for refugee protection and solutions. In addition, and as the authors of those studies admit, there are only certain scenarios where refugees flee *en masse* and such arguments would not apply to individual refugee flows.[79]

Furthermore, the rationale of responsibility for harm is foreign to the Refugee Convention's humanitarian nature and the palliative role of the international refugee law regime. The few refugee law scholars who have engaged with the principle of CBDRRC have also argued that an adaptation to international refugee law should discard the blame-based element of the doctrine and only stick to differentiation on the basis of capabilities understood as capacities and resources.[80] Dowd and McAdam note that commitments to refugee responsibility sharing should not be linked to states' role in creating refugee movements but should only reflect capacities to provide protection and resources to developing states that host large numbers of refugees.[81] They further caution that any adaptation of CBDRRC to international refugee law

75 Ibid.

76 Ibid.

77 ILC Draft Articles on State Responsibility with Commentaries, vol II (Part Two) Yearbook of the International Law Commission 2001.

78 On the responsibility of refugee creating states under the law of state responsibility, See Caroline Nalule, 'Refugee Burden and Responsibility Sharing: Revisiting the Debate on the Right to Compensation to Refugee Hosting State' (2023) 31 Michigan International Law Review 441.

79 Ibid., 451.

80 Wall, 'A New Link in the Chain: Could a Framework Convention for Refugee Responsibility Sharing Fulfill the Promise of the 1967 Protocol?' (n 2) 226, footnote 147.

81 Dowd and McAdam 'International Cooperation and Responsibility Sharing to Combat Climate Change: Lessons for International Refugee Law' (n 12) 182.

should not make existing refugee law obligations conditioned upon international assistance.[82]

4.3 *Responsibility Based on Capabilities*

An adaption of the CBDRRC principle in line with the forward-looking humanitarian character of the Refugee Convention and the palliative nature of the international protection should rightly dispense with the contribution to the problem rationale. Under a CBDRRC guided framework, the institutional responsibility to protect the refugees should reflect states' capabilities understood as resources and capacities. The rationale for responsibility based on capacity would additionally entail greater obligations on the part of wealthier states that have more resources vis-à-vis refugee host states.

Building on the language of the Global Compact on Refugees, the principle of CBDRRC would become the bedrock of the responsibility sharing agreement under the proposed Protocol codified as follows:

States shall share the responsibility for protecting and providing solutions to refugees in accordance with their common but differentiated responsibilities and respective capabilities, in light of their national realities, levels of development and respecting national policies and priorities.

5 The Protocol's Responsibility Sharing Obligations

5.1 *A Legal Compromise: Softening the Obligations*

A treaty on Responsibility Sharing would have to make from the outset a compromise over great legal expectations regarding the character of the codified obligations. The legal design should cater for principle as much as for pragmatism. The study of international environmental law illustrated innovative responsibility sharing arrangements within treaty regimes where obligations are structured against different levels of prescriptiveness. This is not however a feature exclusive to MEAS.

While the VCLT provides that all treaty provisions are binding and must be performed in good faith,[83] not all obligations within a treaty prescribe a certain conduct or result. Certain treaty obligations may have what some scholars

82 Dowd, McAdam 'International Cooperation and Responsibility Sharing to Combat Climate Change: Lessons for International Refugee Law' (n 12) 217.

83 Vienna Convention on the Law of Treaties (adopted 23 May 1969, entered into force 27 January 1980) 1155 UNTS 331 (VCLT), Article 26.

describe as a soft law character.[84] The Permanent Court of Arbitration in the dispute over the Convention for the Protection of the Marine Environment of the North-East Atlantic (1992 OSPAR Convention) between Northern Ireland and the UK made use of the concept of 'cascading standards of expression and levels of treaty provisions'.[85] According to the Court, the drafters of a treaty often make strategic use of 'differential language to provide for stipulated levels of engagement of treaty obligation' to achieve the treaty's objectives.[86] The distinction lies in the formulation of the provision that creates an obligation that may be procedural in nature, such as a duty to report, or prescribe a certain conduct, for example a due diligence obligation, or prescribe a certain result. What is more, there can also be provisions in the operative part of a treaty that merely recommend conduct or contextualise the obligation of each party at the level of implementation. A textbook example of a treaty where some of its provisions are couched in programmatic terms hardly imposing concrete obligations of result is the UN Charter and the relevant provisions on international cooperation in areas of UN concern.[87] Another example of a treaty that uses qualifying or contextual language to differentiate the obligations between the parties at the level of implementation is the ICESCR.[88] Whatever the nature of the obligation, the treaty provisions are still binding on the parties and therefore require performance in good faith in accordance with Article 26 of the VCLT.

The proposed Protocol would codify a minimal package of responsibility sharing obligations that would be implemented bottom-up. These obligations would further be differentiated at the level of implementation guided by the principle of CBDRRC. A bottom-up implementation offers states with the necessary flexibility and reduces the sovereignty costs of entering into a binding framework. The limitation of such legal design is that obligations are admittedly softened in their character. This is however the necessary legal compromise to bring responsibility sharing within international refugee law. To miti-

84 Alan Boyle, 'Soft Law in International Law Making' in Michael Evans (ed) *International Law* (Oxford University Press 2018) 131.

85 Permanent Court of Arbitration, Dispute Concerning Access to Information Under Article 9 of the OSPAR Convention (Ireland v. United Kingdom) Final Award (22 July 2013), para 129. OSPAR Conventions for the Protection of the Marine Environment of the North-East Atlantic 2354 UNTS 67, 32 ILM 1069 (1993).

86 Ibid., para 129.

87 Bruno Simma, Daniel-Erasmus Khan, Georg Nolte, Andreas Paulus, Nikolai Wessendorf (eds) *Charter of the United Nations: A Commentary* Vol II (Oxford University Press 2012), 'Chapter IX: International Economic and Social Co-operation', Article 56, at 943.

88 ICESCR, Article 2 (3). See discussion in Chapter 5, Section 4.

gate this risk, the Protocol would establish a framework of reporting and review that would enhance implementation.

5.2 *An Individual Obligation to Participate in Responsibility Sharing*

The Protocol would codify an individual obligation of responsibility sharing for each state party. Building on existing modalities and practices under the Global Compact on Refugees, the parties to the Protocol would be legally bound to participate to the responsibility sharing effort and publicly communicate their contributions to refugee protection and solutions. The obligation would be structured in the treaty as follows:

> Each Party shall communicate to UNHCR its contributions to refugee protection and solutions in line with its common but differentiated responsibilities and respective capabilities, in light of its national realities, levels of development and respecting national policies and priorities.
>
> Each Party should endeavour to contribute to the financing of refugee protection costs as well as to refugee relocation through resettlement or other refugee admission pathways, taking into account existing contributions to refugees in its territory.

Paragraph 1 of the suggested provision codifies the missing responsibility sharing obligation on the part of each individual state to contribute to the global responsibility sharing effort. The extent and breadth of the subsequent contributions however are left to be determined by the parties in line with their CBDRRC. It would be unrealistic to propose the codification of a legal obligation of responsibility sharing that would prescribe a certain result at the granular level such as the relocation or resettlement of a certain quota of refugees or a financial share.

Crafted as an obligation of conduct, the parties to the Protocol would be required to contribute to responsibility sharing which would no longer be voluntary as well as make their intended contributions public by communicating them to UNHCR as a matter of legal obligation. The weakness of such an obligation is that it does not require the parties to achieve their pledged contributions. Having said this, the fact that there would be a treaty comes with an expectation on the parties that they would implement their pledges in good faith.

Given that responsibility sharing would be guided by CBDRRC, there would also be a normative expectation that a state's contributions reflect its resources and capacities. What is more, existing contributions to refugee protection on a state's territory would be taken into account. To give an example, a CBDRRC interpretation of the Protocol's responsibility sharing obligation would entail that a major refugee host state like Türkiye would not be expected to contribute much to financing protection costs in other countries and a low income or fragile country like Sudan or Uganda that already hosts a disproportionate to its capacities number of refugees would be discharged from contributing to the global responsibility sharing effort altogether. The World Bank's country classification by income is already used in the development sector to determine countries that qualify for aid and UNHCR makes use of it when measuring states' contributions to protections and solutions.[89]

The Protocol on Responsibility Sharing therefore would differentiate between parties at the level of implementation so that resources and existing contributions to refugee protection are taken into account. What is more, by bringing solutions within the obligation of responsibility sharing, the Protocol would ultimately strengthen the legal regime on solutions which under the current legal framework is soft law.[90]

5.3 *A Normative Expectation to Contribute to Both Physical and Financial Responsibility Sharing*

Building on paragraph (1), paragraph (2) of the provision proposed above would set a normative expectation upon each party to contribute to both financial and physical responsibility sharing. Building on Betts and Collier's argument on the need for a 'baseline common commitment' to responsibility sharing, states would be expected to contribute to physical responsibility sharing, namely refugee relocation for the purposes of asylum or resettlement as well as financial responsibility sharing.[91]

For the purposes of securing agreement between states, paragraph 2 of the provision is crafted as a recommendation. Given that refugee relocation is the least popular component of responsibility sharing, perceived by states as an inherently domestic decision, only a provision that recommends it rather than imposes action from the top down could stand chances of acceptance by states. States could therefore decide to pledge resettlement places or comple-

---

89 See World Bank country classification by income level <https://blogs.worldbank.org/en/opendata/world-bank-country-classifications-by-income-level-for-2024-2025> accessed 17 October 2024.

90 Volker Türk, Rebecca Dowd, 'Protection Gaps' In Elena Fiddian-Qasmiyeh, Gill Loescher, Katy Long, Nando Sigona (Eds.), *The Oxford Handbook of Refugee and Forced Migration Studies* 284.

91 Alexander Betts, Paul Collier, *Refuge Transforming A Broken Refugee System* (Penguin Books) 208.

mentary admission pathways. The latter could be pledges towards a number of humanitarian visas, labour mobility schemes or education opportunities for refugees such as academic scholarships and student visas.[92]

Contributions to the costs of refugee protection would include pledges towards humanitarian and development related assistance against real and projected needs. The parties could choose to contribute to UNHCR's funding budget, cover immediate humanitarian assistance programmes in specific refugee situations, or grant refugee targeted development aid through existing multilateral or bilateral channels.[93]

5.4 *A Collective Obligation of Financial Assistance to Host States*

If the Protocol were to change the current inequitable state of the global responsibility sharing effort and set in motion a *process* towards a more equitable one, some modest financial commitments towards refugee host states would be necessary. It is only fair that states hosting a large number of refugees receive the necessary financial assistance from the international community that enables them to secure rights to refugees as well as their citizens.

Despite the well-established nexus between humanitarian protection and development and the importance of development funding to refugee situations, there are certain challenges in the way development aid is channelled that aggravate rather than remedy existing inequalities between states.[94] Those challenges are cross cutting in the development sector and not exclusive to refugee targeted development aid. However, the way aid is structured directly impacts on the international refugee law regime which cannot be isolated from broader questions of fairness in international relations.

The first challenge is structural and relates to the way aid has been traditionally conditioned upon certain kinds of policy reforms in the recipient countries and structural adjustments that have favoured the global markets rather than the local population.[95] In addition, a large majority of aid is given in loans which, even if granted in concessionary terms, namely with low or no

92 Global Compact on Refugees, paras 94–95.

93 Global Compact on Refugees, para 42.

94 Official Development Aid (ODA) can be bilateral or multilateral and includes grants, soft loans and technical assistance. Alexander Betts, 'Development Assistance and Refugees: Towards a North South Grand Bargain?' Forced Migration Policy Briefing 2 (June 2019) Oxford Refugees Studies Centre, 5.

95 Structural Adjustment Lending (SAL) was introduced in the 1980s by the World Bank as finance model for developing countries that entailed a series of policy reforms including deregulation and privatisation that would correct and accelerate the economy's growth rate. See World Bank Accelerated Development in Sub-Saharan Africa Report: An

interest at all, has led to debt accumulation and, in certain countries, debt distress, with devastating impact for the local population and the refugees.[96]

The second challenge is quantitative and is simply about the need to double down on development aid in refugee protection matters. While additional development aid is crucial to host countries so that they can secure refugees with access to rights without overbearing or excluding the local population, donor countries have been reluctant to scale up or even commit to additional aid as a matter of legal obligation. One of the reasons the UN Convention Plus Initiative failed was because donor states were not prepared to bend to the southern host countries' legitimate demand for additional development aid so that refugee targeted assistance would not come out of existing earmarked developmental budgets.[97]

An illustrative example of the negative impact development aid has had on host states and refugees is Tanzania. Tanzania was once amongst the largest and most progressive refugee hosting countries in Africa, offering refugees access to labour market, housing and other socio economic rights.[98] In 2017, it withdrew from the Comprehensive Refugee Response Framework of the Global Compact (GRRF) when, under the International Development Association (IDA), the World Bank's fund for the poorest, it was offered $100 million in aid, split between a loan and a grant.[99] Commentators explained this move at the time as a reaction to the fundamentally unfair system that effectively forces a low-income country and major refugee host state to incur yet another debt when it essentially provides a global public good.[100]

Some progress has been made in meeting those challenges in the refugee protection context. The World Bank IDA-18 Replenishment Regional Sub Window for Refugees and Host Communities offers some favourable terms for refugee development projects. It offers countries at high risk of debt distress

---

Agenda for Action (World Bank 1981),127; Leah Zamore, 'Refugees, Development, Debt, Austerity: A Selected History' (2018) 6 Journal on Migration and Human Security 26, 28.

96 For a history on international loans on refugee assistance and their negative impact, See Eva Eston Calabria, 'Following the Refugees: The World Bank, International Loans, and a Brief History of Refugees and Development' (2018) 37 SAIS Review of International Affairs 3–13 (Summer-Fall 2017), 3–13.

97 See discussion in Chapter 4 Section 4.

98 Zamore, 'Refugees, Development, Debt, Austerity: A Selected History' (n 95) 36.

99 On IDA 18 and its Regional Sub-Window for Refugees and Host Communities, See <https://ida.worldbank.org/replenishments/ida-18replenishments/ida18-regional-sub-window-for-refugees-host-communities> accessed 17 October 2024; Alexander Betts, 'Don't Make African Nations Borrow Money to Support Refugees' Foreign Affairs (February 21, 2018).

100 Ibid.

with 100 percent grant terms, and countries at moderate and low risk of debt distress with 50 percent in grants and 50 percent in applicable credit terms.[101] It should, however, be clarified that the World Bank's financial support is not aimed at compensating refugee-hosting countries or at redistributing resources, but rather on mitigating the medium-term negative impact of forced displacement on host communities and refugees.[102]

Scholars have stressed the need to scale up refugee targeted development aid. Zamore and Betts have stressed the need for significant additionality in aid and inclusion of refugees and host communities in development finance projects.[103] Given that the issue with development aid is not only quantitative but also structural, Zamore has called for a restructuring of the way development aid is granted especially to host states in serious risk of debt distress. She notes:

> Additional support to host countries should be 'untied' and should come in the form of grants, not loans. Just a handful of host governments are home to a majority of the world's refugees. Support for them should therefore be seen chiefly as compensation for a global public good and as a step toward global economic justice. It should not be a secret subsidy for donors or their banks. It should not leave host countries more indebted than they already are.[104]

In a more critical tone, Easton Calabria has questioned the perceived positive role of the World Bank, highlighting the overall negative impact of its involvement in refugee host states.[105] Calls for a restructure of the international development regime are not limited to academic studies. UNHCR has recently voiced the need for reforming the international finance architecture that should be moving towards grant-based or at least long-term concessional de-

101 There are also other eligibility requirements including the population size vis-a-vis the refugee number on the territory, an adequate refugee protection framework and a plan for policy reforms. IDA 18 Replenishment Window.

102 IDA18 Mid -Term Review Fragility, Conflict and Violence (FCV) Annex 5: Refugee Sub-Window: Portfolio Update October 24, 2018, p. 53. <https://documents1.worldbank.org/curated/fr/259151542812499052/pdf/ida18-mtr-fcv-10252018-636762750035047342.pdf> accessed 17 October 2024.

103 Zamore, 'Refugees, Development, Debt, Austerity: A Selected History' (n 95) 48–49; Betts, 'Development Assistance and Refugees: Towards a North South Grand Bargain?' (n 94) 5.

104 Ibid.

105 Easton Calabria, '"Following the Refugees": The World Bank, International Loans, and a Brief History of Refugees and Development' (n 96) 10–11.

velopment finance for refugee situations.[106] UN Reports tracking progress towards the Sustainable Development Goals have also stressed the need for urgent reform in the international finance and development sector.[107]

A CBDRRC guided Protocol would entail greater responsibilities and thus commitments from state parties with more resources. While current challenges in the international development sector require institutional reform, a Protocol on Responsibility Sharing could however contribute, even a little bit, by codifying a collective obligation of financial assistance to refugee host states. Such treaty provision can be structured as follows:

> In line of their common but differentiated responsibilities and respective capabilities, parties shall commit to multiyear refugee targeted assistance, over and above regular development assistance in support of refugees and host communities. Where necessary parties shall secure such funding on a grant basis.

While at first a collective obligation on the part of *all* state parties without distinction might seem counterproductive or even unfair towards developing host states, a careful reading of the paragraph addresses some of these concerns. In practice, official development aid for refugee situations is anyway provided by a core group of states and institutions.[108] Any rigid differentiation within the Protocol between donor and host countries, or developed and developing states, would be unnecessary and would fail to capture the nuances in between.[109] The collective obligation is further guided by the CBDRRC principle which would exclude those parties that are unable to provide aid.

The proposed provision also incorporates a progressive call for financing refugee protection costs on a grant-basis. The qualifier 'where necessary'

---

106 UNHCR Global Indicator Report 2023, 12.

107 The UN Sustainable Development Goals Report 2023: Special edition Towards a Rescue Plan for People and Planet, 12. <https://unstats.un.org/sdgs/report/2023/The-Sustainable-Development-Goals-Report-2023.pdf> accessed 17 October 2024.

108 Two-thirds of ODA assistance comes from the five large providers, the US, United Kingdom, Germany, the EU and the World Bank. Global Compact on Refugees Indicator Report 2023, 29–30.

109 UNHCR has also moved away from the developed-developing categorisation in its reporting adopting the World Bank's regional and income classification. The OECD list of eligible countries for ODA also mirrors the World Bank income classification. See OECD ODA recipient countries, territories and organisations <https://www.oecd.org/en/topics/sub-issues/oda-eligibility-and-conditions/dac-list-of-oda-recipients.html#oda-recipients-list> accessed 17 October 2024.

would reflect countries that are already in or at risk of debt distress for example or countries that host refugee populations disproportionate to their capacities. For these countries, grant-based aid would not only mitigate financial risks but would also serve distributive fairness by compensating those states that make significant contributions to the protection of the community interest.[110]

5.5 *An Individual Obligation of Reporting*

The Protocol's bottom-up implementation would be supplemented by an individual obligation on the part of each state to report on the implementation of its responsibility sharing contributions. In addition, insofar as financial sharing is concerned, parties would be required to account for their direct fiscal expenditures on refugee situations within and outside their territories. In cases where contributions to responsibility sharing are made jointly with other stakeholders such as, for example, a labour mobility scheme in partnership with the private sector, states parties to the Protocol would be bound to report on the clear division of labour between the implementing partners as well as account for any direct fiscal expenditures on their part.

An obligation to report on the implementation of the contributions would bolster the substantive obligation to participate in responsibility sharing enhance transparency of the global responsibility sharing effort and allow for public oversight and review. As the study of international environmental law highlighted, most MEAs codify procedural obligations of transparency and reporting that serve important review functions, especially in contexts where agreement on substantive obligations was either impossible to obtain or undesirable.[111] The core human rights treaties also codify various reporting obligations for the parties, facilitating public scrutiny and review.[112] The Protocol's reporting obligations would facilitate a process of public evaluation and review of the extent and breadth of each party's contributions vis-à-vis other parties.[113] This, in turn, would promote a public discourse on the fairness, as well as the effectiveness, of the global responsibility sharing effort.

---

110 Zamore, 'Refugees, Development, Debt, Austerity: A Selected History' (n 95) 49.

111 Jutta Brunnée, 'International Environmental Law and Community Interests Procedural Aspects', in Eyal Benvenisti, Georg Nolte (eds) *Community Interests Across International Environmental Law* (Oxford University Press 2018), 175.

112 See OHCHR 'Reporting Compliance by State Parties to the Human Rights Treaty Bodies' (15 May 2020) <https://www.ohchr.org/sites/default/files/Documents/Issues/HRIndicators/MetadataReportingCompliance.pdf> accessed 17 October 2024.

113 Daniel Bodanksy, *The Art and Craft of International Environmental Law* (Harvard University Press 2011), 239.

A modest but entirely voluntary reporting mechanism already exists under the Global Compact on Refugees. Before the conclusion of the Compact, there was no central repository system for tracking global responsibility sharing efforts outside UNHCR's annual or midterm reports identifying gaps and needs. UNHCR has highlighted the gap in relation to lack of reporting or inconsistent reporting when it comes to states' refugee related fiscal expenditures.[114] Following the Compact, UNHCR created a digital platform where all actors contributing to refugee protection and solutions can upload their pledges and exchange good practice.[115] The platform includes also a system that tracks the implementation of the pledges. The High Commissioner, however, has clarified that insofar as financial responsibility sharing is concerned, the dashboard 'is not a financial tracking or reporting tool'. The entire tracking of the pledges relies on voluntary reporting by the pledging entities, which include non-state actors.[116]

The obligation to report on the implementation of the commitments made and account for direct fiscal expenditures would ultimately strengthen the Protocol's implementation. Given that the Protocol would be additional to the Refugee Convention, the states' reporting obligations would be a continuation of the reporting duties under Article 35 of the Refugee Convention at least for those states that would be parties to both treaties.

Against the reports submitted by the parties, UNHCR could then be tasked under the Protocol to report on the state of the global responsibility sharing effort, highlight discrepancies in contributions *vis-a-vis* capacities and identify further gaps and needs. This is already done by the High Commissioner in the context of the Global Compact on Refugees so its formalisation under a Protocol would not place an additional burden on His Office.

5.6 *A Global Stocktake*

The Protocol's individual reporting requirements will be complemented by a global stocktake that will assess the collective progress made. This is where the Protocol would integrate the modalities and processes that already take place under the Global Compact on Refugees. The Global Refugee Forum is the institutional forum where states and other stakeholders announce their

114 Harley, Innovations to Responsibility Sharing (n 2) 8.

115 Digital Platform <https://globalcompactrefugees.org/about-digital-platform> accessed 17 October 2024.

116 UNHCR Concept Note Global Refugee Forum – Online Tracking Dashboard on Pledges and Contributions <https://www.unhcr.org/sites/default/files/legacy-pdf/5d6524277.pdf> accessed 17 October 2024.

pledges and where a stocktaking exercise takes place every four years.[117] The Forums can become the Protocol's formal pledging conferences. While these arrangements are largely focused on process rather than outcomes and have been criticised by scholars as 'a bureaucrat's dream'[118] or 'events',[119] they nonetheless constitute 'collective learning processes'.[120] Stocktaking can function as 'a communicative process of constructing shared meanings around new concepts, including normative expectations and identities'.[121] The Global Stocktake under the Paris Agreement plays a key role in assessing collective progress towards the objectives of the treaty and forms an integral part of the treaty's implementation framework.

A global stocktake would play a similar role under a Protocol on Responsibility Sharing as one mechanism for facilitating implementation by tracking and reviewing collective progress. The stocktaking exercise would inform the next round of states' contributions by highlighting gaps, needs and inequities in the global responsibility sharing effort. Combined with the individual reporting requirements of the parties and UNHCR oversight, the global stocktake may even have a normative impact by influencing state behaviour through peer and public pressure.

6 Conclusions

In this chapter, I have sought to flesh out some of the key provisions and a basic architecture of a Protocol on Refugee Responsibility Sharing. Using the prescriptive lens of enlightened positivism, I have explored *de lege ferenda* how responsibility sharing could become the subject of a light package of legal obligations. Under the Protocol, the common institutional responsibility to protect the refugees would be met with an individual obligation on the part of each state to make a baseline commitment to both physical and financial responsibility sharing. A conception of fairness as proportionality is encapsulated in the CBDRRC principle, requiring each state's contributions to reflect its capabilities, defined as capacities and resources. A CBDRRC guided Proto-

117 Global Compact on Refugees, para 103.
118 Hathaway, 'The Global Co-Op out on Refugees' (n 2) 4.
119 Wall, 'A New Link in the Chain: Could a Framework Convention for Refugee Responsibility Sharing Fulfill the Promise of the 1967 Protocol?' (n 2) p 230.
120 Manjana Milkoreit, Kate Haapala, 'Designing the Global Stocktake: A Global Governance Innovation' The Centre for Climate and Energy Solutions (C2ES) (November 2017) 7.
121 Ibid.

col would also serve a conception of distributive fairness reflected in the collective obligation of the wealthier and more well-resourced states to redistribute resources to countries that host large majorities of refugees.

The feasibility of the proposal, as argued in the beginning of this chapter, depends on what is at stake for states in terms of legal obligations. What I have sought to demonstrate is that there can be a legal instrument that optimises fair responsibility sharing between states while addressing vexed matters of prescriptiveness and differentiation in the codified obligations. To this end, I have made use of an important distinction between the binding nature of the Protocol and the subsequent normative force of its constituent treaty obligations. The proposed Protocol would only codify a minimal package of responsibility sharing obligations that are differentiated at the level of implementation. This can be seen as a strength as well as a weakness. If seen as a weakness, the rather soft obligations arguably water down the Protocol. If seen as a strength, they offer states with the necessary flexibility and bring responsibility sharing within international refugee law. The few legal obligations have thus been designed with what is legally desirable but also politically feasible.

The second challenge that I have sought to meet is that the proposed Protocol is not that far away from what is already good practice in refugee responsibility sharing. The Protocol would institutionalise the existing arrangements and good practices under the Global Compact on Refugees under a permanent structure. Institutional forums such as the Global Refugee Forums would become the Protocol's formal pledging conferences where states parties communicate their contributions to protection and solutions. While the legal obligation would only be on the parties to the Protocol, participation to the pledging conferences would be open to non-state parties as well as other stakeholders that may want to join the global refugee responsibility sharing effort.

UNHCR would be endowed with the monitoring of the Protocol. Given that the High Commissioner is the institutional trustee of the community interest and is entrusted with the supervision of the application of the Refugee Convention, it is but natural that it would continue to lead the global responsibility sharing effort in the proposed Protocol as it already does so under the Global Compact.

It goes without saying that what I have proposed is only a Protocol's basic edifice and a rather minimal legal architecture that can and should be supplemented by additional provisions and implementation mechanisms. The frequency of the pledging conferences, the reporting requirements, the accounting rules would have to be further negotiated. The creation of a global refugee fund, as has been proposed by scholars, could also be established. Importantly, the Protocol would not replace regional responsibility sharing structures that operate within regional asylum systems and serve region-specific needs. Crucially, the Protocol would sync the institutional obligation to protect refugees with a concomitant legal obligation on the part of individual states to provide assistance and solutions correcting the existing disjuncture in the legal obligations and filling in the responsibility sharing gap left by the Refugee Convention.

I would like to conclude this chapter with a note on the political capital required to engineer such a multilateral instrument. At the UN level, UNHCR would be best placed to advocate and push for a binding Protocol. Just as it succeeded in concluding the intermediary step, the Global Compact on Refugees, it can now go the full way towards the long-resisted Protocol. A protocol on responsibility sharing would also need 'a champion', a coalition of the willing, as it has been described.[122] This time the coalition of the willing should come from the Global South through a negotiating block formed by major refugee host countries that are mostly and specially affected.[123] The block could put forward the proposal for a Protocol before the UN General Assembly using their majority seats to their advantage.

Political facilitation should also be pursued by campaigning and lobbying at the domestic level. Although international law views the state as one unitary actor, actors at the national, municipal and local levels play an important role in refugee protection. Generating support from individuals, communities, civil society and refugee circles would be crucial in gaining support for a protocol before local constituencies. After all, refugee protection is offered at the national level and is at the local level where refugees and host communities interact and gain from one another.

There is no guarantee that, despite all that has been argued, states, particularly those of the Global North, will see the benefits of concluding such Protocol. Under the status quo, Northern states are free to continue pursuing their externalisation policies whilst contributing well-below their resources and capacities to refugee protection and solutions. The likelihood or unlikelihood of something materialising in the near future, however, shall not stop one from exploring ways to bring about change when it is so much needed.[124] I believe that the proposed Protocol reflects the 'sweet spot', which goes as far as possible, but not beyond, what is politically palatable, offering a principled yet pragmatic legal framework towards fair responsibility sharing.

---

122 Hathaway, 'The Global Co-Op Out on Refugees' (n 2) 12.

123 Alexander Aleinikoff, Leah Zamore, 'The Arc of Protection: Toward A New International Refugee Regime', (Stanford Briefs 2019) 68.

124 Ferracioli, 'The Appeal and Anger of a New Refugee Convention' (n 54) 143.

CHAPTER 8

Conclusions

Despite the enduring relevance of the Refugee Convention, the international refugee law regime is characterised by a responsibility sharing gap that negatively impacts on the quality and availability of refugee protection as well as on interstate relations. The first part of the book examined the law and practice of international cooperation and responsibility sharing for refugees through a comprehensive study of the international and regional frameworks on refugee protection as well as current and past instances of international cooperation in the practice of states. The overarching argument is that insofar the collective responsibility of the international community to protect refugees is not met with a concomitant obligation of responsibility sharing on the part of individual states the international refugee law regime will remain incomplete. Against this premise, the second part of the book advanced a detailed proposal on a Protocol on Refugee Responsibility Sharing that would provide a principled yet pragmatic legal framework. The proposed Protocol would be guided by the principle of CBDRRC adapted to the refugee law regime and codify only a minimal package of common but differentiated legal obligations of responsibility sharing.

Chapter 1 contextualised the negative impact of the responsibility sharing gap on both refugees and interstate relations. The Refugee Convection lacks a redistributive mechanism that corrects the resulting inequities and reapportions responsibilities between states. The absence of a legal obligation of responsibility sharing in the Convention means that any form of assistance to refugee host states is voluntary, while geography and proximity determine which state bears solely responsibility for refugees. Despite recent efforts in the Global Compact on Refugees to revitalise responsibility sharing under new modalities, the current state of global responsibility sharing remains highly inequitable and insufficient to meet the needs of refugees and host states. Since the majority of refugees is hosted by middle and low-income states, predominantly in the Global South, these states face additional strains alongside their existing developmental challenges. What is more, states in the Global North have deployed a range of externalisation measures that seek to minimise and shift refugee related obligations and confine the *locus* of refugee protection in the Global South. Externalisation takes the form of multilateral or bilateral safe third country agreements whereby states of the Global North circumvent their refugee law obligations by outsourcing their

 | DOI:10.1163/9789004547711_009

migration management and asylum functions to partner states in the Global South.

Chapter 1 also introduced enlightened legal positivism as the methodological lens through which the study of international cooperation on refugees is carried out. Enlightened legal positivism is a softer form of positivism, developed by the international law jurist Bruno Simma, who observed at the beginning of the millennium that certain fundamental community values structurally permeate the body of international law and manifest themselves as community interests. Today community interests are protected in the international legal regimes on climate change, law of the sea, biodiversity, human rights. From the vantage point of enlightened positivism, the book puts forward two claims. Firstly, the protection of refugees is a community interest of international law. This is confirmed by the existence of refugees as a distinct legal category of individuals in international law for whom states have enacted a dedicated treaty regime with widespread ratification and participation. Seen from the perspective of community interests, the Refugee Convention codifies a set of universal standards of treatment and rights owed to refugees going over and above the bilateral interests of states. The consensus on the community interest nature of refugee protection is further evidenced by the existence of UNHCR, a specialised UN body tasked with the institutional responsibility for protecting refugees and finding solutions and who acts as the institutional trustee of the community interest. Secondly, questions of fairness between states are not only integral to the debate on how to share refugee protection responsibilities more equitably between states but normatively permeate international law which role is to contribute, even if modestly, to global justice. The international refugee law regime does not operate in isolation and therefore broader questions of fairness in resource distribution acquire salience in the context of refugee protection and the management of forced displacement.

Chapter 2 traced the origins and the legal foundations of international cooperation and responsibility sharing through a doctrinal exploration of international and regional refugee law instruments. The chapter argued that there is a well-established duty of international cooperation in refugee protection matters, which even if it does not concretise into a responsibility sharing obligation, it nonetheless places certain legal parameters on international cooperation. The reading of the relevant provisions of the UN Charter, the Refugee Convention and relevant UNHCR Executive Committee Conclusions suggested that there is a normative requirement that international cooperation in refugee matters aims at or results in fair responsibility sharing. Thus understood, the principle of responsibility sharing that is well-established in international refugee law, is a normative corollary of the duty to cooperate in refugee matters. By the same token, international cooperation that is designed to shift rather than share responsibilities between states goes against a good faith implementation of the duty to cooperate. Within regional refugee law instruments too, there are different approaches to responsibility sharing, with the CEAS of the EU being the most illustrative example of the responsibility sharing challenge that mirrors some of the deficiencies of responsibility sharing at the UN level. All three regional asylum systems in Africa, Latin America and the EU conceptualise the protection of refugees as a common responsibility of states in the region and represent regional expressions of the community interest. Chapter 2 concluded that there is a disjuncture between the institutional obligation of the international community to protect the refugees and find solutions as reflected in UNHCR's mandate on one hand and the subsequent individual obligations of state parties to the Refugee Convention on the other. The only way to correct this disjuncture and fill in the responsibility sharing gap is to sync the institutional obligation of the international community to protect refugees with a concomitant obligation of responsibility sharing on the part of individual states.

Chapter 3 looked at international cooperation in state practice and discussed some of the most questionable safe third country agreements on migration and asylum management. The discussion of third country arrangements between Italy – Libya, EU – Turkey, Australia – Papua New Guinea, Australia – Nauru and US – Canada showed that these arrangements fall short of the prescribed standards on international cooperation for refugees. First and foremost, these agreements have resulted in numerous violations of refugee rights at states' land and sea borders. Secondly, they constitute a bad faith implementation of the duty to cooperate towards fair responsibility sharing under the Refugee Convention. While some of these agreements employ the language of responsibility sharing and international protection standards on paper, in practice the true and primary objective is refugee containment and responsibility shifting. What is more, such arrangements negatively impact on interstate relations for they exacerbate current inequities undermining the fairness of the international refugee law regime. For all these reasons, cooperative arrangements that shift responsibilities onto other states, restrict access to asylum and result in refugee rights violations constitute prohibitive forms of international cooperation under the Refugee Convention.

In Chapter 4 the discussion turned into past examples of international cooperation that have made a positive contribution to refugee protection and responsibility sharing. The Comprehensive Plan of Action for Indochinese Refugees (CPA) and the International Conference on Central American Refugees (CIREFCA) were two overall successful instances of international cooperation, which despite being *ad hoc* and context-specific, they operationalised responsibility sharing against a framework of 'common but differentiated responsibilities' whereby various states in and outside the region assumed different roles with respect to refugee protection and solutions. The chapter also discussed the UN Convention Plus Initiative, which while unsuccessful at the time, its study illustrates some of the broader challenges surrounding responsibility sharing. Among the reasons the Convention Plus failed was because donor states of the Global North excluded refugee host states of the Global South from the negotiations on development aid and rejected the latter's request for additional refugee targeted assistance, ultimately conditioning aid upon readmission agreements.

Chapter 4 concluded with an assessment of the Global Compact on Refugees as framework for international cooperation and responsibility sharing. While the Compact cannot not fill in the responsibility sharing gap, it has set in motion certain processes and modalities that could become part of a Protocol's formal architecture. It reaffirmed the community interest nature of refugee protection and reframed refugee protection as a common but differentiated responsibility. Whether borrowing from international environmental law's principle of CBDRRC was intentional or just a result of negotiations towards a flexible yet tangible responsibility sharing arrangement is not known. What is important to note is that the Compact brought the discourse on the fairness of the international refugee regime at the forefront. On the downside, the Compact endorsed an overtly broad conception of responsibility sharing that goes beyond the provision of international protection and solutions and thus further obfuscated a common conceptual understanding of the term.

The second part of the book turned into international environmental law where the principle of CBDRRC frames responsibility sharing in multilateral environmental agreements (MEAs). Chapter 5 traced the practice of differential treatment in international law of which the principle of CBDRRC is the doctrinal expression. While the principle was explicitly formulated in international environmental law, the wider practice of differential treatment has long been a key feature of multilateral law making. Differential treatment is an application of fairness in international law that requires in certain cases that the material inequalities of states ought to be taken into account within the law's distributive aspects. Elements of differentiation either at the level of treaty obligations or treaty implementation permeate international law and can be found in most multilateral legal regimes on resource and burden allocation. This argument was illustrated by a discussion of differential treatment in international trade law, international law of the sea, international human rights law and international environmental law.

Chapter 6 studied the unique trajectory of the CBDRRC principle in the international legal regime on climate change. As one of the most progressive responsibility sharing regimes in international law, the UNFCCC served as a case study on how vexed matters of fairness and differentiation in responsibility sharing have been structurally integrated within a multilateral treaty through the principle of CBDRRC. The principle's dynamic and changing nature has meant that it has been flexible enough to respond to the changing realities of states. Two of the most widely accepted principles of fairness are obliquely embedded within the doctrine of CBDRRC; the contribution to the problem principle and the capacity or capability to take measures. The principle encapsulates claims of interstate as well as intergenerational fairness as it seeks to fairly distribute the burden of mitigating and adapting to climate change. Distributive fairness under the CBDRRC principle is expressed in the legal obligation of the developed countries to provide financial assistance and help developing states meet their mitigation and adaptation commitments. The chapter examined in detail the legal architecture of the Paris Agreement on Climate Change which illustrated the art of the possible with regards to what legal design could vest a protocol on refugee responsibility sharing.

Chapter 7 contained *a de lege ferenda* proposal for a Protocol on Responsibility Sharing that would complement the Refugee Convention and fill in the responsibility sharing gap. The proposed Protocol would codify three core responsibility sharing obligations. Firstly, an individual obligation on the part of each state to make a common baseline commitment to both physical and financial responsibility sharing, the only two forms of sharing that have the ability to reapportion responsibilities more equitably between states. While participation to responsibility sharing would become the subject of a legal obligation, the extent and breadth of the subsequent contributions would be determined by states in line with their CBDRRC. The CBDRRC principle would also require that states' contributions to responsibility sharing reflect their actual resources and capacities. Secondly, the Protocol would codify a collective obligation on all states to mobilise financial assistance and refugee targeted development aid to host states. The underlying rationale for resource transfer from the Global North to the Global South is distributive fairness so that host states that make an immense contribution to the protection of the community interest receive the necessary assistance from the international community. Thirdly, an individual obligation of each state to report on the implementation of its contributions and publicly account for any fiscal expenditures for refugee protection. This individual obligation of public reporting and financial accounting would enhance the transparency and public review of the global responsibility sharing effort. All three obligations together would put in process a principled responsibility sharing framework that optimises procedural and distributive fairness. Given that UNHCR is the institutional trustee of the community interest, the Commissioner would be endowed with the monitoring of the Protocol in continuance with its monitoring and supervisory duties under the Refugee Convention. Existing modalities and institutional arrangements under the Global Compact on Refugees such as the Global Refugee Forums and the global stocktaking would become part of the Protocol's implementation mechanisms.

I would like to end this study with the following thought. The recent fairness discourse on refugee protection that has prompted questions about the fairness of the international refugee law regime would only prove significant, if seen under the broader fairness discourse that takes place in international law. In the words of Thomas Franck, 'distributive justice is never off the agenda' of international law, 'whether the subject is manganese nodules on the ocean floor, geostationary orbits in outer space, or penguins and the Antarctic's icecap'.[1] If one then looks into the UN Sustainable Development Goals and the recent UN Pact for the Future,[2] one sees that contemporary global challenges are interdependent and interconnected. Poverty, hunger, lack of water and sanitation, gender inequality, climate change are also well recognised drivers of forced displacement. Each single driver, on its own, may not always satisfy the persecution threshold on a given case, but it makes a compelling argument that the global refugee regime cannot be insulated from multilateral efforts to redress injustice and reduce inequalities within and between countries. The journey towards the necessary law reform of the international refugee regime is going to be a long one, particularly in the era of multilateral fatigue and distrust in multilateral institutions by some states. The regime's continued relevance however is already challenged by growing global inequalities which shape states' responses to refugees. It is therefore imperative that the fairness discourse in international refugee law remains alive in both academia and policy.

1 Thomas Franck, Fairness in International Law and Institutions.

2 UN Summit 2024, Pact for the Future, Global Digital Compact and Declaration on Future Generations <https://www.un.org/sites/un2.un.org/files/sotf-pact_for_the_future_adopted.pdf> accessed 17 October 2024.

Select Bibliography

Books, Chapters in Books and Edited Volumes

Acharya A, Dewitt DB, 'Fiscal burden-sharing' in Hathaway, J. (eds) *Reconceiving International Refugee Law* (Martin Nijhoff Publishers 1997) 111

Armstrong D, Farrell T, Lambert H, *International Law and International Relations* (Cambridge University Press 2012 Second Edition)

Austin J, *The Province of Jurisprudence Determined* (1832) (eds) W.E. Rumble (Cambridge University Press 1995)

Barichello S, 'Responsibility Sharing in Latin America' in Juss S (eds) *Research Handbook of International Refugee Law* (Edward Elgar publishing 2019)

Beyelrin U, Marauhn T, *International Environmental Law* (Hart Publishing 2011)

Betts A, Collier P, *Refuge Transforming a Broken Refugee System* (Allen Lane Penguin 2017)

Betts A, *Protection by Persuasion: International Cooperation in the Refugee Regime* (2009 Ithaca Cornell University Press)

Betts A, 'International Relations and Forced Migration' in Fiddian-Qismeyeh, E, Loescher G, Long K, Sigona N, (eds) *The Oxford Handbook of Refugee and Forced Migration Studies* (Oxford University Press 2014)

Birnie P, Boyle A, Redgwell, C, *International Law and the Environment* (Oxford University Press 2009)

Bodansky D, Brunnée J, Rajamani L, *International Climate Change Law* (Oxford University Press 2018)

Bodansky D, *The Art and Craft of International Environmental Law* (Harvard University Press 2011)

Boyle A, 'Soft Law in International Law Making' in Evans MD (eds) *International Law* (Oxford University 2018 Press Fifth Edition)

Boyle A, Chinkin C, *The Making of International Law* (Oxford University Press 2007)

Bregman R, *Utopia for Realists* (Bloomsbury 2017)

Brunnée J, 'International Environmental Law and Community Interests Procedural Aspects' in Benvenisti E & Nolte E (eds) *Community Interests Across International Environmental Law* (Oxford University Press 2018)

Cantor DJ, Rodriguez – Serna N, 'The New Refugees: Organised Crime and Displacement in Latin America' (eds) (ILAS Publications, School of Advanced Studies, University of London 2016)

Cantor DJ, 'Cooperation on refugees in Latin America and the Caribbean The "Cartagena process" and South–South approaches' in Fiddian-Qasmiyeh E, Daley P (eds) *Routledge Handbook of South–South Relations* (Routledge 2018)

Cassese A, *International Law in a Divided World* (Oxford Clarendon Press 1986)

Chetail V, *International Migration Law* (Oxford University Press 2019)

Crawford J, *Brownlie's Principles of Public International Law* (Oxford University Press 2009 Ninth Edition)

Cryer R, Hervey T, Sokhi-Bulley B, Bohm A, *Research Methodologies in European and International Law* (Hart Publishing 2011)

D'Aspremont J, 'Herbert Hart in Today's International Legal Positivism' in Kammerhofer J, D'Aspremont J (eds) *International Legal Positivism in a Post-modern World* (Cambridge University Press 2014)

Evans MD, *International Law* (Oxford University Press 2018)

Franck T, *Fairness in International Law and Institutions* (Oxford University Press 1995)

Gammeltoft-Hansen T, Vedsted-Hansen J (eds) *Human Rights and the Dark Side of Globalisation: Transnational Law Enforcement and Migration Control* (Routledge 2006)

Gibney MJ, *The Ethics and Politics of Asylum: Liberal Democracy and the Response to Refugees* (Cambridge University Press 2004)

Goldstein JL, Kahler M, Keohane RO and Slaughter AM *Legalization and World Politics* (Cambridge, The MIT Press 2001)

Goodwin-Gill GS, McAdam J, *The Refugee in International Law* (Oxford University Press 2007 Third Edition)

Goodwin-Gill GS, 'International Law of Refugee Protection' in Fiddian–Qasmiyeh E, Loescher G, Long Katy, Sigona N (eds) *The Oxford Handbook of Refugee and Forced Migration Studies* (Oxford University Press 2014)

Harari YN, *21st Lessons for the 21st Century* (Vintage 2019)

Hart HLA, *The Concept of Law* (Oxford: Clarendon Law Series 1961)

Hathaway JC, *The Rights of Refugees in international Law* (Cambridge University Press 2005)

Hathaway JC, *Reconceiving International Refugee Law* (Martinus Nijhoff 1997)

Hans A, Surhke A, 'Responsibility Sharing' in J Hathaway (eds) *Reconceiving International Refugee Law* (Martinus Nijhoff 1997)

Higgins R, *Problems and Process International Law and How We Use It* (Clarendon Press 1995)

Honkonen T, *The Common But Differentiated Responsibility Principle in Multilateral Environmental Agreements* (Kluwer Law International 2009)

Hurwitz A, *The Collective Responsibility of States to Protect Refugees* (Oxford University Press 2009)

Jubilut L, *Refugee Protection in Brazil and Latin America: Selected Essays* (Transnational London Press 2018)

Klabbers J, *International Law* (Cambridge University Press 2017)

Krasner SD, 'Structural Clauses and Regime Consequences: Regimes as Intervening Variables' in Krasner S (eds) *International Regimes* (Cornell University Press 1983)

Lambert H, 'Dominant and Emerging Approaches in International Refugee Law' in Armstrong D (eds) *Routledge handbook of international law* (London Routledge 2009)

Lasswell HD, & McDougal MS, *Jurisprudence for a Free Society Studies in Law, Science and Policy* Volume 1 (Brill Nijhoff 1992)

Lehmann J, 'Outsourcing Protection and the Transnational Relevance of Protection Elsewhere, The Case of UNHCR' in Gammeltoft-Hansen T, Vedsted-Hansen J, (eds) *Human Rights and the Dark Side of Globalisation* (Routledge Studies in Human Rights 2017)

McDonald R STJ, 'The Charter of the United Nations as a World Constitution' in Schmitt MN (eds), *International Law Across the Spectrum of Conflict* Essays in Honour of Professor L.C. Green On the Occasion of his Eightieth Birthday (2000) 75 International Law Studies

Moreno Lax V, 'The Legality of the "Safe Third Country" Notion Contested: Contested, Insights from the Law of Treaties' in Goodwin-Gill GS, Weckel P (eds) *Migration & Refugee Protection in the 21st Century: Legal Aspects:* The Hague Academy of International Law Centre for Research (Martinus Nijhoff 2015)

Noll G, *Negotiating Asylum: The EU Acquis, Extraterritorial Protection and the Common Market of Deflection* (Martinus Nijhoff Publishers 2000)

Owen D, *What Do We Owe to Refugees?* (Polity 2020)

Rajamani L, *Differential Treatment in International Environmental Law* (Oxford University Press 2006)

Rawls J, *A Theory of Justice* (Harvard University Press 1999)

Ratner S, 'From Enlightened Positivism to Cosmopolitan Justice Obstacles and Opportunities' in Fastenrath G, Khan P, Von Schorlemer V (eds) *From Bilateralism to Community Interest: Essays in Honour of Bruno Simma* (Oxford University Press 2011)

Redgwell C, 'International Environmental Law' in Evans MD (ed) *International Law* (Oxford University Press 2018) (5th edition)

Sandel M, *Public Philosophy Essays on Morality in Politics* (Harvard University Press 2005)

Sands P, Peel J, Fabra A, Mackenzie R, *Principles of International Environmental Law* (Cambridge University Press 2018)

Sands P, *Principles of International Environmental Law* (Cambridge University Press 2003 Second Edition)

Sharpe M, *The Regional Law of Refugee Protection in Afri*ca (Oxford University Press 2018)

Shelton D, 'Equity' in Bodansky D, Brunnée J, Hey E, (eds) *The Oxford Handbook of International Environmental Law* (Oxford University Press 2008)

Simma B, Khan D-E, Nolte G, Paulus A, Wessendorf N, The *Charter of the United Nations: A Commentary* Vol II (Oxford University Press 2012)

Simma B, 'From Bilateralism to Community Interest in International Law' in *Collected Courses of the Hague Academy of International Law* (Hague Academy of International Law 1994)

Soltau F, *Fairness in International Climate Change Law and Policy* (Cambridge University Press 2009)

Susskind L, *Environmental Diplomacy* (OUP 1994)

Tan N, 'State Responsibility and Migration Control: Australia's International Deterrence Model' in Gammeltoft-Hansen T and Vedsted-Hansen J, (eds) *Human Rights and the Dark Side of Globalisation* (Routledge 2017)

Türk V, Dowd R, 'Protection Gaps' in Fiddian–Qasmiyeh E, Loescher G, Long Katy, Sigona N, (eds) *The Oxford Handbook of Refugee and Forced Migration Studies* (Oxford University Press 2014)

Tzanakopoulos A, Tams C, 'Use of Force' in Kammerhofer J, D'Aspremont J (eds) *International Legal Positivism in a Post-modern World* (Cambridge University Press 2014)

Wood T, 'The 1969 OAU Convention Governing the Specific Aspects of Refugee Problems in Africa' in Satvinder J (eds), *Research Handbook on International Refugee Law* (Edward Elgar Publishing 2019)

Zolberg A, Surkhe A, Aguayo S, *Escape from Violence, Conflict and Refugee Crisis in the Developing World* (Oxford University Press 1993)

Journal Articles

Abbot K, Snidal D, 'Hard and Soft Law in International Governance' (2000) 54 *International Organisation* 421

Abbott K, Keohane R, Moravcsik A, Slaughter AM, Snidal D, 'The Concept of Legalization' (2000) 54 *International Organization* 401

Aleinikoff A, 'The Unfinished Work of the Global Compact on Refugees' (2018) 30 *International Journal of Refugee Law* 611

Aleinikoff A, Poellot S, 'The Responsibility to Solve: The International Community and Protracted Refugee Situations' (2014) 54 *Virginia Journal of International Law* 195

Anker D, Fitzpatrick J, Schacknove A, 'Crisis and Cure: A Reply to Hathaway, Neve and Schuck' (1998) 11 *Harvard Human Rights Journal* 295

Bansak K, 'Improving Refugee Integration through Data Driven Algorithmic Assignment' (2018) 359 *Science* 325

Barutciski M, Suhrke A, 'Lessons from the Kosovo Refugee Crisis: Innovations in Protection and Burden-Sharing' (2001) 14 *Journal of Refugee Studies* 95

Batruch C, 'Hot Air as Precedent for Developing Countries? Equity Considerations' (1999) 17 UCLA *Journal of Environmental Law Policy* 45

Betts A, 'The Global Compact on Refugees: Towards a Theory of Change' (2018) 30 *International Journal of Refugee Law* 623

Betts A, Durieux J-F, 'Convention Plus as a Norm Setting Exercise' (2007) 20 *Journal of Refugee Studies* 509

Betts A, 'Public Goods Theory and the Provision of Refugee Protection; The Role of the Joint-Product Model in Burden-Sharing Theory' (2003) 16 *Journal of Refugee Studies* 274

Bodansky D, 'The Paris Climate Change Agreement: A New Hope?' (2016) 110 *American Journal of International Law* 288

Bodansky D, 'The Copenhagen Climate Change Conference: A Post-mortem' (2010) 104 *American Journal of International Law* 230

Bodansky D, 'The Legal Character of the Paris Agreement' (2016) 25 *Review of European Comparative and International Environmental Law* 142

Cantor DJ, Chikwanha F, 'Reconsidering African Refugee Law' (2019) 31 *International Journal of Refugee Law* 182

Cantor DJ, 'Fairness Failure and Future in the Refugee Regime' (2018) 30 *International Journal of Refugee Law* 627

Cantor DJ, 'The End of Refugee Law?' (2017) 9 *Journal Human Rights Practice* 203

Cantor, D, Tan, NF, Gkliati, M, Mavropoulou, E, Allinson, K, Chakrabarty, S, Grundler, M, Hillary, L, McDonnell, E, Moodley, R, Phillips, S, Pijnenburg, A, Reyhani, A-N, Soares, S, & Yacoub, N, 'Externalisation, Access to Territorial Asylum, and International Law (2022) 34 *International Journal of Refugee Law*, *34*(1), 120.

Carlane CP, Colavecchio CD, 'Balancing Equity and Effectiveness: The Paris Agreement & the Future of International Climate Change Law' (2019) 27 *N.Y.U. Environmental Law Journal* 108

Catalan-Flores A, 'Reconceiving Burden Sharing in International Refugee Law', (2016) 7 *The King's Student Law Review* 40

Chan N, 'Contributions and the Paris Agreement: Fairness and Equity in a Bottom-Up Architecture' (2016) 39 *Ethics and International Affairs* 291

Chimni BS, 'Global Compact on Refugees: One Step Forward, Two Steps Back' (2018) 30 *International Journal of Refugee Law* 630

Chimni BS, 'Third World Approaches to International Law: A Manifesto' (2006) 8 *International Community Law Review* 3

Chimni BS, 'Reforming the International Refugee Regime: A Dialogic Model' (2001) 14 *Journal of Refugee Studies* 151

Chimni BS, 'The Geopolitics of Refugee Studies: A View from the South' (1998) 11 *Journal of Refugee Studies* 350

Cohen HG, 'Multilateralism's Life Cycle' (2018) 112 *The American Society of International Law* 47

Cook B, 'Method in Its Madness: The Endowment Effect in an Analysis of Refugee Burden Sharing and a Proposed Refugee Market' (2004) 19 *Georgetown Immigration Law Journal* 333

Costello C, 'The Asylum Procedures Directive and the Proliferation of Safe Country Practices: Deterrence, Deflection and the Dismantling of International Protection' (2005) 7 *European Journal of Migration and Law* 35

Cullet P, 'Differential Treatment in Environmental Law: Addressing Critiques and Conceptualizing the Next Steps' (2016) 5 *Transnational Environmental Law* 305

Cullet P, 'Differential Treatment in International Law: Towards a New Paradigm of Inter-State Relations' (1999) 10 *European Journal of International Law* 549

Dastyari A, Hirsch A, 'The Ring of Steel: Extraterritorial Migration Controls in Indonesia and Libya and the Complicity of Australia and Italy' (2019) 19 *Human Rights Law Review* 435

Dowd R, McAdam J, 'International Cooperation and Responsibility Sharing to Protect Refugees: What, Why and How' (2017) 66 *International and Comparatively Law Quarterly* 863

Dowd R, McAdam J, 'International Cooperation and Responsibility Sharing to Combat Climate Change: Lessons from International Climate Change Law' (2017) 18 *Melbourne Journal of International Law* 180

Einarsen T, 'Mass Flight: The Case of International Asylum' (1995) 7 *International Journal of Refugee Law* 551

Ferracioli L, 'The Appeal and Danger of a New Refugee Convention' (2014) 40 *Social Theory and Practice* 123

Flory M, 'Adapting International Law to the Development of the Third World' (1982) 26 *Journal of African Law* 12

Fonteyne JP, 'Burden Sharing: An Analysis of the Nature and Function of International Solidarity in Cases of Mass Influx of Refugees' (1978–1980) 8 *Australian Yearbook of International Law* 161

Foster M, 'Responsibility Sharing or Shifting? "Safe" Third Countries and International Law' (2008) 25 *Refuge: Canada's Journal on Refugees* 64

Foster M, 'Protection Elsewhere: The Legal Implications of Requiring Refugees to Seek Protection in Another State' (2007) 28 *Michigan Journal of International Law* 223

Gallie WB, 'Essentially Contested Concepts' (1955–1956) 56 *Proceedings of the Aristotelian Society* 167

Gammeltoft-Hansen T, 'The Normative Impact of the Global Compact on Refugees' (2018) 30 *International Journal of Refugee Law* 605

Gammeltoft-Hansen T, Feith-Tan N, 'The End of the Deterrence Paradigm? Future Directions for Global Refugee Policy' (2017) 5 *Journal on Migration and Security* 28

Gammeltoft-Hansen T, 'International Refugee Law and Refugee Policy: The Case of Deterrence Policies' (2014) 27 *Journal of Refugee Studies* 574

Gibney MJ, 'Refugees and Justice Between States' (2015) 14 *European Journal of Political Theory* 448

Gilbert G, 'Not Bound But Committed' (2019) 57 *International Migration* 27

Gilbert G, 'Indicators for the Global Compact on Refugees' (2018) 30 *International Journal of Refugee Law* 635

Gill-Bazo T, 'The Safe Third Country Concept in International Agreements on Refugee Protection, Assessing State Practice' (2015) 33 *Netherlands Quarterly of Human Rights* 42

Giuffre M, 'State Responsibility Beyond Borders: What Legal Basis for Italy's Push-backs to Libya? (2012) 24 *International Journal of Refugee Law* 692

Goodwin-Gill GS, 'The Movements of People between States in the 21st Century: An Agenda for Urgent Institutional Change' (2016) 28 *International Journal of Refugee Law* 679

Goodwin Gill GS, 'The Language of Protection' Editorial (1989) 1 *International Journal of Refugee Law* 1 17

Grahl-Madsen A, 'Further Development of International Refugee Law', (1965) 35 *Nordic Journal of International Law* 159, 165

Handl G, Reisman M, Simma B, Dupuy PM, Chinkin C, De La Vega R, 'A Hard Look on Soft Law' (1990) 82 *American Society of International Law Proceedings* 371

Harris P, 'Common but Differentiated Responsibility: The Kyoto Protocol and United States Policy' (1999) 7 *NYU Environmental Law Journal* 27

Harley T, Hobbs H, 'The Meaningful Participation of Refugees in Decision-Making Processes: Questions of Law and Policy' (2020) *International Journal of Refugee Law* (*advanced copy*)

Harley T, 'Regional Cooperation and Refugee Protection in Latin America: A "South-South" Approach' (2014) 26 *International Journal of Refugee Law* 22

Harvey CJ, 'Talking about Refugee Law' (1999) 12 *Journal of Refugee Studies* 101

Hathaway JC, 'The Global Co-Op Out on Refugees' (2018) 30 *International Journal of Refugee Law* 591

Hathaway JC, 'A Global Solution to a Global Refugee Crisis' (2016) 1 *European Papers* 93

Hathaway JC, Gammeltoft – Hansen T, 'Non-refoulement in a World of Cooperative Deterrence' (2015) 53 *Columbia Journal of Transnational Law* 235

Hathaway JC, 'Labelling the "Boat People": The Failure of the Human Rights Mandate of the Comprehensive Plan of Action for Indochinese Refugees' (1993) 15 *Human Rights Quarterly* 686

Hathaway JC, Neve RA, 'Making International Refugee Law Relevant Again: A Proposal for Collectivized and Solution-Oriented Protection' (1997) 10 *Harvard Human Rights Journal* 115

Hathaway JC, 'Reconceiving Refuge Law as Human Rights Protection' (1991) 4 *Journal of Refugee Studies* 113

Helton A, 'Refugee Determination under the Comprehensive Plan of Action: Overview and Assessment' (1993) 5 *International Journal of Refugee Law* 544

Howie E, 'Asia–Pacific: Australian Border Control in Sri Lanka' (2014) 39 *Alternative Law Journal* 52

Hurwitz A, 'Norm Making in International Refugee Law' (2012) 106 *American Society of International law Proceedings* 430

Ineli-Ciger M, 'The Global Compact on Refugees and Burden Sharing: Will the Compact Address the Normative Gap Concerning Burden Sharing?' (2019) 38 *Refugee Survey Quarterly* 115

Inder C, 'The Origins of "Burden Sharing" in the Contemporary Refugee Protection Regime' (2017) 29 *International Journal of Refugee Law* 523

Joyner C, Biniaz S, Di Leva CE, 'Common but Differentiated Responsibility' (2002) 96 *Proceedings of the Annual Meeting of the American Society of International Law* 358–366

Jones W, Teytelboym A, 'Choices, Preferences and Priorities in a Matching System for Refugees' (2016) 51 *Forced Migration Review* 80

Juss J, 'Towards a Morally Legitimate Reform of Refugee Law: The Uses of Cultural Jurisprudence' (1998) 11 *Harvard Human Rights Journal* 311

Koskeniemi M, 'The Lady Doth Protests too Much Kosovo and the Return to Ethics in International Law' (2002) 54 *The Modern Law Review* 159

Kritzman-Amir T, 'Not in My Backyard: On The Morality of Responsibility-Sharing in Refugee Law' (2009) 34 *Brooklyn Journal of International Law* 355

Kuosmanen J, 'What (If Anything) Is Wrong with Trading Refugee Quotas?'(2013) 19 *Res Publica* 103

Kucuk E, 'The Principle of Solidarity and Fairness in Sharing Responsibility: More than Window Dressing?' (2016) 22 *European Law Journal* 448

Lacertosa J, 'Unfriendly Shores: An Examination of Australia's "Pacific Solution" under International Law' (2014) 40 *Brooklyn Journal of International Law* 321

Legomsky S, 'Secondary Refugee Movements and the Return of Asylum Seekers to Third Countries: The Meaning of Effective Protection' (2003) 15 *International Journal of Refugee Law* 567

Magner T, 'The Less than Pacific Solution for Asylum Seekers in Australia' (2004) 16 *International Journal of Refugee Law* 53

Magraw D, 'Legal Treatment of the Developing Countries, Differential, Contextual and Absolute Norms' (1990) 1 *Colorado Journal International Environmental Law and Policy* 69

Maiani F, 'The Reform of the Dublin System and the Dystopia of "Sharing People"' (2017) 24 *Maastricht Journal of European and Comparative Law* 622

Maljean-Dubois S, 'The Paris Agreement: A New Step in the Gradual Evolution of Differential Treatment in the Climate Regime?' (2016) 25 *Review of European, Comparative and International Environmental Law* 151

Martin G, 'International Solidarity and Co-Operation in Assistance to African Refugees: Burden-Sharing or Burden-Shifting' (1995) 7 *International Journal of Refugee Law* 250

McAdam J, 'The Enduring Relevance of the 1951 Refugee Convention' (2017) 29 *International Journal of Refugee Law Editorial* 1

McEwen M, 'Refugee Resettlement in Crisis: The Failure of the EU–Turkey Deal and the Case for Burden-Sharing' (2017) 2 *Swarthmore International Relations Journal* 20

Miller D, 'David Owen on Global Justice, National Responsibility and Transnational Power: A Reply' (2011) 37 *Review of International Studies* 2029

Missbach A, 'Doors and fences: Controlling Indonesia's Porous Borders and Policing Asylum Seekers' (2014) 35 *The Singapore's Journal of Geography* 228

Moore AF, 'Unsafe in America: A Review of the US Safe Third Country Agreement' (2007) 47 *Santa Clara Law Review* 201

Moreno-Lax V, 'Solidarity's Reach: Meaning, Dimensions and Implications for EU (External) Asylum Policy' (2017) 24 *Maastricht Journal of European and Comparative Law* 740

Mutua M, 'What Is TWAIL' (2000) 94 *Proceedings of America Society of International Law*, 31–38

Nethery A, Holman R, 'Secrecy and Human Rights Abuse in Australia's Offshore Immigration Detention Centres' (2016) 20 *The International Journal of Human Rights* 177

Nerethy A, Gordyn C, 'Australia–Indonesia Cooperation on Asylum Seekers: A Case of "Incentivised Policy Transfer"' (2014) 68 *Australian Journal of International Affairs* 177

Noll G, 'Why Refugees Still Matter: A Response to James Hathaway' (2007) 8 *Melbourne Journal of International Law* 536

Noll G, 'Risky Games? A Theoretical Approach to Burden Sharing in the Asylum Field' (2003) 16 *Journal of Refugee Studies* 236

Noll G, 'Prisoners Dilemma in Fortress Europe: On the Prospects for Equitable Burden Sharing in the European Union' (1997) 40 *German Yearbook of International Law* 405

Okoth-Obb G, 'Thirty Years On: A Legal Review of the 1969 OAU Convention Governing the Specific Aspects of Refugee Problems in Africa' (2000) 8 *African Yearbook of International Law* 3

Oliva P, 'The International Struggle to Save the Ozone Layer' (1989) 7 *Pace Environmental Law Review* 213

Onuf N, 'International Legal Theory Where We Stand' *International Legal Theory Publication of the American Society of International Law Interest Group on the Theory of International Law* (1995) Volume 1

Owen D, 'Refugees and Responsibilities of Justice' (2018) 11 *Global Justice: Theory Practice Rhetoric* 23

Paulus A, 'International Law After Postmodernism: Towards Renewal or Decline of International Law?' (2001) 14 *Leiden Journal of International Law* 727

Pauw WP, Castro P, Pickering L, Bhasin S, 'Conditional Nationally Determined Contributions in the Paris Agreement: Foothold for Equity or Achilles Heel?' (2020) 20 *Climate Policy* 468

Rajamani L, 'From Berlin to Bali, Killing Protocol Softly?' (2008) *International and Comparatively Law Quarterly* 909

Rajamani L, Werksman J, 'The Legal Character and Operational Relevance of the Paris Agreement's Temperature Goal' (2018) 376 *Philosophical Transactions of The Royal Society*

Rajamani L, 'The Devilish Details: Key Legal Issues in the 2015 Climate Negotiations'(2015) 78 *Modern Law Review* 826

Rajamani L, Bodansky D, 'The Paris Rulebook: Balancing International Prescriptiveness with National Discretion' (2019) 68 *International and Comparative Law Quarterly* 1023

Rajamani, L, 'The 2015 Paris Agreement: Interplay Between Hard, Soft and Non-obligations' (2016) 28 *Journal of Environmental Law* 337

Rajamani L, 'The Changing Fortunes of Differential Treatment in the Evolution of International Environmental law' (2012) 88 *International Affairs* 605

Rajamani L, 'Ambition and Differentiation in the 2015 Paris Agreement: Interpretative Possibilities and Underlying Politics' (2016) 45 *International and Comparative Law Quarterly* 493

Ratner S, 'Ethics and International Law Integrating the Global Justice Project(s)' (2013) 5 *International Theory* 1

Reynolds S, Vacatello JP, 'Building a Lifeline: A Proposed Global Platform and Responsibility Sharing Model for the Global Compact on Refugees' (2019) 21 *The Scholar: St. Mary's Law Review on Race and Social Justice* 325

Ringius L, Torvanger A, Holtsmark B, 'Can Multi-criteria Rules Fairly Distribute Climate Burdens OECD Results From Three Burden Sharing Rules' (1998) 26 *Energy Policy* 777

Roeben V, 'Responsibility in International Law' (2012) 16 *Max Planck Yearbook of United Nations Law* 99

Robinson C, 'The Comprehensive Plan of Action for Indochinese Refugees 1989-1997 Sharing the Burden and Passing the Buck' (2004) 17 *Journal of Refugee Studies* 319

Rutinwa B, 'The End of Asylum? The Changing Nature of Refugee Policies in Africa' (2002) 21 *Refugee Survey Quarterly* 12

Schacknove A, Byrne R, 'The Safe Country Notion in European Asylum Law' (1996) 9 *Harvard Human Rights Journal* 185

Scholtz W, 'Equity as the Basis for a Future International Climate Change Agreement: between Pragmatic Panacea and Idealistic Impediment. The Optimisation of the CBDR Principle via Realism' (2009) 42 *The Comparative and International Law Journal of Southern Africa* 166

Schuck P, 'Refugee Burden Sharing: A Modest Proposal' (1997) 22 *Yale Journal of International Law* 243

Sharpe M, 'The Global Compact on Refugees and Conflict Prevention in Africa: "Root Causes" and Yet Another Divide' (2018) 30 *International Journal of Refugee Law* 708

Shue H, 'Global Environment and International Inequality' (1999) 75 *International Affairs* 531

Shue H, 'Subsistence Emissions and Luxury Emissions' (1993) 15 *Law & Policy Journal* 39

Simma B, Paulus A, 'The International Community Facing the Challenge of Globalization' (1998) 9 *European Journal of International Law* 266

Simma B, Paulus A, 'The Responsibility of Individuals for Human Rights Abuses in Internal Conflicts: A Positivist's View' (1999) 93 *American Journal of International Law* 302

Simma B, Alston P, 'The Sources of Human Rights Law: Custom, *Jus Cogens* and General Principles' (1989) 12 *Australian Yearbook of International Law* 83

Slaughter AM, Ratner S, 'Symposium on Method in International Law, Appraising the Methods of International Law, A Prospectus for the Readers' (1999) 93 *The American Journal of International Law* 291

Smith R, 'Outsourcing Refugee Protection Responsibilities: The Second Life of an Unconscionable Idea' (2004–2005) 14 *Journal of Transnational Law and Policy* 137

Stone C, 'Common But Differentiated Responsibilities in International Law' (2004) 98 *American Journal of International Law* 276

Suhrke A, 'Burden-Sharing During Refugee Emergencies: The Logic of Collective Versus National Action' (1998) 11 *Journal of Refugee Studies* 396

Tan N, 'The Status of Asylum Seekers in Indonesia' (2016) 28 *International Journal of Refugee Law* 365

Taylor S, 'Exporting Detention: Australia-funded Immigration Detention in Indonesia' (2012) 87 *Journal of Refugee Studies* 88

Taylor S, 'Australian Funded Care and Maintain Ace of Asylum Seekers in Indonesia and Papua New Guinea, All care but no Responsibility?' (2010) 33 *University of South Wales Law Journal* 337

Taylor S, 'The Pacific Solution or Pacific Nightmare; The Difference between Burden Shifting and Responsibility Sharing' (2005) 6 *Asian Pacific Law and Policy Journal* 1

Thielemann E, 'Why Refugee Burden-Sharing Initiatives Fail: Public Goods,
Free-Riding and Symbolic Solidarity in the EU' (2018) 56 *Journal of Security and Migration Studies* 63

Thielemann ER, Dewan T, 'The Myth of Free-Riding: Refugee Protection and Implicit Burden-Sharing' (2006) 29 *West European Politics* 351

Thielemann ER, 'Between Interests and Norms: Explaining Burden-Sharing in the European Union' (2003) 16 *Journal of Refugee Studies* 253

Tsourdi E, 'Solidarity at Work? The Prevalence of Emergency Driven Solidarity in the Administrative Governance of the Common European Asylum System' (2017) 24 *Maastricht Journal of European and Comparative Law* 667

Türk V, 'The Promise and Potential of the Global Compact on Refugees' (2019) 30 *International Journal of Refugee Law* 575

Türk V, Garlick M, 'Prospects for Responsibility Sharing in the Refugee Context' (2016) 43 *Journal on Migration and Human Security* 45

Verwey WD, 'The Principles of a New International Economic Order and the Law on General Agreement on Trade and Tariffs' (1990) 3 *Leiden Journal of International Law* 117

Wall P, 'A New Link in the Chain: Could a Framework Convention for Refugee Responsibility Sharing Fulfil the Promise of the 1967 Protocol' (2017) 2 *International Journal of Refugee Law* 201

Wang T, Gao X, 'Reflection and Operationalisation of the Common But Differentiated Responsibilities and Respective Capabilities Principle in the Transparency Framework under the International Climate Change Regime' (2018) 9 *Advances in Climate Change Research* 253

Weisslitz M, 'Rethinking the Equitable Principle of Common but Differentiated Responsibility: Differential Versus Absolute Norms of Compliance and Contribution in the Global Climate Change Context' (2002) 13 *Colorado Journal of International Environmental Law and Policy* 473

Widawsky L, 'In my Backyard: How Enabling Hazardous Waste Trade to Developing Nations Can Improve the Basel Convention's Ability to Achieve Environmental Justice' (2008) 38 *Environmental Law* 577

Williams M, Montes M, 'Common But Differentiated Responsibilities: Which Way Forwards?'(2016) 59 *Dialogue* 114

Zamore L, 'Refugees, Development, Debt, Austerity: A Selected History' (2018) 6 *Journal on Migration and Human Security* 26

Zeick M, 'Doomed to Fail from the Outset? UNHCR's Convention Plus Initiative Revisited' (2009) 21 *International Journal of Refugee Law* 387

Scholarly Working Papers, Reports

Amnesty International, 'The Human Cost of Fortress Europe, Human Rights Violations Against Migrants and Refugees at Europe's Borders' (2014)

Amnesty International, 'Libya: Shameful EU Policies Fuel Surge in Detention of Migrants and Refugees' (16 May 2018)

Arbel E, Brenner A, Bordering on Failure: Canada-US Border Policy and the Politics of Refugee Exclusion (Harvard Immigration and Refugee Law Clinical Program, Harvard Law School 2013)

Barnett L, 'Global Governance and the Evolution of the International Refugee Regime' (2002) *New Issues in Refugee Research Working Paper* No. 54

Betts A, 'International Cooperation in the Global Refugee Regime' (November 2008) *Global Economic Governance Programme GEG Working Paper* No. 44

Betts A, Costello C, Zaun N, 'A Fair Share: Refugees and Responsibility-Sharing' (2017) 10 *Delmi Report*

Betts A, Milner J, 'The Externalization of EU Asylum Policy: The Position of African States' (2006) *Compass Working Paper* No. 36

Betts A, 'Comprehensive Plans of Action: Insights from CIREFCA and the Indochinese CPA' (2006) *UNHCR New Issues in Refugee Research Working Paper* 120

Betts A, 'The Political Economy of Extraterritorial Processing: Separating "Purchaser" from "Provider" in *Asylum Policy' New Issues in Refugee Research'* (2003) UNHCR Working Paper No. 91

Cantor, DJ, 'Responsibility-Sharing in the Refugee Field: Lessons from Latin America', (November 2018) Policy Brief Observatory on European Migration Law, Pisa

Carrera S, Guild E, 'Offshore Processing of Asylum Applications Out of Sight, Out of Mind?' (CEPS Policy Brief 27 January 2017)

Collet E, Ahad A, 'EU Migration Partnerships: A Work in Progress Report' (2017) European Migration Policy Institute

Crisp J, 'A New Asylum Paradigm? Globalization, Migration and the Uncertain Future of the International Refugee Regime' (2003) *UNHCR New Issues on Refugee Research, Working Paper* No. 100

De Bruycker P, Tsourdi E, 'In Search of Fairness in Responsibility Sharing' (2016) 51 *Forced Migration Review* 64

Dimitriadi A, 'The Impact of the EU–Turkey Statement on Protection and Reception: The Case of Greece' Global Turkey in Europe' (October 2016) Working Paper 15

Einarsen T, Engedahl M, 'The Universal Asylum System and the 2016 New York Declaration: Towards a Global Compact on Refugees?' (2016) Working Paper No. 17 Refugee Law Initiative

European Council on Refugees and Exiles (ECRE), 'Sharing Responsibility for Refugee Protection in Europe: Dublin Reconsidered' (March 2008)

Gammeltoft-Hansen T, 'The Extraterritorialisation of Asylum and the Advent of "Protection Lite"' (2007) Danish Institute of International Studies Working Paper No. 2

Grahl-Madsen A, Commentary of the Refugee Convention 1951, Articles 2–11, 13–37 Re-published by the Division of International Protection of the United Nations High Commissioner for Refugees (1997)

Grandi F, 'The Global Compact on Refugees: A Historic Achievement' (2019) 57 *International Migration UN IOM*, 23.

Giuffre M, 'Eurojus from Turkey to Libya, the EU Migration Partnership from Bad to Worse' (2017)

Goodwin-Gill GS, 'International Refugee Law: Yesterday, Today but Tomorrow?' (2016) *Working Paper No. 16 Refugee Law Initiative Working Papers*

Guild E, Costello C, Garlick M, and Moreno-Lax V, 'Enhancing the Common European Asylum System and Alternatives to Dublin' (2015) Study for the LIBE Committee, Brussels

Guild E, Costello C, and Moreno-Lax V, 'Implementation of the 2015 Council Decisions Establishing Provisional Measures in the area of International Protection for the Benefit of Italy and of Greece' (2017) *Study for the LIBE Committee of the European Parliament*

Harley T, 'Innovations in Responsibility Sharing for Refugees' (May 2019) *World Refugee Council Research Paper No. 14 Centre for International Governance Innovation 1*

House of Lords, European Union Committee 11th Report of Session 2003–04 Handling EU Asylum Claims: New Approaches Examined Report with Evidence House of Lords'

Karageorgiou E, *Rethinking Solidarity in European Asylum Law: A Critical Reading of the Key Concept in Contemporary Refugee Policy* (Lund University| Faculty of Law PhD Thesis 2018) * On file with the author

Karageorgiou E, 'The Law and Practice of Solidarity in the Common European Asylum System: Article 80 TFEU and Its Added Value', Swedish Institute for European Policy Studies, European Policy Analysis (November Issue 2016)

Maas, S Jurado, E Capdevila M, Labayle M, Hayward L, Evaluation of the Dublin III Regulation DG Migration and Home Affairs Final report (2015)

Marple N, 'Rights at Risk: A Thematic Investigation into how States Restrict the Freedom of Movement of Refugees on the African Continent' (2016) *New Issues in Refugee Research, Research Paper* No. 281

McAdam J, 'Extraterritorial Processing in Europe Is "Regional Protection" the Answer, and if Not, What Is?' (2015) Policy Brief 1 Andrew & Renata Kaldor Centre for International Refugee Law

Noll G, 'Failure by Design? On the Constitution of EU Solidarity' (26–27 February 2016) Odysseus Network Searching for Solidarity in the EU Asylum and Border Policies, A Collection of Short Papers following the Odysseus Network's First Annual Policy Conference

Noll G, 'Why the EU Gets in the Way of Refugee Solidarity?'(2015) *Open Democracy*

Peers S, 'The Draft EU/Turkey Deal on Migration and Refugees: Is It Legal?' (16 March 2016)

Riera J, Casey D, (principal eds), Regional Parliamentary Conference on Refugees in Africa, 'The Challenges of Protection and Solutions' Outcome of the June 2004 Regional Parliamentary Conference Co-organized by the African Parliamentary Union and UNHCR, in Association with the Inter-Parliamentary Union and the ICRC' (Cotonou Benin 1–3 June 2004).

Refugee Law Initiative Declaration on Externalisation and Asylum 29 June 2022

Schmaltz D, 'The Principle of Responsibility-Sharing in Refugee Protection; An Emerging Norm of Customary International Law' (March 2019) *Völkerrechtsblog*

Swerissen I, 'Shared Responsibility in International Refugee Law' (2011) *SHARES Expert Seminar Report*

Tan N, *International Cooperation on Refugees: Between Protection and Deterrence* Ph.D. Thesis (Aarhus University Department of Law 2018) * On file with the author

UNHCR The Refugee Convention, 1951: The Travaux Preparatoires Analysed, with a Commentary by Dr Paul Weis (1995)

Index

www.ingramcontent.com/pod-product-compliance
Lightning Source LLC
Chambersburg PA
CBHW051358240926
51852CB00001B/62
9789004546691